D0265151

Barwick the big hitter hauls FA from the canv

ESPANA 82

RTV
L/C

of the FIFA World Cup 2006 Organising Committee

The Prime Minister

requests the pleasure of the company of

Mr Brian Barwick

a Reception at 10 Downing Street, Whitehall
rsday 2nd February 2006, from 12·30

Liverpool Football Club
Royal Visit
to
Anfield Stadium
Friday 28th May, 1993

DIRECTORS'
BOX

Nº 1   12

Royal Visit to
FRIDAY 28TH MAY, 1993

DIRECTORS' BOX

ENTRY VIA
MAIN
ENTRANCE

Nº 1   12

National U
of Journal
Member

FOR USE AT ELECTIONS

İstanbul
The Final 2005

Menu/Menü

Turkish "meze" platter / Turk me

Mixed seasonal salad / Me

Beef medallions with eggplant
Dana madalyon (patlican so

"Ekmek kadayıfı" with cherr
Kaymaklı vişneli ekmek ka

BRIAN BARWICK

Anfield Days and Wembley Ways

BRIAN
BARWICK

Anfield Days and Wembley Ways

Sport Media

To my Gerry,

Thank you so much for supporting my
many professional flights of fancy
with such generosity, encouragement
and love. I couldn't do any of it
without you.

Brian x

Copyright text: Brian Barwick.
Published in Great Britain in hardback form in 2011.
Published and produced by: Trinity Mirror Sport Media,
PO Box 48, Old Hall Street, Liverpool L69 3EB.

ISBN: 9781906802769

Photographs/images: Trinity Mirror/Liverpool Daily Post & Echo,
Press Association Images, Brian Barwick collection.
Endpaper design: Lee Ashun.

Printed and bound by CPI Group (UK) Ltd, Croydon, CR0 4YY

Contents

Acknowledgements

I would like to thank my publishers, Trinity Mirror Sport Media, especially Ken Rogers, Steve Hanrahan and Paul Dove for their experience, wisdom and encouragement in getting this project from the inside of my head onto your bookshelf. Care, kindness and professionalism personified.

Thanks also to Summer Harl for her help in getting the manuscript together and reassuring me that the previous six hours' work on the desktop has not 'disappeared into the ether.'

For Louise Whitfield, for helping me find time in my diary to 'sit quietly and write' – and for providing me with a recuperative cup of coffee when desperately needed.

To Dan Wakefield, a proper Red, for reading the manuscript pre-publication and giving it an important and much encouraging thumbs-up. To Andy and Ross Proudfoot, two lifelong friends and 'home and away' Liverpool fans, for unwittingly providing me with some of the book's best content and also supplying the post-publication 'spot the error' service without being asked!

Thanks to Liverpool great Ian Callaghan for so graciously turning up to have his photograph taken with me.

ACKNOWLEDGEMENTS

To all my friends and former colleagues from Quarry Bank School, the University of Liverpool, the *North-Western Evening Mail*, the BBC, ITV, the Football Association and much more for playing your part in making this story worth writing – and, more importantly I hope worth reading. And, of course, for all the laughs along the way.

To the great Liverpool Football Club's players, managers, officials and fans that have made the 50 year experience of watching 'my team' so complete.

To David, my brother, for that cup final ticket and much more.

To my late mum and dad, who would have been so proud of me writing this book – and who provided me with such a loving and happy childhood... and my very first football.

To sons Jack and Joe, my own top team, who have even promised to read the book, whilst bouncing between moments of their busy social life. I am very proud of you both.

To my wife, Gerry, for continuing to feign interest when I discuss with her the likes of Jerzy Dudek's double save in Istanbul and the relative merits of the transfer window.

And finally, to the game of football itself for providing me, and millions like me, with a lifetime's passion, excitement and fun...

Brian Barwick

Introduction

A Privilege and a Pleasure

I am writing these words just a few weeks after witnessing the finest display of club football I think I have ever seen. In fact, I *know* I have ever seen.

It was Barcelona – Messi, Iniesta and Xavi – out-passing Manchester United on a night that defied superlatives. The Spanish champions had put their English counterparts to the sword – and in a manner that enthralled those privileged, like me, to be at Wembley Stadium to see it first hand and for the millions watching on television at home.

It was football on a different level. On a different planet. And it is why the game continues to captivate so many people.

Wembley itself was also a winner that night – a 'coming of age' occasion for a new stadium with a huge reputation to live up to. Given my own personal and professional connection with football's most famous landmark it was a thrill to see it also deliver in such an accomplished fashion – and then be handed the opportunity to do it all again in two years' time. Great.

When I was at the BBC in the 1980s and '90s, I worked with a wonderful man called Albert Sewell.

'Our Albert', as Des Lynam affectionately dubbed him, provided background information and statistics to the *Match of the Day* team to help the programme stay factually correct and informative. Albert loved his football. "The first day of the season is better than Christmas Day!" was a phrase he often used to me.

Well, I am struggling to go that far. I've enjoyed some belting Christmas Days but undoubtedly, football has provided me, like him, with a lifelong thread of interest, involvement and anticipation – from swopping bubble-gum cards in the playground to swopping footballing stories over a pint in the pub.

And I've been especially lucky because the team I have had the pleasure of following all this time is Liverpool Football Club.

I have shared their many great moments and their elevation to world-class status from a truly unique set of perspectives and positions. As a BBC TV sports producer, the editor of *Match of the Day*, the controller of ITV Sport, the chief executive of the Football Association but most importantly to me, as a real fan. Man and boy.

That range of professional roles has given me opportunities to see the Reds' progress – and football, in general – from some very privileged places.

Over the years, I've also met many of the most influential Anfield personalities of the time, and in the pages I share some of those memories and insights with you.

And why the book? Why now?

Well, this autumn marks the 50th anniversary of me watching my first Liverpool game at Anfield – the first of literally hundreds and hundreds of Liverpool games. Home and away, home and abroad.

And, in truth, that first senior game was also the launching pad for me seeing literally thousands of other football matches, of all shapes and sizes both here and across the globe – from Sunday League games in the park played out in freezing rain to World Cup finals hosted in gigantic stadiums bathed in glorious sunlight. And in so doing, I think it has given me an interesting story to tell.

When my dad took me – an impressionable seven-year-old more into children's TV's *Four Feather Falls* than Football – to watch Liverpool play Leyton Orient in the old Second Division of the Football League on October 28, 1961, neither he nor I could have possibly realised it would set me off on a path of such affection for the club and the sport itself. Indeed, a love of football that would become such an enriching and essential part of my daily life and also, ultimately, help mould and define my professional career.

Fifty years on, I am still completely hooked. I am fascinated to know how Liverpool boss Kenny Dalglish – for me the club's greatest-ever player – will weave his managerial magic in the 2011/12 season. His second coming at the club has, so far, been successful in turning around form and fortune. All Liverpudlians are up for the ride.

I also awaited the season's new fixture list with my usual eager anticipation, and then started to plot my own personal journey through the Reds' latest campaign.

I've given up on the league ladders though...

My current working life now enables me to see more Liverpool games than in recent years when professional neutrality was part of what was expected of me. And duly delivered.

These days I run a media and sports consultancy – Barwick Media and Sport – that still keeps me directly involved in both the industries that have brought me such fun and fulfilment over the past 30 years.

The worlds of broadcasting and sport have provided me with some exciting, stimulating, testing and tough challenges in my working life and also provided me with a mixture of both funny and poignant moments and I look forward to taking you on that journey too.

A journey from being a young man, fresh from a happy and lively childhood, a university education and a burning ambition to be a top sports journalist, to walking across the threshold of the Football Association's London headquarters to take up the reins as that organisation's chief executive some three decades later.

And, in between, spending 25 years in the sports departments of two of world broadcasting's most respected institutions – the BBC and ITV – working on some of British television's most iconic sports programming.

Also meeting so many fascinating and talented people en route – as well as having the pleasure of attending so many of the world's greatest sporting spectacles and experiencing them first-hand. I'll share some of those adventures with you.

I now work in many different capacities but especially love my role at the University of Liverpool where as a Visiting Professor of Strategic Leadership in their management school I help young people, many from overseas, develop their own career paths – some into the football industry.

Like many Liverpool fans – all football fans actually – I have my favourite memories, favourite players, favourite matches, favourite goals, favourite Reds 'team', favourite/least favourite opponents, strangest journeys, best food/worst food, best chant, disagreements with mates, been locked out of big games, stuck on motorways, queued for tickets, arrived at a game that's just been postponed, never won the *Golden Goal*, recorded the wrong channel, collected the programmes, the autographs, the souvenir papers and the sweep-stake winnings. Occasionally.

And enjoyed the whole experience.

Unlike others, I have also had the opportunity to personally get to know and meet so many of my sporting heroes, run television's most famous football show, launch the broadcast careers of some of the game's former greats, be part of a musical phenomenon, see the new Wembley Stadium open... and help appoint the England manager.

It hasn't been dull.

I hope you enjoy my affectionate look back at the past 50 years of supporting the Reds and climbing some interesting professional and personal mountains. Please enjoy.

Brian Barwick
July 2011

1

A Tale of Two Finals

May 1st, 1965. FA Cup final day. But not any old cup final day – this one was for real. Liverpool v Leeds United.

And I, for one, was up for it. Early breakfast – snap, crackle and pop – then 'bagging' the armchair nearest the television in good time for the start of BBC's *Cup Final Grandstand*.

And there I would stay, from the first beat of the famous signature tune and David Coleman's rousing introduction from pitch-side at Wembley, until the final note of the self-same tune some six hours later. Football heaven.

'Meet the Teams', 'How They Got There', pre-match pitch-side interviews – all novel, a once-a-year experience, the ONLY live domestic club game on television each season.

And all in glorious... black and white!

The front cover of that week's *Radio Times* was adorned by a silhouette of the FA Cup itself straddled on either side by rosettes of the two competing clubs. Rosettes, eh... sadly they went the way of the football rattle and the bobble hat!

Cup Final Grandstand was an annual national television 'event' and 1965 was no different.

After Coleman's introduction, it was a tour of the empty Wembley dressing rooms with Danny Blanchflower, the iconic double winning Tottenham Hotspur captain turned fledgling broadcaster – an early Alan Hansen if you will.

Liverpool's route to the final was then featured in the programme. A third round win at West Brom, a near-thing against the Fourth Division minnows of Stockport County (an unlikely 1-1 draw at Anfield, before the Reds did the job in the replay), an away win at Bolton, followed by the laying of bogey team Leicester City in a sixth round replay.

A convincing two-nil semi-final win over Chelsea completed the sequence, then Grandstand turned their attention to Leeds United's 'How They Got There.'

All that done, it was off to some highlights from that week's big testimonial match for the retiring Sir Stanley Matthews (aged 50!) before Grandstand, in typical fashion, laced the pre-match air-time with all manner of Cup final features – not forgetting the golf from Sandwich, racing from Ascot, swimming from Portsmouth and rugby union from Twickenham.

All that, and still back in time for the community singing with Frank Rea at Wembley. Of course, we all sang along at home.

The two teams emerged from the tunnel to be greeted by rain-leaden skies and a Wembley crowd going bonkers. It was Leeds United's first-ever FA Cup final appearance and Liverpool's first Cup final appearance since 1950 – the club had still to lift the coveted trophy – and the Kopites were out in force to help sing and shout them to victory in their own inimitable style.

Of course, in those days the FA Cup could genuinely boast of its position as the world's most famous cup competition and really mean it.

The annual televising of the final itself had literally stopped the nation in its tracks since its first showing in 1938 – when a young Preston North End wing-half named Bill Shankly had enjoyed his first taste of Wembley success.

The famous Lancastrians won that particular 'War of the Roses' against Huddersfield Town via a last-minute penalty from George Mutch.

Twenty seven years on and at 15 Eastham Close, our family home in Childwall, the household was in a state of expectation – and preparation, for the afternoon ahead.

Curtains were tightly drawn to exclude any offending daylight, sandwiches were prepared (pilchard my particular and peculiar favourite – no fancy pizza or Big Macs in those days), the *Liverpool Yeah Yeah Yeah* newspaper special had been read from cover to cover – and, of course, there was no house-room for the casual 'take it or leave it' neighbour who wasn't besotted by the prospect of the forthcoming afternoon's entertainment.

Back at Wembley itself, Her Majesty the Queen was gracing the game with her presence, and before kick-off, the Duke met the King – Prince Philip met Bill Shankly.

* * * * *

Prince William waited nervously in the tunnel at the Millennium Stadium in Cardiff. It was his first official duty as the new President of the Football Association and the 24-year-old future heir to the throne was in unfamiliar territory.

Guiding him through the afternoon of May 13th, 2006, was my duty, in the capacity of chief executive of the Football Association. It was my second FA Cup final in that role at the top of the game. The first had been the previous year's match between Manchester United and Arsenal.

That had been an unremarkable match with a penalty shoot-out clinched by Patrick Vieira's winning spot-kick – his last competitive game for the club.

But this year was different. The 2006 FA Cup final, the 125th, was between West Ham United and Liverpool. My professional neutrality was going to be severely tested... again.

In fact, that was the case throughout my four-year term of office at Soho Square – a rich period of form for Liverpool. A famous Champions League win, an FA Cup final success, an FA Community Shield bagged plus two FA Youth Cup final wins – the second at Old Trafford. Football insiders were getting suspicious!

Liverpool's route to the final had been lively. I had been at their third round tie at Luton with the home team having a 3-1 second half lead and on course to send the Reds out of the cup, before a comeback was sealed with a Xabi Alonso goal scored from his own half. 5-3 the final score.

An away win at Portsmouth followed and a memorable Peter Crouch goal knocked out Manchester United. I saw a spectacular 7-0 away win at Birmingham and then an exciting 2-1 semi-final victory over Chelsea at Old Trafford – once again, the diminutive Luis Garcia proved to be the Reds' match-winner – and the Blues' nemesis.

And so to Cardiff... and the Reds' 13th appearance in the FA Cup final.

The appointment of Prince William as President of the Association had been deemed a bold and positive move, as I believe it has been, and now he was ready to make his first public impression in the role. Taken down by lift into the bowels of the stadium, we both stood at the back of the tunnel as the teams emerged from the dressing rooms. Prince William quietly said to me: "Oh, look, there's Stevie G.".

Liverpool captain Steven Gerrard raised an inquisitive eyebrow when spotting the Royal guest quietly standing in the background and then broke into a broad smile. Prince William shyly returned the compliment.

It was fascinating to watch these two famous young men from completely different walks of life, acknowledging each other. Both men slightly in awe of the other.

Walking along and greeting the two lines of players on the pitch before the game was a surreal experience for me. Sure, I had done it before – it was part of the role as CEO of the FA but this was different. This was Liverpool in the FA Cup final and this was me, an ardent Reds supporter man and boy trying to act impartially – and hopefully managing it.

Mind you, just for a moment I was truly tempted to depart from expected protocol and, instead of a 'good luck' message, hit the Red line with: 'Carra don't let Ashton get a sniff', 'Stevie, bomb through that midfield son', 'Sami, make a nuisance of yourself at corners', 'Harry, any chance of finishing the game?' and 'Djibril, wrong hair dye mate!' If only...

By the way, I don't think any of the West Ham players truly believed the positive sentiments I imparted their way whilst completing my pre-match duties but I did act in accordance to protocol. However, any illusions of neutrality went skyward for television viewers when BBC commentator John Motson told the watching world... 'Brian Barwick there, a staunch Liverpudlian who has supported the team all his life!'

*   *   *   *   *   *

A boring first-half at Wembley, notable only for a bone-crunching assault by Leeds' hard man Bobby Collins on Gerry Byrne, leaving the Liverpool full-back with a dislocated shoulder and a long and brave afternoon ahead of him. No substitutes in those days, of course.

My dad had joined the viewers at 15 Eastham Close midway through that first half, straight from finishing 'morning' duty as a police officer in Liverpool's G division.

A big, gentle man with a real passion for sport, he headed straight for his favourite armchair and was brought up to speed on what he had missed so far. Nothing.

The second half produced little much more and the final whistle brought proceedings to a timely halt and the prospect of the first FA Cup final extra-time since 1947.

* * * * *

A different story at Cardiff, the game had positively bristled with action. West Ham had taken an early two-goal lead through a Jamie Carragher own goal and a Dean Ashton tap-in. A super finish by Djibril Cisse had pulled one back for Liverpool and Steven Gerrard, in typical determined style, had evened things up early in the second half.

Both teams seemed bent on all-out attack on a day when defences looked vulnerable. The match was developing into a classic and Paul Konchesky, West Ham full-back and a future Red, would be next on the scoresheet when he hit a cross which bamboozled Reds 'keeper Pepe Reina – and the Hammers were back in front.

Over lunch before the game, Prince William had asked me and my fellow FA executive and West Ham legend Sir Trevor Brooking how we would contain our enthusiasm if and when 'our' team scored given, as he pointed out, our official roles and duties on the day and our lifelong commitment to the respective finalists.

'We've learnt how to do that' we both said unconvincingly – and Trevor's reaction as West Ham went ahead again just momentarily betrayed his normal cool calm exterior and his professional implacability. He was chuffed. And why not?

Mine too was also about to be tested...

*   *   *   *   *

Extra-time at Wembley, the skies now releasing what they had promised all afternoon – and then finally a goal. And a Liverpool goal...

Gerry Byrne and Willie Stevenson combined to give Roger Hunt a chance to stoop low and head home. Our front room went crazy... yes, even mum, who seemed to have unexplained leanings towards Everton at that time, went mad. This was it, Liverpool were about to finally win that most coveted of trophies – the FA Cup.

But hold on, what's this?

Jack Charlton is up-field. He heads across the box and that ginger-haired fire-ball Billy Bremner crashes a volley home. 1-1.

Despair at 15 Eastham Close and the best biscuits were removed from the new coffee table. No time for self-indulgence and custard creams. And no time for penalties either, they were not to be introduced for another 20 years. An FA Cup final replay, the first since 1912, loomed large.

Then, in the second half of extra-time, Ian Callaghan crossed brilliantly and 'the Saint'– Ian St John, wrote himself into Liverpool football folklore with an acrobatic and decisive diving header. A goal worthy of winning any cup final – and of clinching Liverpool's first.

No resistance this time from Leeds, job done.

*   *   *   *   *

The clock had tipped over into the 91st minute as Liverpool still trailed 3-2 in Cardiff. A cracking cup final was in its last throes and Liverpool seemed destined to be on the wrong end of the result. West Ham had been the better team. But wait...

Just as many times before, and since, the Reds' super-skipper came to the rescue. Steven Gerrard crashed home an improbable yet unstoppable 25-yard shot to burst West Ham's bubbles. It was an absolute screamer of a goal and half the stadium erupted; I was chuffed... super chuffed, and spontaneously reflected that emotion.

A brief leap out of my seat, a gentle punch in the air, then a quick kiss for my wife, Gerry, before I resumed my air of presidential calm and coolness. But not before I had been spotted by Prince William, who greeted my reaction with a warm smile. Football fans will always be football fans wherever they sit or whatever they wear, it's in the blood – red and blue.

On BBC Television, John Motson was describing the game as the 'best cup final of modern times'. 3-3. Extra-time drew no more goals and so it was to penalties. Something Liverpool were past masters of, not least as illustrated in Istanbul the previous year.

This time, a Pepe Reina save from an Anton Ferdinand penalty was the clincher and Liverpool were FA Cup winners for the seventh time in their history.

*   *   *   *   *

Ron Yeats and his team walked proudly up the 39 steps to the Wembley Royal box – and the Queen and the Cup! Liverpool's Captain Colossus lifted the trophy and half of Wembley went berserk. *'Ee-aye-addio, we've won the cup'* came ringing from the terraces – and from the whole of Eastham Close – well, nearly all, there was the odd Evertonian and football non-believer washing their cars and trimming their hedges as if little or nothing historic had passed their way that afternoon. As if...

Time for me, a mad-keen 10-year-old to get out into the street and replay the final – including running around the Close with a silver cup, courtesy of nicking a bit of my mum's silver baking foil.

Bit one-sided the game – ten delirious Liverpudlians against a couple of Evertonians, three Subbuteo players, a Magic Robot, two Pinky and Perky puppets, an Action Man and a *Z-Cars* annual.

Then dragged reluctantly back indoors for tea and an evening in front of the television – *Juke Box Jury, Doctor Who* – with William Hartnell, the original and some argue the best-ever 'Doctor'. His battles with the infamous Daleks were destined to go into their own extra-time for many decades to come.

The *Dick Van Dyke Show*, Roy Castle and a bit of Sherlock Holmes rounded off the night's viewing. Both BBC1, and the brand new BBC2, closed down shortly after 11 o'clock – sending the nation to bed.

The following day, after church parade with the Cubs – never my favourite event as I had to carry the flag with all my mates on the pavement winding me up – mum drove me and my brother, David down to Liverpool city centre to see the Reds bring the cup home.

Mum had just passed her driving test (at the fourth attempt) and this was her FIRST solo drive. Dad was on crowd control duty in the city centre and so the journey to and from town, on incredibly busy roads, full of impatient motorists, and a deadline to make, was as memorable as standing five deep, and only five foot tall, trying to get a glimpse of our returning heroes and that famous trophy.

These were the days before the carefully-staged tour around the city was established, and some 250,000 people crowded into the city centre. People were literally hanging from buildings, standing on top of bus shelters, anything to get a better spec.

My brother and I actually saw very little, had to contend with mum having driving hysterics and witnessed the first embryonic signs of that later phenomenon 'road rage' from her ungracious fellow motorists – but despite all this, we can always say that we were there to see the cup come home!

* * * * *

Twenty-four hours on from Liverpool's dramatic win over West Ham in the FA Cup final in Cardiff, I found myself, ironically, at Upton Park itself attending another final – the FA Trophy Final between Grays Athletic and Woking.

Once again on official duty, but this time without the twinkle in the eye a certain result would give me.

The West Ham club officials offered their FA guests their usual warm hospitality and their 'what might have beens' from the previous afternoon. I, of course, responded with a statesman-like air, nodding in all the right places.

In many ways, those two FA Cup finals, some 40 years apart, gave me as a Liverpool supporter, be it as boy or 'blazer', the same fantastic feeling of being part of another chapter in my club's illustrious history.

2

An Unlikely Victory

It's July, 2005 and eager children are just days away from breaking up for their well-earned school holidays.

During that summer, tennis superstar Roger Federer had won his third consecutive Wimbledon title with a straight sets victory over American Andy Roddick. And Venus Williams had finally overcome fellow-American Lindsay Davenport in the longest women's final in the history of Wimbledon.

In golf, another sporting supremo, Tiger Woods, was on the eve of his attempt at winning a second Open Golf Championship. The venue was St Andrews and the main challenger Scotland's Colin Montgomerie.

Tiger would emerge victorious five days later but not before Montgomerie had tested both his nerve and his talent.

Oh, and one of the most celebrated Test Series in living memory was still a week away from actually starting!

The 2005 Ashes Test Series was *the* highlight of the summer – a memorable set of matches which roared into life from the very first morning of the series at Lords.

Controversially back-loaded to take place in the middle of the season, the Test, when it finally got underway, produced some of the most thrilling cricket, inspiring sportsmanship and dramatic moments in over a century of the two great nations facing each other in this special piece of sporting combat.

Tennis, golf and cricket – the staple diet of the English summer – but in the second week of July – July 13th, to be precise – football was back.

Just seven weeks after winning the UEFA Champions League final in spectacular fashion, unsurpassed in the competition's history and just as people were rummaging around for last year's sun cream ahead of their annual two-week sunshine break, Liverpool, the new champions of Europe, were back in action defending their glittering crown.

Total Network Solutions may not be the most unusual opponents Liverpool Football Club have ever faced at Anfield but I am struggling to name a more unlikely match-up.

Liverpool had been drawn to meet the Welsh champions in the very first stage of the 2005/2006 competition for reasons that will unfold. Used to crowds in the hundreds, they now faced a night in front of the Kop.

Total Network Solutions, or TNS as they were more handily known, had actually clinched their Welsh Premier League title on the same night that Liverpool had produced a magnificent draw in Turin against Juventus to move into the semi-finals of the Champions League and that remarkable all-English match-up with Chelsea.

Having received the Welsh Premier trophy in front of a crowd of just 417, the boys from Llansantffraid went on to clinch their domestic double with a cup final win over Carmarthen at Llanelli the following month.

TNS had competed first in Europe as Llansantffraid FC back in the 1996/97 season. Their complete record in European competition would not have given Liverpool's all-conquering coach, Rafa Benitez, too many sleepless nights.

Played 12, Won 0, Drawn 2, Lost 10. Goals for – 6; goals against – 41. It was not the stuff of champions – or European champions shall we say.

But they did have the Welsh League all-time leading scorer, Marc Lloyd-Williams in their ranks, as well as a player who would find the thought of playing against Liverpool to be the stuff of dreams.

John Lawless, TNS winger, and scorer of the winning goal in the previous season's cup final win over Carmarthen, was an out and out Red. A genuine fanatic.

John, a Kop season-ticket holder, had Liverpool's crest proudly tattooed on his arm, and had been in Istanbul on that special night when the Reds defied the odds to claim victory in such dramatic fashion.

"To think I was there, watching Liverpool against AC Milan and now they're playing TNS in the first game since that night. It's just mad."

Mad but true – and for both clubs this was a tie that neither had expected to happen.

For TNS, because "these things don't happen to teams like us" and for Liverpool, because a berth in that season's UEFA Champions League competition had been the stuff of controversy since, and indeed before, the Reds had produced the ultimate comeback to clinch their fifth European crown – and the accompanying bragging rights as the continent's footballing top-dog for the next 12 months.

Bragging rights yes but guaranteed entry into the following season's competition? No. There was no automatic entry into the following season's Champions League for the winners – and there never had been.

And so the tussle off the field to give Liverpool their rightful opportunity to defend the title went right down to the wire, with many different twists and turns.

Let me take you on them.

Context: Everton had been having a stonking season – and, for once, were outshining the Reds in the Premier League. Despite sharing the spoils in the two derby matches – a win apiece – it had become clear as the season entered its final stretch that Everton were about to gatecrash the 'big four' and gain entry into the UEFA Champions League for the first time.

And that could present a really delicate problem for the Football Association, the FA Premier League and most chiefly UEFA as the team they were likely to replace were their arch-rivals, Liverpool.

Unedifying for all Reds fans but those more fair-minded Kopites accepted if the Blues finished ahead of their own heroes the place was rightly theirs. Except...

Liverpool were still marching on through the UEFA Champions League – and could still win it.

Pre-Christmas the likelihood of that would have seemed slim, until a special European night at Anfield had seen Liverpool scale a remarkable second-half assault against Olympiakos and another Steven Gerrard special helped clinch a place in the competition's knock-out stages.

Past Bayer Leverkusen and then Juventus and onto a semi-final to savour with Chelsea.

By now, as CEO of the FA, I had put UEFA on red alert that they were faced with an unprecedented and ultimately tricky situation. And one they may need to resolve in double-quick time. I was also hugely aware of a potential personal conflict of interest that lay ahead of me.

I had joined the FA that January as its chief executive – a job with a chequered history and a short shelf-life!

Appointed following a tabloid expose of a complicated love triangle between the then England coach Sven- Goran Eriksson, the FA's Chief Executive Mark Palios and a staff member, Faria Alam. It put the FA on the front pages – and the back-foot. Result? Palios out, Alam gone – Sven stayed put.

The real consequence of what in truth was a tame affair was that the FA and all matters pertaining to it were now fair game.

So, when the job advertisement for a new chief executive popped up in the *Sunday Times* the assumed logic was to ignore it.

And I did for several weeks. I was happy and successful at ITV in my role of Controller of their sports output. We had big contracts and top talent.

The year 2003 climaxed in the channel broadcasting the sporting moment of the decade – (up to then!) – Jonny Wilkinson's famous drop-kick to clinch World Cup victory for England in Australia and 2004 also delivered a good mix of programming – Champions League, Formula One, Tour de France and the European football championships.

It was during a coach journey – on the aptly named *Desmobile* – between Euro 2004 venues in Portugal that ITV's presenter and good mate, Des Lynam and I had idly engaged in a conversation about the future. He was about to retire from front-line live sports presentation. An iconic broadcaster, Des and I had spent many years together and made literally thousands of hours of programmes at both the BBC and ITV.

Indeed, when I left the BBC in 1997 after 18 years service, we had thought the successful partnership was ended. Then, two years later, I signed him for ITV – a big money transfer that filled the front, middle and back pages for days.

Anyway, over a coffee, Des reflected on his own career and then said:"What are you going to do next?"

"I am happy where I am Des," I countered. "No, you have one more big job in you," he said. The conversation drifted away.

As I filled in the application form for the "big job", the FA, I knew what he meant. It was a role that had become thrust into a public spotlight – no longer just a 'suit' but a suit with a very public profile.

I got the job. Offered and accepted – and off and running. There was microscopic investigation into my ability to do the job in the media – some with me, some not. I made a mental note of the 'anti-brigade'.

I enjoyed a splendid send-off from my colleagues at ITV, a short break in Dubai and then into the job – via an impromptu photo-shoot outside the FA headquarters at Soho Square.

I settled in quickly – felt at home actually. The staff welcomed me, the football family did too – well, most of it.

Things moved along swiftly. I realised very quickly that this was a relationship business more than anything else. And those allegiances shifted on a daily basis.

The Liverpool/Everton/FA/Premier League/UEFA puzzle on a potential shift in the rules of qualification on entry to the Champions League was an early indication of how my working life would now be.

An added problem was that I was known as a dyed-in-the-wool Liverpudlian – never hidden the fact, pointless trying.

Now, as we faced the last few weeks of the 2004/5 season, that lifelong support for the Reds could possibly blow up in my face if I was not able to steer a positive and neutral course though the quagmire of football politics and do what was right for all sides. An early and near impossible task.

And a task the press had also spotted! Explain the issue to their readers, sit on the sidelines and watch the FA cock it up... seemed to be the context of their stories.

As the season entered April, Everton's ascendancy in the Premier League remained and Liverpool had beaten Juventus over two legs. Things were hotting up.

The UEFA Congress in Tallinn, Estonia, gave me a chance to get the 'issue' in front of the European administrators – and I did so quietly at a mid-session break. I homed in on UEFA General Secretary Lars-Christer Olsson, a typically phlegmatic Swede and explained English football's dilemma:

"If Everton get the fourth place in the Premier League and Liverpool win the Champions League then we, the FA and you, UEFA will be in the tightest of tight corners because dropping one Merseyside club out of the competition for another – Everton for Liverpool – would be simply impossible to handle and deeply unfair."

I was also very conscious of the fact that when Everton had qualified for the senior European Club competition in the mid-eighties they had been prevented from actually competing in it because of the ban on English clubs following the events at the Heysel Stadium in 1985.

I, therefore, spoke from both my head and my heart. His reply was not encouraging:

"Brian, you know there are rules already in place – and if that situation happened the FA would have to decide which four clubs it would enter in the Champions League. Not five... four! And, anyway, you know how football is – things will happen on the pitch and the problem will go away. Trust me"

I did not share his confidence. As I saw it, Liverpool could beat Chelsea in the Champions League semi-final and then could win the final – Everton I thought were certainties for fourth place.

I left Tallinn disappointed and more than a little concerned by UEFA's complacency.

Liverpool's draw at Stamford Bridge in the semi-final first leg set up a huge game at Anfield. The papers were full of it. Chelsea were the new headline makers of English football, combining Abramovich's Russian roubles and Mourinho's tactical genius.

The atmosphere at Anfield that night was simply remarkable – shiver down the spine remarkable. I remember watching the Chelsea players warming up before the game and huddling in groups, their attentions unavoidably focussed on the Kop and the battle-hymns already coming from that hallowed football choir.

Now, every Liverpool fan has their favourite 'Anfield big night' – and I had been denied two major previous occasions – Inter Milan 1965 (too young) and St Etienne (locked out) but there had been plenty of other biggies including those of Bruges, Barcelona and Borussia Monchengladbach to savour.

But Liverpool v Chelsea on May 3rd, 2005, was right up there. And the Londoners were rattled – and conceded a goal from an early piece of opportunism from Luis Garcia.

He nipped in to beat Cech, the ball was cleared as it crossed the line but Garcia, his team-mates and every single Liverpool fan in the stadium called 'GOAL' – and so, critically, did the Slovakian referee, Lubos Michel.

Bedlam. Anfield rocking, Mourinho enraged, Benitez focussed as always.

Fast forward to deep into injury time and Liverpool now hanging on, a ball breaks to Chelsea's Eidur Gudjohnsen inside the penalty area. As he struck the ball, the whole crowd held its collective breath – his shot headed goal-ward… was this to be the cruellest of European exits for the gallant Reds?

No, the ball went inches wide.

The crowd inside Anfield went berserk – BERSERK – the final whistle soon followed. Liverpool were back in *the* European final. Back where they believed they belonged.

Mourinho described his Anfield experience – and praised the Liverpool crowd. "I felt the power. It was magnificent."

I was in the directors' box, playing neutral, thinking partisan. I was absolutely thrilled but contained my excitement. But what a night – for Liverpool first and English football second

Indeed, the Reds' place in the competition's climax began a run of five consecutive finals with English participants – including an all-English final in 2008.

I also knew on my way back to London that we were a step nearer the 'impossible' problem... how to get five into four.

We had already formally written to UEFA to add weight to my informal discussions with their top-brass in Tallinn.

But still no movement from UEFA. Not for the first time or the last the Swiss-based footballing bureaucrats felt England wanted to be treated differently and more favourably than the rest of their member states. It was, they felt, a recurring theme and, I sensed, a constant source of irritation in UEFA headquarters in Nyon.

By the time the big night in Istanbul came around there was still no resolution to the issue. By now it was on the media's radar, albeit a journalistic side-bar to building up Liverpool's first appearance in Europe's major club final since that fateful night at the Heysel Stadium in 1985.

Everton had clinched the Premier League's fourth place to great acclaim, three points clear of fifth-placed Liverpool.

AC Milan – European champions on six occasions – up against Liverpool, European champions on four occasions. This was a real match-up.

Istanbul was the venue – at the Ataturk Olympic Stadium – out of town and barely finished.

It was to be the venue of Liverpool's greatest ever victory and the illustrious competition's most remarkable match.

As I headed to the stadium in a VIP coach, I allowed myself a smile and a quick trip down memory lane.

I had been to all five of Liverpool's previous European Cup finals – as a 'real' fan. Train from Lime Street to Rome in 1977 and back two days after the final had finished; 1978 Lime Street to Wembley Central; 1981 – a flight from London to Paris; 1984 – this time a flight, not a train, from London to Rome. Happy memories – and the sad ones of that fateful day in Brussels and the aftermath that followed it.

Now, as chief executive of an association providing one of the finalists, I was accorded all the privileges.

I never took it all for granted. I had done the hard yards as a genuine fan but I would also be lying if I didn't say a little of bit of luxury went a long way.

Before the game, I was mixing with the footballing world's great and good – something I always enjoyed. Talking football was never an issue for me. I could do it all day long.

And the room was full of great former players, the likes of Michel Platini and Franz Beckenbauer, both of whom had crossed swords with Liverpool in European competition in times past.

I had watched Platini in action first-hand at the 1982 World Cup in Spain when he captained his French team to the semi-finals and that remarkable tussle against West Germany in Seville.

I was literally sitting behind the goal, on broadcast duty, that night in Seville and watched Platini sweat blood for his country, ultimately to no avail.

Beckenbauer was simply one of my all-time favourite footballers, who I'd seen play twice for Bayern Munich at Anfield in the early Seventies. The classiest defender I'd ever seen... ok, this side of Alan Hansen! Both Platini and Beckenbauer were now becoming football power-brokers – and Platini would make it to the top.

Also there, another face that was to become very familiar to me a few years hence, former AC Milan player and coach, Fabio Capello (I'd see a lot more of him in the future).

After the small talk, I hit on a few UEFA officials again with the 'what happens if' argument. Again they said there was no provision for the winners of the competition to be parachuted into the following year's entry – unless the home association was prepared to substitute one team for another.

They also referenced a precedent that had actually happened in 2000 when the Spanish Federation, simply and autocratically, replaced fourth-placed Real Zaragoza with Real Madrid who had finished fifth in La Liga but won the Champions League.

I did not see a repetition of that solution in England, not with Everton and Liverpool as the potential winners and losers. No chance.

Finally it was time for the match to start.

Now thousands of words have been written about Liverpool's tumultuous win over AC Milan that night. I'll keep mine brief.

It was the most remarkable comeback you will ever see – and in a game of such importance. Stunning.

We were played off the park in the first half – it was 3-0 and it could have been more – many more.

The second-half – or six minutes of it – were the stuff of folklore. Driven on by the Reds' travelling contingent's half-time show of belief and defiance, Steven Gerrard started the ball rolling.

Something was afoot, confirmed for me when Vladimir Smicer scored – from OUTSIDE the box – followed by the Gerrard tumble and Alonso's penalty rebound goal.

Throw in Dudek's save, Shevchenko's penalty shoot-out miss and it all added up to something that is enshrined in the hearts and minds of those who witnessed it first-hand, or the many millions who had it beamed in to their front rooms.

At half-time, Michel Platini had said to me a little apologetically "Well, Brian what happens next?"

"Well," I said, "you are either going to witness the heaviest defeat in European Cup final history or the greatest comeback."

And, as I celebrated – and celebrated – as the European Cup was lifted by Steven Gerrard and my team – Platini came over and gave me that trademark Gallic shrug and smile, muttered "well done, what a game, what a comeback, fantastic... but now a problem, yes?"

Fleet Street's finest weren't slow in recognising here was a piece of football politics which would test the often fragile relationship between Liverpool, London and Geneva – and would be an early and very public test of my own negotiating skills.

The following day back in London my time was split between congratulating Liverpool on seemingly every TV and radio outlet imaginable, whilst also trying to position the argument to help Liverpool and Everton both get in – and stay in next season's competition. One team had just won the trophy itself and the other had recently gained their deserved qualification for Europe's top contest. And me, a Scouser and a Liverpudlian, had to deflect any argument of bias, whilst trying to turn around an intractable UEFA.

Rick Parry, Liverpool's CEO, threw the problem both the FA's and UEFA's way. And so we began a period of hasty negotiations with key people in Geneva. FA Chairman Geoff Thompson's quiet diplomacy and FA Executive David Davies' energy helped as did the phone calls and political pestering but the clock was ticking.

'You must have the Champions defend the trophy' we said, 'yes, and English football must only have four entrants, so make your choice of who they are,' they said.

At least, UEFA President Lennart Johansson himself seemed to be catching the wider mood. "The winner should have a chance to defend the title. We must sit down as a matter of real urgency to see if there is a fair way to make it happen."

Encouraging, but some way short of a slam-dunk. Other members of his executive board were concerned at having more than four teams from one country or changing rules in mid-flight.

The English press went on full-scale attack at UEFA's intransigence. Good copy but not particularly helpful. We, meanwhile, kept the pressure up. Phone call, followed email, followed visit – and eventually UEFA cracked.

On June 10th, they announced that Liverpool FC would be allowed to defend the title in an 'historic' one-off decision which would allow five English clubs to enter the following season's Champions League.

And that, from now on, the European Cup winners would gain automatic qualification, if need be, at the expense of the side that finished fourth in the Premier League.

William Gaillard, UEFA's obdurate spokesman described the decision as 'exceptional' because in the upcoming season England would be the only association ever, and for the last time, to have five clubs.

He also pointed out that the financial pot for English clubs would be spread five ways rather than four.

Victory in Europe – again. This time off the pitch but with it the earliest start to a season in Liverpool's history. Why? Because they were forced to begin their defence of the title at the very start of the competition – the first qualifying round.

And in the draw for those uncharted waters, Liverpool drew the minnows from Llansantffraid.

So, the story of how Welsh part-timers TNS rolled into town to play European champions Liverpool was complete.

The matches themselves were marked by a hat-trick from Steven Gerrard in the 3-0 first leg win. Gerrard had actually spent his post-Istanbul break contemplating a move away from Anfield before a twelfth hour change of mind.

Everyone connected with the club drew a collective sigh of relief – Gerrard himself added a further goal to his European tally in the 3-0 second leg win held at Wrexham's ground.

Ultimately, Liverpool weren't able to complete a successful defence of their title, being eliminated in the last 16 of the competition by Benfica, but as a Reds fan, with a rare seat at football's top table, I had helped them qualify for it – from sitting behind a desk!

3

The Second Coming

The return of Kenny Dalglish as manager of Liverpool Football Club in January 2011 just seemed timely. The club was going through a remarkable dip in form and confidence and Roy Hodgson's position had become increasingly untenable.

A good man – a proven coach – Hodgson just couldn't get it right and the Kop had seen enough. What had started as an awkward murmur in the crowd at the Northampton Carling Cup exit had become a louder cry of 'help' by the time the team was struggling through December into the New Year.

I was actually sitting next to Kenny Dalglish the first time the 'Dalglish' chants rang out and his awkwardness was palpable.

A decent man himself, Dalglish was aware of how that chant, however well-meaning, would sound, and feel, to another decent man, Hodgson.

And the chant wouldn't go away despite some fans feeling it wasn't quite the 'Liverpool way'. In the end, a miserable away defeat at Blackburn did for Hodgson and Dalglish was called back from a holiday cruise in the Middle-East to save the club from further indignities.

The rest is history. Recent history. Kenny Dalglish galvanised the whole club on his return. The players by responding with great enthusiasm and the crowd, by just underlining their affection for him. The relationship between Dalglish and the Liverpool supporters is unique and everybody is now on the same side. Liverpool is now on the right road.

My own reaction to his January comeback?

Originally, one of nervousness. I just didn't want Liverpool's best-ever player, Liverpool's Double-winning manager (and throw in scoring the title-clinching goal for good measure) and a man who'd shown immense compassion through the dark days of Hillsborough and beyond, to have that unsullied reputation cheapened by a run of indifferent football results.

Too good a man. Too good a Liverpool man. A proud family man with genuine and heartfelt respect for his adopted city.

I needn't have worried. Kenny took up the reins again like he had never been away and that trademark smile that greeted every subsequent Liverpool goal was just priceless – and a return to earlier and better times.

When Kenny arrived from Celtic in the summer of 1977, he was joining the reigning champions of Europe and replacing another Anfield great Kevin Keegan. Keegan was off to Hamburg where he would continue to impress, picking up two European Player of the Year titles.

Kenny was already 26 when he came to Anfield but he would play on until he was nearly 40. He would win silverware, lash in memorable goals, create more for others with a sweetness of touch, coax great performances out of his team-mates when elevated to his managerial post, bamboozle opponents, confound critics, confuse journalists, and leave us all just a little incapable of understanding his every word!

I have dropped in and out of Kenny's life for off and on 30 years but always felt that bit happier for having spent some time in his company. And I have been the beneficiary of numerous acts of kindness from him and Marina, his wife and rock.

As I was making my way through the ranks at the BBC it coincided with his special time at Anfield. He was a man who wouldn't suffer fools gladly, could be obtuse, answer a question with a question – he still does – BUT once you had won his trust he was on your side. And I managed to do just that.

Like many other Liverpool fans, I watched his early games for Liverpool and realised Bob Paisley had pulled off a master-stroke bringing this Scottish maestro to England.

His winning goal against Bruges in the 1978 European Cup Final was a typical piece of cool clinical finishing and his celebration – jumping over the advertising hoardings – typical of his unbridled joy at scoring.

I watched Kenny's early games for the Reds from the terraces and he very quickly convinced me that he was a special football talent. I have had the privilege of watching up-close players of the calibre of Pele, Maradona, Cruyff, Best, Platini, Van Basten, Zidane and Messi and I am comfortable in putting Kenny in that type of elite company.

The other remarkable thing about Kenny was he turned out match after match. The only rotation Kenny was involved in was turning his marker inside out. If fit, he played. Period. That meant a remarkable unbroken run of 180 games in the opening three and a bit seasons of his Liverpool career.

An early goal he scored at Anfield was against Chelsea. He had already found the net on his league debut at Middlesbrough but I remember thinking 'wow – that was a special strike' when he scored against the Londoners.

He went on to score 172 goals – goals of all shapes and sizes, with plenty more 'wows' and special strikes.

He was also a master goal-maker and his combination play with serial goalscorer Ian Rush was something to behold. The Welshman's goal against Watford from a Dalglish precision pass in the early Eighties is burnt into the memory.

By 1980, I was working at the BBC in its famous sports department – this was life before SKY and satellite television – and as a rookie, any 'edge' I possessed had to be used.

I knew Liverpool, I said, and was close to the players I said. The former was true, the latter wasn't, but I sounded convincing enough to be sent on every assignment to Anfield either for *Match of the Day* or its Saturday lunch-time preview *Football Focus*.

I lapped up my time at the BBC, worked hard, learnt from the best and turned up for everything. This was my big break and I wasn't going to blow it. One minute I was watching *Match of the Day*, next thing I was working on it. Incredible.

A burning ambition to work in the field of journalism had led me down to London and a six-month contract with the BBC. I actually stayed 18 years.

My career with them began as an assistant producer, then as producer of *Football Focus* and onwards to the highly-valued and influential role of editor of *Match of the Day* – all inside 10 years – and Kenny and Liverpool were top-dogs during this period.

I will devote some time to my spell as Editor of *Match of the Day* in later pages but whether it was choosing their fixtures to broadcast, editing their games to the right length, selecting the right interview or crafting the programme's closing images with them featured, Liverpool were 'the' television team of this era and Dalglish the main attraction.

Indeed, Kenny was always popping up on our screens.

I remember filming a lengthy feature on Bob Paisley's retirement for BBC's Sportsnight. Bob's style of verbal delivery – quite confusing at times – became a gentle, affectionate and running observation from his players, past and present.

Reporter Alan Parry raised it with Kenny.

"I believe Bob is difficult to understand."

"Pardon?" countered Kenny in a flash, who then threw his head back in a spontaneous burst of laughter!

Alan, like many defenders before him, wrong-footed by Kenny's quick wit.

*   *   *   *   *

Kenny officially moved from a player to player-manager in the immediate aftermath of the Heysel Stadium tragedy, although the news had leaked out on the morning of that ill-fated European Cup final between Liverpool and Juventus. Dalglish was to take over from Joe Fagan, who himself had brilliantly kept Paisley's winning ethos in place.

The choice of a managerial rookie instead of an experienced old-hand was a piece of inspired thinking by that powerful Liverpool duo, chairman John Smith and chief executive Peter Robinson.

And just as cannily, Kenny appointed Bob Paisley as one of his advisers. Energy and experience wrapped up in that managerial duo. He also looked to Tom Saunders for his wisdom, and Ronnie Moran and Roy Evans for their dyed-in-the-wool Liverpool 'nous'.

What Liverpool had in Dalglish, the manager, was a man with an encyclopaedic knowledge of the game, both here and abroad. He would occasionally come into the Sportsnight offices in London, where we had broadcast feeds from football all over Europe. He would watch six games at a time and have the uncanny knack of never missing a goal scored in any of them. And he seemed to know every player on every pitch.

Kenny's first season as player-manager ended gloriously as Liverpool became only the third team, to that point, to win the domestic Double – league championship and FA Cup – emulating the earlier achievements of Tottenham Hotspur and Arsenal.

He had left himself out of the side for much of the season but as the run-in began he slotted seamlessly into the team and Liverpool finished the campaign at full pelt.

On the final Saturday of the 1985/86 season, the Reds had a tricky away match at Chelsea knowing if they won it they would pip Merseyside neighbours, Everton, to the title – and just a week before they would meet each other in an FA Cup final.

Of course, it was Dalglish himself who chested the ball down and volleyed the ball into the Chelsea net. He celebrated that decisive first-half strike in typical fashion, arms outstretched and a smile as wide as the Mersey.

On the final whistle the Liverpool players celebrated in front of the visiting supporters. And I too was on the pitch. My BBC brief was to grab some of the key players for interviews live into *Grandstand*.

I was able to do just that as the team wanted to share their big moment with anybody and everybody.

As the players headed down the Stamford Bridge tunnel in triumph I followed them and knocked on their dressing room to continue my post-match brief. Suddenly a voice cried out. "Brian, come in, what do you need?" It was Kenny from inside the team's private quarters.

I took him up on his offer and found myself the only 'outsider' in the inner sanctum. Kenny gestured to me to sit next to him and I just let my professional face slip for a few moments and enjoyed a unique opportunity to share in my own team's post-match celebrations. This was the team of great characters, the likes of Bruce Grobbelaar, Alan Hansen, Mark Lawrenson, Craig Johnston, Jan Molby and Ian Rush.

And the players were absolutely cock-a-hoop with having clinched the title with a strong run-in which ultimately out-paced their chief rivals Everton and West Ham.

The atmosphere in the dressing room was electric.

Amidst all the revelry I nearly left with the ultimate souvenir. As Kenny, himself, celebrated with his team-mates he joyously ripped off his famous number seven red shirt and hurled it at me.

These were the days before shirt-swapping and the collecting craze of football memorabilia had really got underway. However, I had always been a keen collector of all things Liverpool since the early '60s – albeit mainly programmes and books.

I caught Kenny's shirt and held it for a few moments – then just as I had designs on taking it with me out of the dressing room, Ronnie Moran, the Boot Room's sergeant major, took charge of gathering all the sweat-soaked jerseys, spotted the errant shirt in my possession and swiftly took it from my grasp. Just so it could be part of the laundry probably!

Even now, over 25 years later, I still kick myself for not having vacated the Liverpool dressing room seconds earlier with *that* shirt on *that* special day.

The following week was dominated by the build-up to the all-Merseyside FA Cup Final. Everton were determined to bounce back from losing the league title in the home stretch and Liverpool were on the verge of winning the coveted Double.

I filmed a 'Merseyside week', complete with a Beatles sound-track, to open the traditional BBC *Cup Final Grandstand*.

Twenty-five minutes to try and capture the essence of the

remarkable football fever that had struck my home town as it looked forward to a 'first' all-Merseyside FA Cup final.

Yes, they had met each other at Wembley in the 1984 Milk Cup Final but coming up on Saturday was *the* final.

I had even written to Paul McCartney to suggest that it was a fantastic opportunity to re-form the Beatles for a one-off and have them perform on the pitch before the game – football and the Beatles, the ultimate Scouse occasion. No luck on that one I'm afraid.

The match itself was that well-worn cliche, a game of two halves; Gary Lineker put Everton ahead in the first half, before in the second stanza, Liverpool got back into the game with an Ian Rush short-range effort. Aussie Craig Johnston, who had allowed me to film footage of his newly-born daughter born in Cup Final week, got their second and Rush went on to score the game-clinching third, the goal that famously knocked over the camera in the net.

On the final whistle the BBC cameras still standing, zoomed into a big close-up of Kenny, on the centre-spot, arms outstretched, a huge smile – and job done!

*   *   *   *   *

The following day I joined both teams as they shared the same Boeing aircraft to travel back to Liverpool. A good idea in prospect, pre-planned in part to continue to try and publicly heal the wounds between the clubs and their supporters following Heysel and Everton's resulting exclusion from the European Cup. And, no doubt, because it was also financially prudent.

On the actual day, however, it's a fact that there was one team on board who had won the Double – and another that had lost it in the previous eight days.

The plane landed at Speke Airport and as the teams disembarked they were met by the sounds of a school band and a welcome from the Deputy Mayor of Liverpool and rabid Evertonian, Derek Hatton. The teams did the traditional tour of the city – both teams honoured by their fans who lined the whole route. Everton led the procession. There was remarkable turn-out from both sets of supporters.

I was on the Liverpool open-topped bus as it made its way slowly around the crowded streets. Once again my professional brief was to grab reactions from the players as they were feted by their supporters.

As we reached the outskirts of Childwall via Queens Drive I told Kenny how my mother stood at the same spot at the Fiveways each time either Liverpool or Everton brought the cup home.

Typically mischievous, Kenny waited his moment and as we approached he pushed me to the front of the bus and there I was next to Liverpool's all-conquering heroes and the FA Cup itself. And yes, I did then spot my mum and it took all of what was left of my professional discipline not to lift the famous trophy as she waved us by!

*   *   *   *   *

Dalglish's positive influence on Liverpool's fortunes continued – with another title in 1988 and another cup final appearance, a losing one, at the hands of the Crazy Gang of Wimbledon.

My abiding memory of the game is watching Kenny sweltering in his coat as Wembley basked in temperatures in the high 80s – and Wimbledon celebrating their unexpected victory.

Liverpool had reached that final via a semi-final win over Nottingham Forest; a comprehensive 2-1 win in front of a capacity crowd at Sheffield Wednesday's Hillsborough Stadium and a seemingly over-packed Leppings Lane end.

In an ultimately devastating twist of fate, the two teams were matched up again in the following year's semi-final – and the same stadium was allocated the match. Despite the lessons that could have been learnt from the previous year, the clubs' supporters were allocated the same ends.

The incidents that followed on that spring afternoon in 1989 are now burned into the collective consciousness of English football, and will remain a tragically defining chapter in the Anfield club's history.

I will add my own thoughts in due course but this is the moment to reflect on the compassionate and deeply-caring response to the tragedy by one man, Kenny Dalglish – and, indeed, his family.

In the aftermath of that painful day, Kenny led from the front, superbly aided by his wife, Marina. He made himself available to the bereaved and injured and did everything he could possibly do to somehow stem the pain and suffering. He was faultless in his dedication and selflessness. Whether it was spending hours listening to those who had lost loved ones, visiting the injured or attending heart-breaking funerals, Kenny was there.

His ability as a world-class footballer had never been in doubt but now he showed the more important quality of being a world-class human being.

It cemented his place in the hearts of Liverpudlians forever.

And it ultimately took its personal toll on Kenny itself – so much so that in February 1991, despite more silverware the previous season, the stresses and strains of non-stop commitment hit home and he surprised the football world by resigning from his much-coveted role at Anfield. Putting himself and his family first for once.

I phoned the Dalglish home on hearing the news and Marina took the call. Kenny had gone to the golf course with chief scout, Ron Yeats. She accepted my good wishes and I left her with a thought for Kenny that if, after a break, he wanted a platform to explain his reasons for quitting a little more fully I could provide it.

Three weeks later I got a phone call in the Sportsnight office – it was Kenny saying he was ready to go on television and explain a little more about his unexpected departure from Anfield.

He came in to the London studios, shared the first ten minutes of the programme with Des Lynam. It was an old-fashioned 'scoop' – and an illustration of the trust that had been built up. He also knew I wouldn't let him, his family or the club down by pulling a cheap stunt – and he was right.

Twenty years on, Kenny is now back at the helm of the club he is so much part of and Marina has recovered from the trials of breast cancer so positively in aiding the suffering of others.

Unassuming and totally committed.

The Anfield crowd now bellow the Dalglish chant three or four times each half and each time he returns their adulation with a salute. And a smile.

There is no need for any awkwardness now.

He is where he believes he belongs, on the touchline driving his Liverpool players on to greater things. And the Kop has got a smile back on its face.

4

Red and white in black and white

The choice of which football team you support has an air of serendipity about it... or did. When I first became aware of football, at the very start of the 1960s, your team, like your school uniform, was passed down to you.

None of this, 'I live in Cornwall but have always followed Spurs...' you became a fan of your local team, whoever it was. And that allegiance was for LIFE.

Now, I accept that idea is a little easier to bear if born and raised in one of the great footballing cities of Britain – Liverpool, Manchester, Sheffield, Birmingham, London and Glasgow and so on. But, even then, there are still choices to be made – big choices – And they too are for LIFE.

God had given me a good start by sending the stork up to Merseyside before it hit the ejector button.

However, the choice of whether I would be a Red or a Blue was still up for grabs... or nearly.

I was born in Croxteth during the close season of 1954 but before I had juggled – and burst – my first Frido ball, the Barwick family were off to live in a council house in 'leafy' Childwall.

Eastham Close became our new home and the strip of grass at the end of the road became Anfield, Goodison Park, Wembley or the Maracana, depending on which game me and my mates were replaying. Full on, no quarter asked or given, until your mum called you in for your tea!

Football was just main-lined into us all. We played it, talked about it, argued about it, fought about it… all of us under 10, but already under the spell of the great game.

This was Liverpool in the early '60s, just before the Beatles sent the city into orbit and made it – and us – world famous. It was already a city with a rich maritime history, a thriving port industry and a ready line in wit. Liverpool people were – and still are – genuinely funny.

It was also the home of two major football clubs – Everton and Liverpool, the latter having been created from the remnants of the former, when a dispute over rent sent the original team over the park to a new site called Goodison Park.

For the 70-odd years that followed, the two teams each enjoyed their own respective periods of local and national domination.

Everton, one of the original founding members of the Football League, had subsequently secured that championship on five occasions and had won the FA Cup twice; Dixie Dean, their legendary centre-forward, scoring in their 1933 FA Cup final win over Manchester City. Liverpool, founded in 1892, also had won the championship on five occasions but still had to nail 'the big one' – the FA Cup. Billy Liddell, Liverpool's post-war great, having been in the side that had lost the second of their FA Cup final appearances in 1950 to Arsenal.

When I became first cognisant with the fortunes of the two Merseyside giants, it was Everton who were enjoying the better of it.

The 'Millionaires Club' or 'School of Science' as they had become known, were in the First Division. Backed by the Moores family, and guided by manager Harry Catterick, Everton were upwardly mobile and about to enter a decade of high achievement.

Liverpool were in the Second Division and had been since 1954. They were a club that had settled for second best too – until a thunderbolt hit them.

*   *   *   *   *

Bill Shankly joined Liverpool as manager in December 1959.

His impact was simply seismic; he was a one-off, a football nut, dedicated, determined and decisive. He wanted the best for his new club, and nothing – nothing – would stop him in that quest.

He also had a unique rapport with the fans. Indeed, he was one of them, and reminded his players of their responsibility to those self-same people every day of his working life.

The Merseyside scene was set for a period of high drama, high excitement and high expectation.

All I, Brian Barwick, aged seven, of Rudston Road County Primary School, had to do was to pick which team was going to be mine.

My father, John, was a sports fan, Liverpool-born and a follower of the Reds – but in a gentle way. He didn't go to every game and didn't turn every conversation in our home around to football. He also loved his boxing, horse-racing and had even taken in a bit of speedway in his early life when watching the Liverpool Chads and Pirates scorch around the red shale track at the Stanley Stadium back in the 1950s.

One claim to fame my dad did have was that he ultimately made more appearances at Anfield than the collective total run up by the likes of Jackie Whitham, David Speedie, Salif Diao and Paul

Konchesky, because part of his regular police duties were to walk around the pitch with his fellow officers as the Reds played out their home league and cup games.

Spotting my early interest in the game, he would often bring me home that day's programme, an errant rosette and rattle or a set of away team's autographs – in so doing he inadvertently started me off on a collecting bug that has never gone away.

My dad would also be on duty at Liverpool (and Everton's) reserve team home games. Much less well attended than their senior equivalents, these games often provided him with an opportunity to take my older brother, David and I, with him.

Having checked in with his senior officer, my dad would then have David and I stand in the same spot every time and just before kick-off he would come out from the Main Stand and say: 'Oi, you two, come here... I want a word with you!'

On that command, we would walk slowly towards him in well-rehearsed fashion and then in an instant we would be spirited down the players' tunnel and into the ground to watch the match. It probably made me and my brother a very unique pair because, departing from normal convention, we were actually being escorted INTO the ground by the police!

When off work, my dad would occasionally take us to either Anfield or Goodison to see the city's top two teams. It is difficult to pin down the actual first game I saw at Anfield but everything points to it being Liverpool v Leyton Orient on October 28, 1961. Final score 3-3. I was a little bit spoilt and must have left the stadium thinking every game had six goals in it!

I just about remember sitting in the old Main Stand watching that game and I still have the match programme. Mind you, that's not anything special because I now have the programme from every home game Liverpool have played since that match – nearly 50 years worth. Collecting football programmes – Liverpool's games home and away – has become a pastime that has brought me lots of satisfaction.

I now have a formidable collection including all the various cup finals they have played in down the years, as well as many issues from games played all over the world.

I have also obtained some of the club's earliest programmes dating back to the opening seasons of their 119-year existence, including a copy of the programme printed to mark Liverpool's first-ever home game against Rotherham Town on September 1st, 1892.

Thousands of programmes, hundreds of books, autographs, balls, and shirts – my collection has mushroomed over the years and represents an instant history and colourful reminder of the major moments in the Reds' illustrious past.

Back in 1961, it was still unclear whether that collection was going to be Red or Blue. But something clicked during that season, the dye was cast red and whether through dad's quiet influence or my own early gut instinct I plumped for Liverpool – despite the team being in an inferior league to their Merseyside rivals – and I've never had cause to regret it.

*   *   *   *   *

I chalked up another league game in my debut season – against Preston North End – before celebrating Liverpool's much-awaited promotion back to the top-flight. The Reds were back in the big time after an eight-year absence.

By then, I had already caught the school playground craze of collecting ABC bubble gum football cards (...I'll swap you my Kevin Lewis for your Ronnie Moran...), started putting together my first scrapbook, kept my 'League Ladders' bang up to date, was becoming a dab hand at blow football (*Subbuteo* was to follow later) and, of course, tuned in to the end of *Grandstand* every Saturday at 'twenty to five' to hear the click, click, click of the teleprinter as David Coleman guided us through the day's final scores. It was compulsive television and a precursor of everything similar that has followed it.

I still remember the first Saturday in January, 1962, when this FA Cup third round scoreline came stuttering through... *Liverpool 4... Chelsea...* (Barwick family holds bated breath!) ...*3* (phew!). It all sounds terribly twee now, but then it was edge of the settee stuff!

Armed with a pair of football boots crowned with huge toe-caps, shin-pads that could stop a silver bullet and a flimsy red shirt, V-necked and short-sleeved – just like Roger Hunt's – I was ready for action in whatever game our strip of grass would replicate.

I was already completely and utterly hooked.

Just like the young teenager who is brought into the first team to get some vital experience and then dropped back into the reserves to continue his football education so it was for young Liverpool supporters like me in the early '60s.

Sure, there were those who short-circuited the system and went straight to Anfield's famous boys' pen but equally there were plenty, like the rising young stars, who mixed a regular diet of reserve team football with the occasional outing with the first team.

Liverpool were now back in the First Division and the much-awaited first league derby match for eight years was upon us. There had been odd FA Cup ties, Lancashire and Liverpool Senior Cup ties, matches to mark the new era of floodlit football, but the first league derby was the real deal.

Seventy two thousand fans crowded into Goodison Park to watch the Merseyside rivals play out an exciting 2-2 draw – Roger

Hunt popping up with a last gasp equaliser. Big black and white photographs of that game from Monday's *Daily Post* found their way straight into my latest scrap-book.

My own Saturday afternoon had actually been spent at Anfield watching the 'mini-derby' as it was called – Liverpool Reserves v Everton Reserves – all part of the 'education'. I'd watched the Reds beat the Blues 2-0 with goals from George Scott and Alf Arrow-smith.

George Scott never quite made it at Liverpool, but as he left Anfield to continue his career at Aberdeen, he was boosted by Bill Shankly's view that George was "the 12th best player in the world... there's the Liverpool first team then you, son, because you are leading scorer in the reserves at the greatest club in the world." With such wonderfully absurd logic, Shankly could have run the country let alone a football club.

I had become something of a regular at Liverpool's reserve games and whilst revering the marquee names of Hunt, St John, Callaghan and Yeats, the signatures going into my autograph book were the likes of Scott, Bobby Graham, Phil Ferns, Gordon Wallace and a couple of up and coming youngsters named Smith and Lawler!

I watched the second strings of the likes of Manchester United, Bolton Wanderers, Wolves and West Brom and at the end of the season chalked up my first cup final, as Liverpool and West Ham met in the two-legged FA Youth Cup final.

My attendance at the first leg at Anfield completed my first full season's 'education'. I'd followed the first team through mono-chrome television clips and newspaper back pages – my black and white Reds if you like – but watched the reserves in full glorious colour.

Bill Shankly had taken Liverpool through a comfortable first sea-son back in the top-flight. They finished eighth in the league, and in a season ravaged by the harshest winter for years, went close to reaching their first FA Cup final since 1950.

Wins over Wrexham, the previous year's FA Cup finalists, Burnley, Arsenal and West Ham set up a semi-final against Leicester City, a side that were to become our 'bogey team' in the early days of our return to top-flight English football.

These were the days when both semi-finals were played alongside each other with Saturday three o'clock kick-offs – and no live television coverage. So, once again, it was to David Coleman, *Grandstand* and that blessed teleprinter we turned to with trepidation to hear the vital outcomes.

Click, click, and click... FA Cup semi-final. Manchester United 1 Southampton 0... FA Cup semi-final. Leicester City 1... click, click and click... Liverpool 0.

Close but no cigar. Liverpool had fallen at the final hurdle on their Road to Wembley. Two years later they would make no mistake.

Another rather interesting by-product of that season's visits to Anfield was my first introduction to the art of full-blooded swearing!

As the crowds at the reserve games were small, I usually parked myself near the dug-outs trying to advance my football education – and usually spent 90 minutes listening to a whole new version of the English language!

Whilst I wasn't conversant with every word I just knew if I repeated those same words – adjectives, verbs and nouns, at home I'd be sent straight to bed without my nightly drink of Ribena and copy of the Beano...

B*****ks!

5

The King's Speech

Doing justice to Bill Shankly in print is the ultimate challenge. Like trapping the North Wind in a bottle... or actually being that snowball in hell – it is an impossible task.

Shankly was Liverpool, Liverpool was Shankly. For me, the gritty Scottish genius from Glenbuck in Ayrshire is the defining figure in Liverpool Football Club's history.

That, in itself, is a statement of intent from this writer because it places in his wake all those that went before him – the club's visionary founding fathers, great players either side of two World Wars, inspirational team managers and unique supporters – and also all those that have followed him; record-breaking managers, local and foreign; world-class footballers, local and foreign, the club's owners, local and foreign and, of course, the new generations of the Reds' loyal supporters, also local and foreign.

Bill Shankly was unique. From the moment he arrived at Anfield in 1959, his determination was to shake the club from its lethargy, its lack of ambition – indeed, its lack of running water at the Melwood training ground!

Shankly was simply a complete football man, a one-off, a larger than life disciple of the game – and a man about to embark on a mission to make Liverpool great again. Shankly had spent his playing career at Carlisle United and Preston North End, where he made nearly 300 appearances. He had also been a very proud Scottish international.

His managerial career had begun in March, 1949 at Carlisle United and then had taken him to Grimsby Town and Workington before he landed the job at Huddersfield Town in December 1955. He spent four years there, and had a young Ray Wilson and a precocious Denis Law under his wing, before Liverpool showed their interest in him.

Law would ultimately be a major star for Manchester United but, at the time of Shankly's departure from Huddersfield, may well have thought he would follow his fellow Scotsman to Anfield – and thus have re-written history. Wilson, of course, did make it to Merseyside, but to Everton, not Shankly's Liverpool.

It is believed that Everton chairman, Sir John Moores, who also had a soft spot for Liverpool, and Manchester United manager and ex- Liverpool star Matt Busby, had guided the Liverpool board towards the appointment of Bill Shankly. And so Reds chairman, T.V. Williams went to see Shankly at Huddersfield and asked him to help make Liverpool great again.

And Shankly agreed. His last match in charge of Huddersfield was, ironically, a 1-0 home win over Liverpool on November 28, 1959. Two days later he was appointed by Liverpool and soon his vision for the future and his scale of ambition for the club was unveiled.

"My idea was to build Liverpool into a bastion of invincibility. Napoleon had that idea. He wanted to conquer the bloody world. I wanted Liverpool to be untouchable. My idea was to build Liverpool up and up until eventually everyone would have to submit, give in."

No sense of purpose then!

His early signings gave the football world a feeling of where Shankly wanted to take his new club. Two young Scotsmen came south of the border and delivered a combined service of nearly 900 games for their new club.

The acquisition of Ron Yeats, tall and strong, and Ian St John, compact and clever, stamped Shankly's passport for a brighter future at Liverpool.

In Eric Sawyer, Shankly critically, had a like-minded individual sitting on the Anfield board and he also led from the front in supporting the new manager's expansionist plans.

Sawyer's famous response to the board's cautious view on the prospective Yeats and St John's deals: "Can we afford to do it?" was clinical. "We can't afford not to do it!" he exclaimed.

There have been many famous words and phrases borne of life at Anfield, Liverpool 4, but not many as far-sighted as that sentence from Sawyer.

As well as bringing in top talent from elsewhere in the football family, Shankly also nurtured the best of what was already there. The likes of Gerry Byrne, Ian Callaghan and Roger Hunt were all given a chance to blossom and ultimately to collectively play over 1,600 games for Liverpool.

A near-miss in 1960/61 was followed by promotion the next year and Shankly had achieved the first objective: the return of First Division football. On route to becoming Second Division champions they scored 99 goals and finished eight points clear of Leyton Orient.

It gave Shankly a chance to lock horns with the other leading managers of the time – Double-winning Bill Nicholson at Spurs, canny Harry Potts at high-flying Burnley; his long-time friend and Manchester United legend, Matt Busby and Everton's own new man, Harry Catterick.

Catterick himself got off to a great start with the Toffees, winning the League Championship in 1962/63 and what followed over the next few years was a period of joint high achievement on either side of Stanley Park.

With Tottenham slowly relinquishing their domestic supremacy, it was left to the two Merseyside clubs, the two Manchester clubs and Don Revie's rising Leeds United to broadly contest the top honours over the rest of the Swinging Sixties.

And the two managers at the Merseyside clubs cut very different characters. Shankly, track-suited, Catterick, lounge-suited; Shankly, a man of many words, Catterick, a man of few; Shankly an extrovert, Catterick an introvert. What they had in common was the ability to pick good players, field strong and consistent line-ups and win football matches. Plenty of them.

It was a good habit to share. The local and national press also built up the rivalry between the two men – and both did little to quell the fire. They respected each other... 'liked' is probably too strong.

The atmosphere in Liverpool in the early '60s was electric; the Beatles had become a pop phenomenon. Having honed their stage-craft in The Cavern and during long- playing stints in Hamburg, the Fab Four were now the biggest name in the business and still are nearly 50 years later.

The success of the Beatles spurred a whole new export industry from the port of Liverpool – the Mersey Sound. Group upon group chased the Beatles up the charts and off around the country. The Searchers, the Merseybeats and Gerry and the Pacemakers were just three groups who stormed the new music scene.

The latter, of course, would become enshrined in Liverpool legend by turning a Rodgers and Hammerstein musical torch-song from Carousel into the finest and most enduring football anthem in the world.

Football, music and also comedy were helping lift Liverpool above the crowd. Ken Dodd played a record-breaking season in London's West End and Jimmy Tarbuck 'borrowed' the theatre once a week to compere one of ITV's most iconic shows, *Sunday Night at the London Palladium*.

Liverpool was a city with a swagger to it, and Bill Shankly, with his Jimmy Cagney stance, just fitted the space and time.

And although he seemed keen to work without a contract he was building the foundations of a dynasty at Anfield. When he eventually put pen to paper so had the likes of Willie Stevenson, Gordon Milne and classy winger Peter Thompson.

The club's first league championship title since 1947 was landed in the 1963/64 season. The landmark success was clinched with a 5-0 win over Arsenal in April.

As well as over 48,000 spectators, a camera crew from the BBC's prestigious current affairs programme *Panorama* was at Anfield to capture the new 'Mersey Sound' – the Kop, at full belt, with its growing repertoire of songs and its swaying, tumbling and unique exuberance. A truly amazing sight and sound.

Thirty years later I made a documentary on the history of the Kop as it was closed as a 'standing' terrace. Amongst all the archive film I dug out from the BBC archives was that original *Panorama* report with its arcane narration and slightly patronising delivery. The pictures and sound of the Kop were mesmeric – and during hours of spooling the film footage backwards and forwards I spotted a very young Stan Boardman giving 'She Loves You' all he could. For the documentary I took the comedian back to that exact spot and captured his memories of those special times.

By now, my own interest and commitment to Liverpool was total and the balance of first team to reserve team games was growing steadily. I had almost earned my first team place.

And I was also totally bought into Bill Shankly – and still am.

Nowadays, I quite often get asked to speak at business conventions and such-like about leadership and management and I always talk about the different styles of those skills I have come across in my own personal and professional life. Shankly is always one of a select group of people I talk about.

The Scotsman, with that rasping vocal delivery, inspired both players and supporters alike to believe that Liverpool were the 'greatest football club in the world' and we all talked that little bit more proudly about our team.

Achievements on the field backed up his confident appraisal. FA Cup winners in 1965, the club's first season in European competition, the Anfield humbling of the great Inter Milan, the League Championship of 1966, and a first European final – the European Cup Winners Cup final, his eye for a future great player – the likes of Emlyn Hughes and Kevin Keegan – all these things gave Shankly and his team an air of invincibility.

And I, like many others, had become a supporter of, and was influenced by, the swagger of Bill Shankly. His style, his focus, his respect for the fans – and, most importantly, his team were making being a Liverpool fan great fun.

One of the unusual features of that period was the opportunity we had to get close to the star players and key staff. Sure, the days of the players and the supporters sharing the same bus to the match were well-gone but compared to the relative chasm that exists now between the game's stars and their followers, things were far more accessible and accommodating.

For instance, each half-term holiday over several seasons, my mate Andy Proudfoot and I would head off to the West Derby district of Liverpool, on the 68 Corporation bus, and arrive at our destination: Melwood, Liverpool's training ground. Without fail, we would be allowed in to watch the club's playing staff train.

Surprisingly, there would probably be only another 50 or so youngsters who shared the same idea and so with those manageable numbers we were able to watch our heroes arrive at the ground by coach from Anfield and then go through their training drills, shuttle runs, heading practice and five-a-sides before they jogged off for a welcome cuppa, an eager posse of autograph hunters on their trail, then the coach back to Anfield.

Shankly had turned Melwood into one of the most advanced training centres of its time. "Melwood means more to me than any other part of Liverpool" he would say. It was where he honed his team's attitude and ability, put them through their paces and sent them to the 'sweat-box' – a four-sided wooden shooting range used to sharpen up their touch and technique. It was his 'office'.

For youngsters like Andy and me being in and around it all for a brief time was just fantastic and made all the more special because without fail Bill Shankly, himself, would come out of the dressing room area and walk over to us have a quick chat, sign an autograph or pose for a photograph. "Morning, boys," he would say, "Thanks for coming to see the lads train. Been a good session so far. Get yourselves over to the sweat-box and see how they're doing for me. Now who wants what?"

To this day, I use those small gestures of a great and busy man, as an illustration of how making a special effort for people will be paid back time and time again.

Those brief interchanges with Shankly took place over 40 years ago but they are still amongst my childhood's most endearing and vivid memories.

I would race home with a book full of autographs, a head full of dreams and a conversation for tea-time. "What did you get up to today?" my mum would say. "Oh, went to Melwood and had a chat with Bill Shankly." I would say with a casual air...

Shankly was not just a master of small-talk but a quite brilliant orator. His public utterances were pure gold-dust whether made to the local newspaper, national television and radio or just the man in the street.

His value to today's media would be simply priceless. "Fifty million for Torres? Christ, son, at today's prices that wouldn't have been enough to buy Tom Finney's standing leg!"

And I think his view of football agents, foreign ownership of clubs, the size of transfer fees and the scale of players' wages would be worth listening to – and, no doubt, somebody is, and getting both barrels in that Boot Room in the sky!

Shankly was at his best when he was talking to the people he cared most about – his family, his players and his public.

A most vivid recollection of mine is hearing first-hand his simply magnificent speech to the 250,000 Liverpool fans who cheered the team home after their 2-1 FA Cup Final defeat against Arsenal in 1971.

This was the first big test for Shankly's 'second' team who were a new side put together following the Reds' critical FA Cup quarter-final loss at Watford the previous year.

If Shankly had a fault it was that his loyalty to his players meant he had probably kept some of them in his first team longer than other managers would have. He found it difficult to make those decisions which would effectively end the careers of players who had served him and the club so well.

A year on, the team of Lawrence, Yeats and St John had become a team of Clemence, Lloyd and Toshack (and Keegan's arrival was around the corner).

Add a couple of graduates, Brian Hall and Steve Heighway and you could sense a new era was taking shape.

Shanks tried everything in his power to help his young side in their first big test, the FA Cup final against Arsenal. My former broadcast colleague and Arsenal great, Bob Wilson, told me how the Gunners went to Wembley Stadium the day before the final – and while they were there it started raining heavily.

They left the pitch quickly but not before a guy standing on his own in the Wembley tunnel had managed to say: "Hi Bob, how's it going, terrible surface for goalkeepers isn't it?"

The man, Bill Shankly, just trying a bit of psychological one-up-manship ahead of the following day's game.

The team ultimately came up just short at Wembley but the Liverpool public still came out in huge numbers to see them when they returned to the city. And Shankly didn't miss his opportunity.

Hushing a singing, chanting and boisterous crowd by simply putting his arms out for quiet – he got it in an instant – his speech was then brilliantly well-measured.

"At Wembley we lost the Cup. But you, the people, have won everything. I have always drummed into my players time and time again that they are playing for you, the greatest public. If they did not believe it then, they will now.

"It's questionable if Chairman Mao could have arranged such a show of Red strength as you have shown yesterday and today."

It was simply brilliant. The King's Speech.

* * * * *

A couple of years later I was studying for an Economics degree at the University of Liverpool, and one term Bill Shankly was booked in as a guest speaker at the Law Faculty Society's monthly meeting. It is fair to say that I wasn't a regular attendee at the Law Society meeting. In fact, I had never been before and have never been since.

But I wasn't going to miss Shankly in full flow and nabbed a front row seat for my one and only appearance.

The lecture theatre was absolutely full to bursting for the Liverpool manager's appearance – and, to be fair, not everybody was a fan – or indeed a law student! But this was a session that usually had a great legal 'star' at the lectern not a mere sporting mortal.

Shankly sensed this too, and trod his way carefully through the opening few minutes of his talk and gradually won his doubters over. Mind you, the rest of us were cheering his every word and soon he had the whole room eating out of his hands.

He was a unanimous hit. Shankly had delivered a typical virtuoso performance.

He talked about his childhood, his early days in football, his work ethic and gave his views on team building, team spirit, and team bonding – only he used real words not the corporate jargon of today. Shankly was there for two and a half hours, and by the end, you could hear a pin drop and the doubters were his biggest fans.

Peter Robinson once said that what shone through in Shanks was his gleaming honesty – and on this occasion this was clearly the case.

Many modern politicians would have loved his grasp of how to deliver a strong and emotive message to an audience. But how many politicians would have received such a positive response?

On the field his new team was going places. Kevin Keegan was proving an inspirational signing and his combination with Toshack was becoming deadly. Emlyn Hughes, Tommy Smith and Ian Callaghan added experience – and others played their part too.

Finally, it all came together in April in the space of six days, with a vital win over close rivals Leeds United and a goalless draw with Leicester City confirming Liverpool as the league champions for 1972/73. It was the club's first silverware for seven years – a long wait.

The rapturous reception for the team that day was only topped by one other – the reception for Bill Shankly when he walked out onto the pitch at the end of the Leicester game. The crowd roared *'We want Shankly, we want Shankly'* until he finally emerged.

His post-match celebratory appearance was always a highlight – I admired the players but I 'loved' Bill Shankly. I struggle to think of anybody who has made a similar impact on me. He led from the front, a lesson I took from him and tried to use in my own working life.

He walked around the ground with his players, arms outstretched – and as he finally reached the Kop it went into total frenzy. Famously he picked up a scarf that was on the ground, pointing out to an adjacent police officer that "it isn't just a scarf, it's somebody's life!"

UEFA Cup final success followed closely behind the championship win. Shanks had got 'his' own double – and his first European trophy. A year later, it was Wembley and an FA Cup final win over Newcastle United. Well, I say a win – an annihilation more like – three second-half goals and a fourth dubiously ruled out gave Liverpool and Shankly a second FA Cup success. He out-smarted his great old pal, Joe Harvey, the Newcastle manager, who in unique Wembley cup final style was sitting alongside him on the bench.

They had featured earlier in the day on *Cup Final Grandstand* from their respective hotels and Shankly had given an ebullient performance.

A split-screen of the two men had a Kennedy/Nixon moment

about it – Shankly all smiles, Harvey, distracted and agitated. It set the tone for the day.

During the match itself one brilliant camera shot caught Bill sweeping his arms to the left and right with great and positive purpose. Here was Bill conducting his orchestra, making his players follow his mental baton and directing them to victory. Sweet music.

At the end, the players did the traditional lap of honour and we all went mad at the tunnel end of the stadium, but the cameras sought out shots of Shankly, Liverpool's unique manager and they were rewarded when two supporters leapt across the barriers and were captured kissing the great Scotsman's feet.

A little bit excessive sure at this distance now, but then Shankly stirred these emotions in his loyal followers.

As always the fans' adulation for Shankly was genuinely heartfelt and the homecoming triumphant. An estimated 500,000 people came out to welcome him and his team home and, once again, the trophy cabinet was replenished as he addressed his followers with great warmth and presence.

"We have had many great moments at Liverpool Football Club during the last few seasons. I think today I feel prouder than I have ever done before."

Then came one of football's big shocks.

* * * * *

I was busy doing a shift at my summer holiday job in the famous Schofield's Lemonade factory in Dalrymple Street off Scotland Road. It was a daily test of personal bravery as the regular employees tested their student 'casuals' by hurling fully loaded crates of fizzy pop at them at the pace of Dennis Lillee!

'Catch 'em and then stack 'em,' was the foreman's simple instruction followed by a broad wink to his staff – armed and ready for the day's first over.

One by one these crates would come whizzing at you full pelt and you had to 'catch 'em and stack 'em' on the top of a lorry for hours on end and, of course, show 'no fear or no pain' even if you thought your head, hands or arms were going to fly off with the crates at any time. Character building stuff, as they say...

I left that factory later that summer to re-join university life vowing never to drink another glass of lemonade in my life ever again, such were the painful memories! Anyway I digress.

On one July lunch-time – July 12th, to be exact – I was on board the out-going lorry, ducking the fizzy bouncers being hurled at me when a bloke raced in and shouted: "Have you heard... absolutely amazing... Bill Shankly has retired."

A crate of dandelion and burdock hit the deck...

"He's done what?!" I said.

He repeated his bit of genuinely sensational 'breaking news'. Another crate of dandelion and burdock smashed on the floor!

I was simply stunned, speechless, saddened and thousands of other Liverpool fans were the same. Shankly was Liverpool and Liverpool was Shankly.

And it was true. Shanks and the Liverpool board had just ended a press conference and the craggy Scotsman, honorary Scouser, had taken the walk, as he framed it, to the 'electric chair' and stood down from the manager's job at Anfield.

I took the rest of the day off. I just couldn't get my head around it. There was only one subject in the pubs of Liverpool that Friday evening.

It would seem Shanks had just got to a point in his life where he was tired of the stresses, strains and expectations of being Bill

Shankly, football manager. He was 60.

He was also keen to put his wife, Nessie, first for once. And we reluctantly accepted we had to slip back in the pecking order.

Earlier that summer, Shankly and his wife had been down to Buckingham Palace where he had deservedly received his OBE – in truth, nothing but a knighthood – ok, sainthood, would have satisfied his adoring Red public. Now he was in the headlines again for a completely unexpected reason.

There had been attempts to keep Shankly from stepping down. Certainly Liverpool's brilliant administrator Peter Robinson had tried everything, including a range of options, from him having a rest and returning refreshed, or being retained as a consultant or even as General Manager. Anything to keep him in 'the family' but Shankly's mind was made up.

It probably wasn't just one thing, but his own tiredness, and his known ambivalence for boardroom politics and politicians were contributory factors. Anyway, whether it was a single reason or a combination of circumstances, Liverpool were losing their greatest asset – the ultimate game-changer.

As Peter Robinson expected, and indeed had told Shankly, the self-confessed football nut found his post-Anfield time personally and professionally difficult, as did the remaining Anfield hierarchy. His daily trips to Melwood slowly diminished. They were awkward for those he had left behind – and things had to move on.

Whatever the rights and wrongs of it, Shankly became a man who, more often than not, chose to watch his football away from his spiritual home rather than be there to witness 'his' team – no longer under his spell. Indeed, he often felt he got a warmer welcome when visiting other clubs – certainly 'upstairs'.

Shankly's fame and fervour obviously did cast a long shadow for those who followed in his footsteps. They had to get on with the job. And they did. And did it rather well.

Shankly led the team out at the FA Charity Shield, had an emotional testimonial, took time out to actually stand and watch a game from the Kop and kept busy talking football with all his old and new friends in the game. But his great influence gradually and naturally diminished.

Poignantly, in 1977 when the Paisley-led Liverpool brought their first European Cup back to an exultant city-centre, Shankly was on the extreme edge of the victor's balcony, left of centre-stage.

Bill Shankly died on September 29th, 1981, aged just 68 – one of football's giants taken far too early.

I had the privilege of attending his memorial service held at Liverpool Cathedral and it was a fitting mix of the famous and the fans. Former team-mate Tom Finney spoke, as did some of his former players and Ian St John gave the address. Gerry Marsden's emotional rendition of the Kop's own hymn of hope, 'You'll Never Walk Alone', fittingly closed the service.

At Anfield itself, the Shankly Gates and the life-like statue erected outside the Kop are two fitting lasting memorials to his greatness as a Liverpool manager.

Perhaps more important is that every time a Liverpool team takes to the field they take a little bit of Bill Shankly on the pitch with them.

His legacy of what is expected from a LIVERPOOL team lives on. And, no doubt, will for many years to come.

Liverpool was Shankly, Shankly was Liverpool. His standards, his honesty, his energy, his enthusiasm, his integrity and his love for the club – and, most importantly, for the people who follow it, will last forever.

6

Faints, feints
and fumbles

September 1965 was a big month in my life. Firstly, I started at a new school – Quarry Bank High School for Boys – and secondly, I started to go and watch Liverpool's home games on a regular basis.

The new school was a whole new adventure. From being the eldest boys at our primary school, Rudston Road, we were now the youngest; clearly visible by our gauche looks, short trousers and brand spanking new school uniforms.

My brother David was already at the school and was about to start in his fourth year, so via garden fetes and school plays I had been a regular visitor to my new academic home but now it was for real. I was a pupil.

Quarry Bank was a famous school with a formidable list of old boys, the best known being the late, great John Lennon.

His time at Quarry had been lively, and it is fair to say, he hadn't always been the model pupil but when I arrived at the school's premises in Harthill Road to begin my secondary education, having a Beatle as one of the school's former pupils was seriously sexy.

As well as John Lennon, no less than three Labour cabinet ministers in the 1970s have hailed from the school and in sport, Joe Royle, the great Everton centre-forward scored goals for fun for the school first XI whilst being denied a chance to play for Liverpool Schoolboys. Steve Coppell, of Manchester United and England fame, would follow in Joe's footballing footsteps.

Getting used to a new school was a challenging experience. New mates, new teachers, new subjects and new experiences. Like the journey to school.

Quarry Bank's day started with school assembly at 8.30am which meant a super early start in the Barwick household. Breakfast was followed by a short walk, two buses and another short walk – about 45 minutes in all on a good (and dry) day. Longer at other times.

It is only now I reflect on the fact that every school day must have involved a wake-up call well on the 'wrong' side of seven o'clock in the morning.

The upside of an early start was an early finish – shortly after 3pm – which meant that, transport permitting, I'd be back home an hour later.

Anyway, my secondary education was underway. As was a greatly increased number of visits to Anfield to see my heroes.

As a youngster, you are never party to the conversations that your parents have that help 'direct the traffic' in your life but undoubtedly there had been one such conversation about my growing desire to be a 'regular' supporter of the Reds. Not just the reserves and an occasional first team game but a commitment every other week at Anfield.

Conversations were had (I think the fact I was now in secondary school was key) and so it was decreed I could start going regularly, accompanied by my dad, my mum or my brother. Fine.

Next – where in the stadium. The boys' pen was ruled out. No complaints from me on that one. The Kop was considered too dangerous for me. No complaints from me on that one either. The decision, after much careful aforethought, was a slot in the Paddock, the low-level terracing that ran the length of the Anfield pitch. Spot on. And so from September, 1965, through until the early 1970s and a move to the Kop, my 'spec' was established.

And because of my route to the match – bus from Bowring Park to the Rocket, bus or walk to Old Swan and then a 'Football Special' bus from Old Swan to Anfield, I came up to the ground from the Priory Road end and therefore entered the Paddock nearer the Anfield Road than the Kop.

My 'spec' – on the edge of the 18-yard box at the Anfield Road end of the Paddock – halfway up, halfway along, was sorted. And became special to me.

And my matchday routine was also taking shape. Play football for the school on Saturday morning (occasionally in the first team, invariably not); race home, gobble down lunch – sausage roll, chips and beans followed by a cream cake; watch BBC's *Football Preview* with Sam Leitch, don my beloved red and white scarf, with attendant sewn-on patches and pin badges, grab my quarter pound bag of wine gums – an ever-present – enough pocket money for entrance fee, bus fares, match programme and a hot or cold drink. And then off to the match...

It was the real start of a Saturday afternoon love affair which is still flourishing today. I loved going to 'the match' – and always will do. It is a constant in an ever-changing world.

A single football season straddles all four seasons and the changing weather this country throws up – you'd start the season in a T-shirt, then move to a light jacket, then a mac, then a 'great bear' of a coat, then a mac, then a light jacket, then a T-shirt... before a pair of trunks on holiday before the football started all over again!

And, of course, you develop your matchday habits, your superstitions, your likes and your dislikes, your favourite and least favourite players, your favourite and least favourite opponents, your favourite (or least favourite) referee, your favourite chants, your favourite grounds and so on and so forth.

Great isn't it?

And so in 1965, my world of watching my 'black and white heroes' was about to burst into colour – RED.

Everything about a match day was exciting. All the games kicked off at 3pm and by 'twenty to five' we had a new league table. These were the days of a ten minute half-time, one substitute apiece – for injury only – and very little added time. And nobody moaned.

No live TV games, limited TV highlights, goals you saw scored were locked away in your own memory bank and not replayed a thousand times and heroes were moulded by you and not by a marketing team creating their brand.

Listen, I am a huge advocate for many of the changes that have taken place in modern football and the way it is brilliantly captured live on television.

I have also been a beneficiary of the game's remarkable growth. Equally, I'm about to hit on a bit of nostalgia so please allow me that indulgence.

*   *   *   *   *

I am glad I watched my football as a lad when I did. It wasn't in your face 24/7 – but my love of it was – and still is.

There are many differences on the 'then and now' register and that's before we get into the price of admission!

My memory is of arriving at the stadium about 90 minutes before the kick-off, finding your place (remember we were standing up) and then contributing to the racket around the ground as the time passed towards kick-off.

You got to know the guy who stood next to you, knew what time he would arrive and what his view would be on certain players, good, bad or indifferent. The atmosphere would be special and at Anfield, sometimes simply spectacular.

It was part of the sheer theatre of the occasion. One of the things I really do miss now is the crowd's own build-up. Sure, the players warm up but the fans don't.

And that bit of football has been lost forever.

These days supporters scuttle to their seats minutes before or, indeed, after the game gets underway. Forty-odd years ago the crowd had been in the ground for well over an hour singing and swaying to their favourite songs and chants – and at Anfield that was truly, truly special.

Back then, the first time you saw the players of either side was at five to three; no shuttles, sprints, twists and turns, bibs and cones, 20 minutes before. And the two teams would come out at different times for the match itself.

The away team would invariably emerge from the tunnel first to good-natured booing (and, in truth, less good natured if they turned towards the Kop end).

Then, like a world heavyweight boxing champion awaiting his moment, the home team – Liverpool – would emerge, resplendent in all-red, confident, committed, a crack squad with Shankly's final words of encouragement swirling around their heads. It was the best moment of the week – until they scored the first goal that is!

And, of course, all we youngsters were green with envy as the same lad got stripped to his Liverpool kit in the dugout every week and came out with the team as their mascot.

Warm-up was also a slice of cabaret, laced with the pungent

smell of liniment. Ian St John played keepy-uppies juggling the ball on his head; Peter Thompson continually repeated the thigh/ knee/foot routine with a willing leather ball; Roger Hunt and Ian Callaghan would practise their short sprints whilst captain, Ron Yeats, would try and stretch his shirt sleeves over his wrists and hands before making his way up to the halfway line for the toss-up.

This, too, was part of the theatre because if Yeats won the toss we knew the Reds would attack the Kop end in the second half. If the opposition won the toss they had a choice. Attack the Kop in the first half and keep the natural order of things or get Liverpool to attack the Kop in the first half and throw the home team's equilibrium. Either way we were ready with our observations!

The game would then get underway and if Liverpool kicked off they would start the same way every time – two short passes and a long ball to the left wing. I never saw us score a goal from that move in all the time I watched it happen.

As the first half progressed, the guy selling *Wrigley's Spearmint* and *Doublemint* from a tray would walk along the touchline – and like a slip fielder, catch coins thrown from the crowd before propelling a pack of chewing gum back in the same direction with unerring accuracy. A modern-day quarter-back could not have topped this performance.

At half-time the scores were displayed on either side of the ground via alphabetical wooden boards, one running alongside the wall of the Paddock, the other along the Kemlyn Road. Each letter signified a specific game, with the code in the programme – but the real fun came when a goalless first half at a game depicted by a letter M gave us MOON and, of course, a 0-0 half-time score elsewhere could give us a POO. Small things amuse...

During half-time two little guys – former fly-weight boxers I presume – would be either end of an elongated sandwich board which advertised the coming attractions at the famous Liverpool Stadium, whether it was the latest Johnny Cooke or Alan Rudkin fight or extolling the virtues of the coming week's Friday night *All-Star Wrestling* programme featuring the likes of Mr Jackie 'TV' Pallo or the legendary Kendo Nagasaki – mask 'n' all.

The ten-minute half-time was made for a cup of hot sweet tea in a wafer-thin plastic cup which guaranteed you scolded fingers and a burnt tongue, and a bag of Smith's Crisps with a blue paper twist of salt to liven them up. If you got two bags of salt it was deemed lucky, if your bag had no salt the reverse was true and you fretted through the second half, hoping you hadn't brought bad luck upon the team. It was all part of the ritual.

Then, on again, second half with Liverpool kicking towards the Kop. It was a piece of theatre itself to see 28,000 fans tumbling down towards the pitch as the Reds turned the heat on the day's opposition. Wave after wave of fans – and of forwards – until opposition defences were breached.

At twenty to five, the final whistle would blow and we would cheer the team off the pitch – victory secured – before moving at pace to get an early Football Special back to Old Swan. Onwards by bus to home, then tea, followed by a walk up to the top shops to buy that Saturday evening's copy of the *Liverpool Football Echo*.

It was a ritual every Saturday evening. Me, Andy and another mate, Stephen, would make the half-mile trip to the 'top shops', pick up the pink paper and quickly check all the final scores, the league table, and, if Liverpool were away from home, look out for the paragraphs set in bold type in the running match report from their game which signified a description of a goal – hopefully a Liverpool goal!

This was invariably the first proper information we had about an away performance and those 'bold 'paragraphs were always hugely significant. Even more so if they ended up in the newspaper's *stop press* as the game had over-run because of injuries and such-like.

Equally important was to see the newspaper's cartoons of the 'Kopite' and indeed 'the Toffee Lady' and see whether they too were in celebratory pose to mark their respective clubs' wins.

Armed with that night's *Football Echo,* me and my group of mates would walk back to our respective homes and once inside our own houses, the arguments would start over who in the family got first dabs at reading the paper, invariably cover to cover.

The final piece in the Saturday masterplan was to try and persuade mum and dad to allow me and David to stay up to watch that evening's edition of *Match of the Day* – either by emotionally twisting their arms ('everybody else is allowed to do it') – or by keeping schtum and hoping that we hadn't been spotted hiding behind the settee as the time for the programme came around.

There seemed to be no rhyme or reason behind which Saturdays I was allowed to stay up and those I wasn't (although I'm sure there was).

Anyway, a Saturday evening with the first look at the Footy Echo and a front row seat for *Match of the Day* was a win double and a rare occurrence.

The 1965/66 season gave my Anfield attendance figures a real boost. The list of matches mounted up – Fulham, Aston Villa, Nottingham Forest, Burnley, Arsenal, Sunderland, Blackpool, Tottenham Hotspur and more. Three games that did stand out included that season's Anfield derby match, which was my first experience of 'not getting a ticket' – I missed out on watching the Reds' famous 5-0 win over Everton which inspired the evergreen chant '1,2…1,2,3…1,2,3,4…5-0!' All part of the education.

Mind you, I was at another 5-0 demolition seven weeks later, this time of Northampton Town, a team that went up four divisions and then came straight back down the same four in eight consecutive seasons, which I still believe is a record.

I was mindful of that particular game when I attended the recent Carling Cup match between the two sides which ended in such an upset with the Cobblers beating Liverpool in a dramatic penalty shoot-out.

I wondered at the time how many people in the ground had seen that other Anfield encounter, all those years ago... answer, not many of us!

The third notable game for me that season was in October when Newcastle United came to town. As always they brought a large travelling support and the game was played in early autumn sunshine. Those factors, plus bolting down my lunch, may well have contributed to my only experience of 'fainting' at a football match!

Yes, halfway through the first half I suddenly felt light-headed and the next thing I knew I was at the corner of the Anfield Road end being escorted gingerly to the St John's Ambulance. Inside the vehicle I remember being given what seemed a nuclear blast of smelling salts which fully brought me around, and indeed, stayed in my nostrils for days. Such was the over-powering effect of the extravagant dose I'm surprised I ever got off to sleep for the next few days. Every time I nodded off, a large inward sniff would seem to re-activate the medicine and I would be wide awake again.

The following season I continued to get along to Anfield on a regular basis and favourite matches included Liverpool's home game against the world champions, or three of them at least, West Ham's Bobby Moore, Martin Peters and Geoff Hurst.

We, of course, had our own World Cup star in Roger Hunt, but on a gloomy January afternoon it was a player, ultimately left out of the World Cup squad, who lit up the afternoon with a virtuoso performance.

If Roger Hunt was my favourite Liverpool player at that time Peter Thompson ran him a very close second. Thompson, who Bill Shankly had signed from Preston in 1963, was such an entertaining player. He was a winger with fantastic twists and turns, feints and flicks and a master in the art of dribbling. There are those who felt he over-did it on occasions, and I'm sure that was probably true but when he was on his game, he was absolutely terrific to watch. On that winter's afternoon he was on his game, scoring both goals in a 2-0 win, cutting in and hitting two similar yet unstoppable shots from the edge of the box.

Two interested spectators that day were Warren Mitchell aka Alf Garnett and Tony Booth aka Mike 'Scouse git', two of the leading stars of the smash-hit comedy series *Til Death Do Us Part*.

The two actors – both in character – filmed a cameo piece for the show – one a West Ham fan the other a Red, whilst sitting in the Kemlyn Road Stand watching the action.

A couple of months later, Anfield welcomed a new young player who was destined to be one of the club's most decorated players. He played over 650 games for the club, scoring 48 goals, and won almost every honour in the game.

Emlyn Hughes made his debut against Stoke City and I was among the near 49,000 fans who watched this all-action bundle of enthusiasm and energy start his Liverpool career. Shankly had signed him from Blackpool – he had only played a handful of games – and later said it was one of his greatest captures.

Forty years on, I was honoured to be asked by his widow, Barbara and family, to help unveil a statue honouring him in his native Barrow-in-Furness. The sculpture perfectly caught Emlyn's unique all-action style. He was a Liverpool great.

That season also saw that remarkable FA Cup fifth round cup tie against Everton at Goodison – and Anfield!

We, of course, had heard about the latest clash of the Merseyside titans by smuggling a transistor radio into school on a frosty February Monday morning and mid-way through 'Double English', lifted the desk-lid concealing the radio, and ever-so quietly tuned into that day's FA Cup draw. It was, and still remains, absolutely brilliant radio, and yet only 'so-so' television (too many graphics – but sponsors rightly want their air-time).

Back in the Sixties, we tuned in and were told we were about to enter that day's FA Cup committee meeting and join them for Item 5 on the agenda: the 'Draw for the Fifth Round Proper of the Football Association Challenge Cup'. It did make you wonder what items 1-4 were! I would find out in later years.

Anyway, draw over, BBC representatives removed themselves from the room, the committee moved on to Item 6 – lunch – and our radio was switched off, desk-lid lowered and it was back to *Much Ado about Nothing*... seamless!

Of course, these were before the days of wall-to-wall live television and so the only way to satisfy the demand for tickets for this game was to move it to the evening, a 7pm kick-off, and beam the action from Everton's ground to Anfield. In so doing, the match became the first FA cup tie ever to be relayed from one ground to another. This was breaking new ground.

The Liverpool matchday programme for the event covered the club's backside by saying that 'whilst neither club had control over the technical side of the evening's innovation, we are assured that there is no reason, no matter what the conditions that reception should not be perfect...'

Except that, on the night, a howling gale meant one of the eight screens – 30' by 40' – briefly came free of its rigging and it, like

Liverpool's chances, was blown away. The result 1-0; the scorer Alan Ball. The combined attendance a staggering 105,000!

If weather played its part in Everton's winner that evening the following season saw one of Anfield's most bizarre goals on a snowy winter's afternoon.

Just under 40,000 were in the ground when Leeds United, fourth in the league table, came to play second-placed Liverpool. Already keen rivals, this match was to add another unforgettable chapter.

Liverpool, kicking into the Kop, were a goal to the good – Roger Hunt on 18 minutes – when, with seconds ticking down to half time, Jack Charlton, the lanky Leeds United stopper, passed the ball back across the snowy surface to the Yorkshire team's goalkeeper, Gary Sprake.

The young Welsh keeper was already gaining a reputation for being able to be both brilliant and bad in the same 90 minutes – and the next few seconds cemented that reputation forever.

Sprake picked up Charlton's back-pass and was about to throw it out to his full-back Terry Cooper. However, at the last moment, he spotted Ian Callaghan closing down Cooper and fatally changed his mind but not his momentum and instead threw the ball over his shoulder into an empty net – at the Kop end!

I remember immediately looking at the referee, Gordon Hill, a well-respected official, and for a moment you could see him just working out himself what had actually happened before signalling a goal. Unbelievable... pandemonium. Within a matter of seconds, the half-time whistle was blown and Leeds United's Sprake was cheered off the field by the fans... the Liverpool fans!

At the interval, the man in charge of the half time entertainment put on Des O'Connor's latest release, the appropriately titled 'Careless Hands' – priceless – and the Kop also serenaded the Leeds goalkeeper on his return after half-time with their own version of the Scaffold hit – 'Thank U Very Much'. So the second half began with nearly 20,000 fans singing: 'Thank u very much for throwing the ball in... thank u very much, thank u very, very, very much!'

Unforgettable.

That was the season, 1967/68, when I made 'my' European debut – watching Liverpool hammer TSV Munich by EIGHT goals to nil. The German team, who had been Cup Winners Cup finalists at Wembley two years before were just beaten out of sight. It was a different experience for me. Foreign players, foreign names, and foreign tactics... but, that night, Liverpool were irresistible.

I have a German business colleague now, who used to play in goal for TSV Munich and he says for all the club's important victories before or since that game, it is their 8-0 drubbing at Anfield that is the result that people – German and others – most easily recall.

Mind you, it could be worse; you could be a Stromsgodset fan – the Reds beat the Norwegian part-timers 11-0 some seven years later. Interestingly, Shankly named the same eleven players for the second leg against Munich – no rotation then – and the Reds lost narrowly 2-1.

The next round was against Ferencvaros and the games fell either side of Christmas, both being played on a carpet of snow. Not surprising in Hungary perhaps, but a rare snowfall in Liverpool had given me the dilemma of earning a few bob or missing the match.

Me and my mate, Andy, both 13 by now, had hit on the handy seasonal trade of snow-clearing whenever an Arctic chill hit Merseyside – which was about every ten years!

Slightly dodgy work ethic sure, but the moment the snow started falling we would grab a couple of shovels and go door-knocking to see if people wanted their paths cleared. A shilling a path – two bob with 'salt', but not any old salt – our mums' best Saxa salt, which we had both spirited out of the kitchen.

Not sure how the salt would compare with today's big 'gritters' but back then, shovel and salt was the game. And what we didn't shift for our customers, their pet dogs would, as they licked the newly-tastily seasoned snow off the path! In fact, every Butch, Snudge and Dandy was following us around adding their canine encouragement! It worked a treat – and a new snowfall meant fresh business – perfect. Bit light April to October, mind.

On the day of the Ferencvaros second leg in January, a fresh snowfall meant more work for us. But we were both big Reds and also wanted to go to the match, snow or no snow. So it was down tools at 6pm, salt back on the larder shelf, dogs back in their yards and off to the game.

A two-inch layer of snow also fell on the Anfield pitch, which the Hungarians waltzed across as the Liverpool players slid about. In due course, Laszlo Branikovits hit a wintry winner for Ferencvaros and we were out of Europe, albeit a very snowy Europe.

Me and Andy were disappointed but I did wonder what might have happened if Shanks had given us a call earlier in the day – and asked us to get across to Anfield with our spades and 'magic' salt before the game and do our finest. We may just have saved the day and brought our own husky pack with us for good measure.

*   *   *   *   *

The following season Liverpool had surprised the football world by paying £100,000 for the Wolves teenager, Alun Evans.

We'd seen Evans score for Wolves as a 16-year-old at Anfield and now he was in the Reds' line-up for his debut against Leicester City.

One thing about going to the match more regularly was you got to know the people who stood around you. Just as you had your spot on the terrace, so did everybody else – and you shared all the banter, bias and bullsh*t with them.

So imagine the scenario yourself. Liverpool are playing Leicester City, it's Saturday afternoon, 3pm, and our new record signing is making his debut. No live television, of course, and indeed the game has not even been picked for *Match of the Day* or ITV's regional Sunday highlights show.

What you'd see on that afternoon is what you'd remember from that particular match.

Now, there was one guy who always stood just behind us in the Paddock. And he always turned up just before quarter past three, having finished his shift at work a few minutes before that.

Every match, we would collectively give him an update. 'No goals yet', 'you haven't missed much', 'two good saves and Hunt missed a sitter', 'their keeper's dodgy'... that sort of stuff.

Only, on this occasion, when he turned up at his normal time, his usual query: "Have I missed anything?" was met by an embarrassed silence from his normal comrades-in-arms...

"Well... have I missed anything?"

It was at that moment I realised life isn't always fair – a judgement that has stood me in good stead since – because, as the youngest and smallest guy in the group, I was encouraged, nay called upon, nay helped by a sharp push in the back, to bring our friend up to date.

"Well, actually, it has been a bit of a lively start for once – and, in fact, (...long pause... embarrassed cough) it was... erm... four-nil to Liverpool after 12 minutes. Mind you, you haven't missed anything in the last three minutes..." I muttered unhelpfully.

It registered on him slowly. "Four-nil, four-nil... four f*!?*n' nil... and I suppose you are going tell me I've missed young Evans, our new record signing, score his first landmark goal for Liverpool?"

Another push in the back. "Erm, yes, actually he got the third... a bit of a fluke. Took a deflection from twenty yards... you didn't miss much... fancy a wine gum?"

The match finished, you've guessed it... four-nil. Or four f*!?!*n'-nil, as our mate continued to call it throughout the remaining 75 f*!?!*n' minutes!

And we all trooped out of the stadium that afternoon trying not to catch the eye of our matchday mate. After all, his nightmare had barely started because, of course, later that night, and without the aid of moving pictures, he had to describe all the goals from Liverpool's 'best start to a game in 50 years' to his drinking pals who he regularly told: "You don't know what you're missing not going to the match." Funny, we never saw him again!

*   *   *   *   *

Although Liverpool was my first, and only football love, I must now admit to a teenage flirtation with another target for my affections. In true Jeremy Kyle show-fashion I now own up to being the man who briefly led a two-timing love-life – sporting love-life, that is – in the mid-Sixties.

Whilst my relationship with LFC was already close to being at the 'undying love' stage, I had a little room left for my midweek passion and regular bedroom companion, Melchester Rovers!

Led by the ultimate sporting hero, centre-forward Roy Race, Melchester would beat everybody put in front of them, from fellow humans, circus animals, stilt men, to a team of robots from Mars – both home and away legs mind – as the comic strip heroes from *The Tiger* made many a youngster's life that bit much more fun.

I was a convert from about the age of nine and read the stories for another five… ok, ten… ok, fifteen years… and counting.

Roy Race, the most successful footballer ever ever ever, and his team-mates Blackie Gray, Tubby Morton, Bomber Reeves and Buster Brown took us on a weekly footballing journey which was never less than extraordinary.

Three-nil down with 90 seconds left of a big cup tie, Roy would conjure up a hat-trick in 60 seconds which left him and Melchester enough time to score a fourth. Gray, on his birthday, notching with three seconds to spare. And, of course, everything would be right with the world.

The Tiger comic, the new *Kop* paper, the weekly copies of *Goal* and *Shoot* magazines and *Charles Buchan's Football Monthly* were now my required reading literature along with the odd Latin text-book (oh, and a well-thumbed copy of *Parade*!)

I was hooked and read about football cover-to-cover, even better if the stories featured Liverpool players or the big full-page colour photographs were of the Reds' great stars, prime real estate to be autographed. *The Kop* paper came along in the mid-Sixties and gave the club another print vehicle to position its business but in truth was cartoons, caricatures, player features and the odd report – nowadays the sell would be a little harder!

As well as the weekly magazines each Christmas brought along the possibility of getting a football annual as a present. *The Topical Times, Football Champions* or my favourite, the *Roy of the Rovers* annual. Read cover to cover by Boxing Day, those annuals still have pride of place on my bookshelves and are still frequently sought out on eBay.

Once again, the first job was to skim through the book and see how many stories, pictures or features there were on my Anfield favourites, and then see whether Roy had saved the planet again, this time by heading in a close range injury-time winner against an unbeaten team of Androids from the far-off planet, Ulopiak before piloting a stranded spaceship back to Earth in time to play Athletico Thortino in the European Cup final. Then win the Grand National, the Boat Race and the Wimbledon men's singles title (as if!)

After the reading came the board and miniature football game playing, and as a boy in the Sixties, you moved along a well-beaten track – blow football, magnetic football, *Shoot*, dice football, *Wembley*, *Chad Valley Football* to the real 'daddy' – *Subbuteo*. I played them all. Got huge chunks of enjoyment out of them, and have never regretted a second of the time absorbed in those games.

For others it was train sets, *Meccano* or *Scaletrix* but for me it was anything that could replicate the game of football. I tried the lot – even if they each had their difficult moments. In blow football, the pitch would get waterlogged with you and your opponent's spittle as the game got increasingly exciting; in magnetic football the two connecting rods would get stuck to each other under the table; in *Shoot* the little round counters would get chipped, and in *Chad Valley Football* the players would come out of their rubber suckers and lose their thrust. (That sounds a bit dodgy actually!)

Subbuteo also had its problems, especially if you trod on your new star striker who had just fallen off the dining room table without you noticing, but it was the 'king' of football games for me and many fellow 'flickers'. In truth, I would have probably happily played it forever, if puberty, girls and all that other stuff like exams hadn't kicked in.

In fact, my mate, Andy and I's obsession with 'flicking' took a big hit one Saturday evening when mid-match, his doorbell rang, and our close pal Greg arrived with his new GIRLFRIEND.

It may well have been the moment that marked the end of our childhood as Andy lifted 'Wembley' off the living room carpet in a flash and scrambled around for his brother's latest Led Zeppelin album. We went from Jimmy Greaves to Jimmy Page in an instant. Somehow the joys of *Subbuteo* were never quite the same again.

My lads, Jack and Joe, now play computer games like *FIFA 11* on PlayStation, with all their incredible life-like graphics and synched-up commentary and they play them with amazing mental and physical dexterity – and play them all night, it seems to me.

But tell me, is it a patch on laying down a ruffled cloth *Subbuteo* pitch on the lounge carpet, getting the iron red hot to flatten out all the creases (and singe the touchlines and the shag-pile), have the game's duration counted down with an egg-timer and provide the running commentary yourself whilst trying not to kneel on your full-back?

Come on, call me old-fashioned...

Ok, call me old-fashioned!

7

'Sir' Roger and the Medal Hunt

In July 1966, football fans laid down their club scarves and rattles to become united in their support for England and their quest for the World Cup. This was our chance to win the trophy that Kenneth Wolstenholme so beautifully described when we ultimately lifted it.

"Its twelve inches high, it's solid gold and it means England are the world champions."

That famous, famous day was July 30th, 1966 – a Saturday never-to-be forgotten if you were one of the lucky 98,000 privileged to watch the game at Wembley, or as the Barwick family, and millions of others did, glued to television coverage and the twists and turns of that remarkable match – extra time and all.

The most famous game in English football history.

The country went mad when we finally shook off the sturdy resistance of the West German side... we had won the World Cup on home soil. Party time!

It remains the country's finest sporting moment. Indeed, one of this country's finest moments, sport – or non-sport – period.

When I was at the FA, like many before me, I allowed myself the dream that we would win the World Cup again and on MY shift.

And, like others before me, my 'turn', 2006 in Germany, ended in disappointment and another set of what might have-beens.

One of the reasons for wishing success on ourselves was to just imagine the party that would have followed any such victory. It would have been simply sensational. Ah well, dream on!

In 1966, the World Cup had got off to a rather inauspicious start when we actually lost the trophy itself! It may have been twelve inches and solid gold but we had managed to lose it.

On display at a London exhibition in March, the trophy had been taken away 'by person or persons unknown' and the FA was faced with the deep embarrassment of losing the Cup before even having a chance to win it.

Only in England! And, only in England would Scotland Yard's best detectives be beaten to recovering the missing bauble – by a dog!

Pickles, a loveable mongrel, became the most famous canine in the world when, whilst out on his daily walk, he sniffed excitedly at a parcel wrapped in newspaper – and when his inquisitive owner, David Corbett, opened the package he was astounded to find it contained none other than the famous Jules Rimet trophy itself. Dog biscuits all 'round!

Forty years on, and just before England set off to challenge for the 2006 World Cup, England played a warm-up game against Hungary at Old Trafford. My guest at the pre-match dinner was the self-same Mr Corbett.

He told me he had dined out on the story of finding the trophy for the past four decades and bought the house he still lived in from the reward he earned. And why not? After all, he did get to lift the World Cup before even Bobby Moore got his hands on it!

Alas, Pickles died the year after England won the World Cup. His story had taken the General Election off the front pages and he even attended the winners' banquet – a story I'm sure he is still regaling upstairs in doggy heaven!

England's build-up to the opening of the tournament had been less dramatic but had seen Liverpool star striker Roger Hunt staking his claim to being in the starting line-up for the opening game of our World Cup campaign against Uruguay.

Despite being an innocent party in the Jimmy Greaves v Roger Hunt debate – the Fleet Street press favoured the Southern-based star – Roger combined two vital assets. He scored goals and his hard work made it possible for other players to score their share too.

Roger was one of seven Liverpool players who made (Sir) Alf Ramsey's original 40 selected in early spring alongside the names of Tommy Smith, Chris Lawler, Gordon Milne, Peter Thompson, Gerry Byrne, Ian Callaghan and Roger Hunt.

That number was whittled down to 28 by June and ultimately the England coach's final 22 man squad included three Anfield players – Callaghan, Byrne and, of course, Hunt himself.

Their squad numbers suggested they may be part of the supporting cast rather than leading players – Hunt would have the number 21 shirt, Callaghan 20 and Byrne 15 – but history tells a different tale.

Roger Hunt had made his debut for England in a 3-1 win over Austria at Wembley in April 1962. Hunt actually scored in the second half which was a good thing for two reasons. Firstly, in those days, the midweek Wembley internationals would be played in the afternoon and the BBC would only show the second half. And secondly, I had raced home to see Roger's televised full England debut – or half of it!

Hunt had made enough of an impression to make the squad that travelled over to Chile for the 1962 World Cup and, whilst he never made an appearance, he was gaining invaluable experience around the international scene. Four years later he was on course to securing his place in both the squad and the team. Hunt had played in seven out of the 12 England games leading up to the World Cup finals, scoring twice against Scotland and, indeed, England's final warm-up goal, a winner against Poland. And on that pre-tournament tour Hunt had continued to impress, his work-rate catching Ramsey's eye.

Bill Shankly used Hunt as an out-and-out striker for Liverpool; Ramsey's wingless wonders meant his role had to be a combination of goals and graft.

Roger admitted the England job was unremittingly tough. "My role in the 1966 World Cup was up front in a 4-4-2 formation. Geoff Hurst and I were the battering rams for the midfield players and the overlapping full-backs, running up front, taking a lot of stick from defenders and taking them away to leave gaps for others.

"It is a difficult role to play. You are a workhorse and to shine in that sort of position in most games is impossible. It didn't flatter me as a player, even though I was probably doing a good job for the team."

And he was. So, when England came out to play the opening game of the 1966 World Cup against Uruguay at Wembley, Hunt was in the starting line-up. And he never lost his place for the next memorable five games.

The opening game itself was a huge anti-climax. 0-0. But five days later, again at Wembley, Bobby Charlton hammered home a first half thunderbolt against Mexico and then, in the second half, Hunt scored from close-range to secure the vital win.

The way the other England players celebrated Roger's goal underlined both their respect and affection for him.

For the third group game against France, Hunt was joined in the England team by Liverpool team-mate Ian Callaghan.

And once again, Hunt was in scoring form. He got both goals in a 2-0 win, the second of them set up beautifully by Callaghan.

England were through as group winners and next up would be tough as teak Argentina.

And with an uncanny sign of things to come, as England played their games I would type out a brief report on their progress on my *Petite* typewriter, just stopping short of shouting 'copy!' to my Dad as he left to go on his night-shift. But he would take my notes and bring them home the following morning freshly reproduced on a proper typewriter. I so wish I still had those reports.

For those reading this book under the age of 50, this may all seem an age ago, but for those of us privileged to have watched that World Cup, albeit on the small screen, it was simply sensational.

Only a 16-team tournament and three weeks in length, every evening the nation was glued to the box watching the game of the day. For three weeks the World Cup *was* the only game in town.

And that was how we saw it in the Barwick household. We never missed a match and even actually got to see one live!

Goodison not Anfield had been chosen to host some matches from the competition's Group 3. It contained the reigning world champions Brazil – Pele et al, and the rising stars of Portugal and their young superstar, Eusebio. So, on the evening of July 8th, courtesy of my Dad getting us last minute tickets, I had the privilege of watching those two great footballing nations compete for the right to progress in the tournament. Brazil v Portugal; Pele v Eusebio.

Pele, a supreme talent, came under intense and unjust attention from the Portuguese defenders and he was brought down heavily and had to be helped off the field. He came back on but to little effect. Eusebio, meanwhile, was simply irresistible, scoring twice in the match on his way to being the outstanding player of the tournament.

Above: With my Auntie Joan... trying to hear if Billy Liddell's scored yet

Simple pleasures... me and Dad on a family holiday

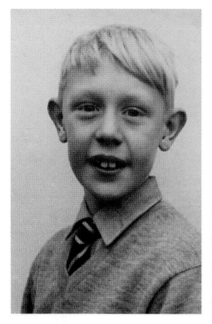

Me at nine years old - modelling the FA Cup!

Graduated... and I demanded it was a red ribbon for the scroll

Our school team. I'm on the back row, far left with the long blond hair... oh, happy days!

*Away day...
On holiday with
mum and my
brother David*

*My own special
Box Brownie
photos from
those half-term
Melwood training
sessions - Ron
Yeats (left), Larry
Lloyd (right) and
Chris Lawler,
(below) among
my victims*

Me and my mate Andy after the 1984 European Cup final in Rome... we did eventually give the cup back

On the playing fields of England, our pub team is born - the Evertonians eventually agreed to wear the kit

The best Match of the Day I was ever involved in... with Gerry on our wedding day

The FA show off the family silver to the new President, Prince William. Also pictured are Executive Director David Davies and Chairman Geoff Thompson

Great double act. With Kenny (top) sharing a pre-match joke and at the game with Rushie

Anyway, Rick, this is how I would do it...!
With Rick Parry at Anfield (top) and (above)
with former ITV colleague and current
Liverpool FC Head of Press Paul Tyrrell in 2001

With Alan Hansen at a charity dinner.
Having given him his big break, I'm
delighted to see how he has made such a
success of being a television pundit

Life in the fast
lane... me at
McLaren

Worth the wait! With Liverpool legend Ian Callaghan and that very special World Cup winner's medal

The game, played in front of a capacity crowd under floodlights remains one of my footballing highlights and whilst I have had the pleasure of seeing many other World Cup matches since – and actually meeting both men in person – the game itself remains a favourite memory. I was 12 and I was at the World Cup… which just happened to be a six penny bus ride down the road!

The other great thing about the 1966 World Cup was that WE – us Liverpool fans – had a player in the England team.

Club v country has always been a contentious debate. I've seen both sides of the argument but in July 1966 everybody was behind the national team – and club favours were widely spread around on the day of the final. No less than eight clubs were represented in England colours that famous afternoon.

Argentina had been beaten in a close and bruising encounter, and then Portugal put to the sword in a memorable semi-final – a game in which Roger Hunt was goal-maker – again.

The build-up to the final itself was all-pervading and the key subject of debate centred around the national press boys' favourite Jimmy Greaves. Would the Tottenham star have recovered enough from an injury he had picked up against France and would Ramsey be prepared to leave out the energetic Geoff Hurst or the hard-grafting Roger Hunt to fit him in?

It was the sort of subject that our 24/7 media of today with its phone-in programmes, tweets and blogs would have imploded about!

Ramsey dealt with it with subtlety and certainty. He took Roger aside on the night before the final – his 28th birthday actually – and told him he was in the side for the following day.

When the team was revealed on the day of the game, the Greaves v Hunt v Hurst debate was put to bed and Liverpool had a player in football's biggest match. And West Ham had three.

The match itself is part of football folklore – and Roger Hunt's contribution is perhaps best remembered for what he DIDN'T do rather than what he did do. It was Hunt who was on hand to nudge the ball over the line when Geoff Hurst's shot famously crashed off the underside of the bar and across the line – probably! But Roger didn't complete the job.

He was already convinced the ball had crossed the line and, by turning away with his hand held up in celebration, Roger may well have helped the 'Russian linesman' – Azerbaijani Tofik Bahramov – make up his mind so decisively for England against West Germany. After all, Roger could have slammed the rebound home – in theory.

The irony of the situation was painfully illustrated 44 years later when Germany benefited in a similar situation.

Frank Lampard's strike late in the first half of England's last 16 match with our European rivals, hit the underside of the bar and clearly crossed the line but was spirited out and back into play by the German goalkeeper. No goal was given and Germany, who seconds before had just conceded a first England goal, went on to romp home.

It was a World Cup accident waiting to happen – and must be the turning moment in FIFA's unsustainable resistance to the use of goal-line technology. I am a huge advocate for it – understand the best technologies – and even assist one of the companies trying to move things forward. Cairos have invented a ball with a micro-chip in it that instantly can tell the referee whether a ball has crossed the line or not. Not in a few seconds – INSTANTLY.

On the day of the England v Germany match last summer Cairos had two reasons to be pleased. One, the incident reinforced the clarion call for goal-technology and secondly, and more simply, they are German!

Back in 1966, Geoff Hurst's goal had actually put England ahead again after West Germany had scored a last-gasp equaliser in normal time. At that very moment Hunt's Liverpool colleagues, Ian Callaghan and Gerry Byrne, had been making their way down from their seats in the stand to be part of the post-match celebrations.

In the space of that short journey, the Germans had made it 2-2, and so Callaghan and Byrne watched extra-time action up-close from the trainer's bench.

Callaghan was also guarding a valuable item in his pocket... Nobby Stiles' false teeth! In all the kerfuffle on the final whistle, he was unable to get the precious cargo to Nobby which meant when the Manchester United star did his famous victory jog it was 'sans dents'.

Geoff Hurst's third goal and England's fourth had clinched a famous victory and set the country up for the wildest street party of the Sixties.

As Liverpudlians, we were proud that one of our men was in the England team that had won the World Cup – it added that extra sense of enjoyment. And whatever the subsequent club v country arguments have been I can assure you on that day we were just proud our national team – with one of OUR players – had landed the ultimate prize.

Two weeks later, I was at Goodison Park to witness an unforgettable moment when Hunt and Everton's Ray Wilson paraded the World Cup around a rain-soaked stadium before the start of the FA Charity Shield match between the two Merseyside rivals. It brought the house down.

Hunt, Wilson, Callaghan and Byrne were also presented with mementos – and Ron Yeats and Brian Labone and the two teams then followed Hunt and Wilson's lap of honour by doing a similar spin with the League Championship trophy and FA Cup respectively. Memorable moments, captured in a photograph that still hangs on my office wall.

In keeping with the occasion it was Roger Hunt who scored the game's only goal, receiving a pass from Peter Thompson and driving a left-foot shot into the corner from 20 yards.

One interested, and interesting, spectator that day was a 15-year-old Scottish lad, a certain Kenny Dalglish. On Merseyside for a week's trial at Liverpool, Kenny was getting an early taste of the atmosphere of an Everton v Liverpool derby match ahead, in future years, of both playing and scoring in them. Then, indeed, managing his own players in one of British football's big match-ups.

Roger Hunt's England career gradually faded, Gerry Byrne had played his last international and bizarrely Ian Callaghan would earn his next England cap some 11 years after winning the one from his single appearance in the 1966 World Cup.

When the great Bobby Moore was fittingly awarded on OBE in the 1967 New Year Honours List, the Kop responded good-humouredly by bestowing a 'knighthood' on their own man... Ee-Aye-Addio 'Sir' Roger Hunt!

Hunt remained a Liverpool hero throughout his career. Still on target for the Reds on a regular basis, including three in two days when in 1968 Liverpool had the strange affair of playing at Anfield on both Good Friday and Easter Saturday – the first against Sheffield United, the second Sunderland. For good measure he had scored the winning goal at Old Trafford the previous week. I went to both Anfield games, the highlight of which was a fantastic goal from Hunt who carried the ball from the half-way line before unleashing a shot from some 25 yards which literally flew past the Sunderland goalkeeper, Derek Forster into the Kop goal.

A tremendous goal, celebrated in a typically modest way by Hunt – no great leap, no somersault or crazy antics of any kind. He just wheeled round with one arm raised and acknowledged the ecstatic crowd.

The following season saw a rare show of pique when, on being substituted by Bill Shankly in an FA Cup fifth round replay against Leicester City, Hunt angrily ripped off his shirt as he left the pitch. It was so out of character that it made back-page headlines but Hunt was back in the team for the next match. He accepted he had made an uncharacteristic mistake but, as he pointed out, he didn't have a bad record: 'eleven years at the club and just one incident.'

Hunt played on for Liverpool until December 1969, and beat the club's existing scoring record with a close-range effort at Chelsea. He went on to play 484 games for the club and score 285 goals, and his 34 England caps brought a further 18 goals.

His testimonial match at Liverpool in 1972 drew a crowd of 56,000 with thousands locked out. This in itself was testimony of his place in the heads and hearts of Liverpool fans.

I've had the pleasure of meeting 'Sir' Roger many times since those days in the Sixties, at all manner and means of functions, and three things remain constant – one, Roger, now an MBE, is always the perfect gentleman; two, he never looks a day older and three, I blush every time I meet him! He will always be Roger Hunt of Liverpool and England –World Cup winner – to me.

*   *   *   *   *

Fast forward some 40-odd years, and I was now at the helm of the Football Association. When I settled into my office I had a large colour photograph of England's greatest moment mounted on the wall.

A regular visitor to Soho Square then was Jimmy Armfield, the great Blackpool and England full-back who helped me out in all sorts of ways while I was at the FA. Jimmy had dropped in for a coffee and chat and I caught him looking at the big photo on the wall of Bobby Moore lifting the World Cup. Armfield had been another member of the squad – but like Gerry Byrne hadn't played a match.

It was always a delight talking to great old players – a genuine perk of the job – and I was intrigued at what the 'other' eleven – the ones who didn't play in the final – got in terms of a memento.

"Nowt," Jimmy essentially informed me. In those days only those selected in the final eleven got medals. England captain Bobby Moore had made sure that the £22,000 given to the players by the FA after the final had been equally distributed between all the members of the squad, but only the starting eleven got the price-less medals.

Over the intervening 40 years, various people had tried to get that iniquity changed but with no luck.

Finally in 2005, a newspaper, the *Mail on Sunday*, started a campaign which made some head-way. Richard Caborn, the then Minister of Sport got behind it, as did other sporting notables, and I also made sure that the FA started to lobby FIFA in earnest too.

I'm not sure what had gone on before my time at the FA but I was always keen to make sure that the organisation properly respected its former greats – I suppose it was 'the fan' in me – and had been part of the group that supported the sculpting of both the Bobby Moore statue and the Sir Alf Ramsey bust which are now proudly on show at the new Wembley Stadium.

I had also been keen to make sure that at England home games we had a sprinkling of former England players as our guests – something that we achieved and that still happens today.

Anyway, over the next couple of years, the pressure was kept up on FIFA to grant our 'other' 11 (plus the late Sir Alf Ramsey and his coaching staff) their richly-deserved and long-overdue winners' medals.

FIFA looked back at this sporting injustice and Sepp Blatter himself promised to put this one right for us – and, indeed, for all the other countries that had won the World Cup in an era before EVERY squad player got a medal.

I was also personally keen to help make this happen and had said so in the press. It was important to me.

No problem... other than every time I went to see a match at Anfield, I would, without fail, bump into Ian Callaghan and Gerry Byrne in the corridor before the game and they would never fail to ask me where their World Cup medals were.

It became a bit of a joke between us – and if I spotted them first I'd be off like a flash!

No news was, in this case, no news!

The FA, and others, were delighted when FIFA finally announced the medals were ready for distribution.

And so, in June 2009, some 43 years after that famous Saturday at Wembley, Ian Callaghan, Gerry Byrne and all the other 'other' World Cup heroes got their medals.

They were presented to them by Prime Minister Gordon Brown at a 10 Downing Street lunch-time reception.

By this time I was no longer working at the FA but watched the television pictures from Downing Street with a sense of pride.

Later that day, the former players attended England's World Cup qualifier against Andorra at Wembley.

The players, who had been delayed on route to the stadium because of traffic problems, went down on the pitch at half-time and rightly received rapturous applause from fans who themselves had got caught up in the 'romance' of the story.

At the usual Wembley function, I spotted a table of VIPs I just had to speak to. They were the 'other boys' of '66 – and as I walked up to the table Liverpool greats, Ian Callaghan and Gerry Byrne, spotted me and started waving and laughing.

"We've got them. At last!" they said.

And, with smiles as wide as the Mersey, and looking as proud as punch, they each opened their respective leather cases to show me the gleaming gold medals.

They were chuffed, I was chuffed. A good day.

8

Me and
Match of the Day

Early last season a national newspaper rang me up offering 'some decent space' to write a critique of *Match of the Day*. The news--paper felt the programme was suffering an unusual dip in form and I suppose they wanted to give the show a constructive 'shellacking' from somebody with the credentials to do so.

I accepted the offer and in 500 words gave what I believed was a fair and objective appraisal of the programme's editorial style, content and impact. I was critical where I needed to be – and supportive where the subject warranted it. There were things that were still the programme's strengths and bits of the programme that needed refreshing.

What I was sure of was the programme's continued validity and relevance and that even in a broadcast world awash with live football, a well-constructed highlights programme with such a strong and established brand was still a big winner.

"Form is temporary, class is permanent" was my closing remark and it came from both the head and the heart.

I have had a 45 year association with *Match of the Day* – the iconic football programme – both personal and professional – and remain one of its huge advocates. Despite once or twice threatening its future existence!

Whether as a young armchair viewer, a starry-eyed assistant producer, the actual editor, the programme's chief broadcast rival, a rights negotiator for and against it, an on-screen talent developer or back now where I started, as an armchair viewer, *Match of the Day* and I have a special relationship, as does the football club I support. And that relationship goes back to the programme's very first day.

It is now a well-known piece of television trivia that *Match of the Day* began its life at Anfield on August 22nd, 1964. On that day, the opening day of the season, Liverpool, the reigning league champions met Arsenal, the team that they had beaten 5-0 in the corresponding fixture the previous season to clinch the title.

But there was a third team on show that day. The new *Match of the Day* team there to capture the action and capture a little bit of television history.

Those of us who have been alive long enough to have been able to see the first *Match of the Day,* all claim we saw the programme.

However, the reality is likely to be very different. It is believed that only about 20,000 watched the first programme, transmitted on the new BBC2 and in the London region only.

In fact, there was more than double that number of people at the match itself!

However, down the years, we have all seen the goals from that first broadcast so often we all believe we saw it first time up.

The BBC's caution in placing it on their new channel was understandable. Up until then any football highlights show had contained filmed excerpts rushed to a studio on motor-bike. Now technological advances in both electronic cameras and video-tape meant the games could be edited swiftly and centrally and then put directly on the air. Having a weekly football programme was also useful for the production and camera teams with a little thing called the World Cup less than two years ahead.

With the show's original theme tune, 'Drum Majorette', and the show's opening words – "Welcome to *Match of the Day*, the first of a weekly series coming to you every Saturday on BBC2 and as you can hear we are in Beatleville for today's Liverpool v Arsenal match" – a piece of television magic was underway.

The show's first presenter was also its first commentator, Kenneth Wolstenholme, and the programme only contained one match.

And, on a day of firsts, it fell to Liverpool scoring-machine Roger Hunt to claim the historic first goal, looping in a volley at the Kop end after just 11 minutes.

The match would ultimately finish 3-2 to Liverpool with Gordon Wallace scoring two second half Liverpool goals, the second, just three minutes from time. Liverpool had claimed the programme's first win.

Interestingly, one of the Arsenal's scorers that day was Geoff Strong who ended the season playing for Liverpool in that season's FA Cup final against Leeds. Another famous on-screen performer that day was the programme's first pitch invader; a black cat that ran onto – and around – the pitch for several minutes, delaying a corner and becoming part of the show's rich history.

I think that Scouse moggie brought the new programme good luck, because it was truly off and running and about to become part of the nation's Saturday night viewing habit for decades to come.

The need to give everybody a fair crack of the whip and the Football League's insistence of a spread of venues meant Liverpool was only featured a further two times on that season's programmes, with away defeats at West Ham and Manchester United.

And despite being champions the following season, the Reds were only featured on five occasions. Home and away against Chelsea, both wins, and away matches at Arsenal and Fulham, and a home win over Tottenham Hotspur. A home game appearance against Sheffield Wednesday was cancelled because of snow – in April!

What you can see developing is the programme liking for a North v South clash. In the days when you could only pick one or, at the most, two games for the programme, geography became significant in the choice along with form and position in the league.

Also in the programme's second season the Football League, mindful of the growing influence of televised football – and their deep suspicion of it – reduced the length of the edited highlights of the chosen match by 10 minutes. What had been 55 minutes in '64/65 was now down to 45 in '65/66.

But *Match of the Day's* big lift-off was just around the corner.

For just three weeks after England had won the World Cup, *Match of the Day* was back and Kenneth Wolstenholme's opening remarks clearly set the out the new agenda.

"Welcome to those who have followed us from BBC2 to BBC1, but a special welcome to those viewers who have been won over by the World Cup."

Yes, off the back of a triumphant World Cup and a sense they had a ratings winner on their hands, the BBC moved the programme to its senior channel and to a new late evening slot – and a new broadcasting habit was born. Audience figures went through the roof and suddenly the programme was being watched by eight or nine million.

By the early Seventies the show was drawing audiences well over ten million, rising even higher on FA Cup weekends.

And the programme was to have a new piece of title music – the theme now known the world over – and recently voted British TV's no.1 most recognisable theme music was introduced.

Written by Barry Stoller, the piece of music called 'Match of the Day', imaginatively, became as much part of the programme as Hunt, Greaves, Best and Summerbee.

By 1968, ITV had joined the party with regional highlight shows on Sunday afternoons – and these became a further part of the self-respecting fan's commitment to the cause. Sunday lunch with Gerald Sinstadt became the norm.

In Granada, the Sunday highlights regularly featured Liverpool in what was, after all, a football-rich area.

The club were also chosen for *Match of the Day's* next major landmark when in November 1969, Liverpool v West Ham was the first match transmitted in colour. Viewers watched the vivid red shirts of Liverpool overcome West Ham with goals from Chris Lawler and Bobby Graham.

I was at that game and we were all very excited to be part of a new venture. Mind you, it would be another three years before a colour television was installed in the Barwick household!

Why choose Liverpool as the venue? Well, the producer of the programme, Alec Weeks, said: "We wanted a colourful place and Anfield seemed the obvious choice."

I later worked for Alec Weeks when I joined the BBC and found that he had a soft spot for Liverpool – and especially Anfield. He knew that even if the game was boring, the crowd wouldn't be. He loved zooming in on the Kop when they were going full blast – and now in full colour.

Three weeks after their latest innovation, the BBC cameras were back on Merseyside for the Merseyside derby and, once again the serendipity of football showed its face.

Gary Sprake's famous own goal at Anfield remains confined to the memories and memoirs of those people who saw it live on the day – there are no moving pictures of the remarkable incident.

Unfortunately for Everton's Sandy Brown the same could not be said. Brown who had scored a header against Liverpool in 1966, sent another flying home in the Goodison derby match of 1969 – but this time for Liverpool!

And the incident was watched that evening by ten million *Match of the Day* viewers. Sandy Brown was a good solid professional and ended that season with a league championship medal but on December 6th, 1969, he scored an own goal so striking that, for decades to come, an own goal in the local Liverpool leagues was often referred to as a 'Sandy Brown'.

In full BBC Outside Broadcast Colour, Brown diverted a Peter Thompson cross spectacularly past Everton goalkeeper, Gordon West – as unexpected as it was unstoppable.

It was the second goal of a three goal hammering for the Blues at the hands of their closest rivals – and I, for one, having seen it all happen live at Goodison Park in the afternoon, was in front of the telly that evening to see it all over again. My viewing habits were becoming sorted out on a Saturday evening – and having won and lost in even measure the argument over whether I could stay up or not in previous years – I had now reached the age when it was not an issue.

As the 1970s decade got underway I was in front of the box ready and waiting for that familiar opening music to start – and also to see whether Liverpool were one of the now two matches to be screened that night.

As had been the practice from the start, the whereabouts of the BBC cameras used to remain a pre-match secret so as not to have an adverse effect on the attendance at the chosen games.

The football authorities were still paranoid about the potential damaging effect of television on the future welfare of the game.

In 1971, Denis Follows, the Secretary of the FA – a variation of the role I subsequently held in the sport's administration, said: "In future there is very little chance of the public seeing any more football on television. In fact, they might indeed see less."

Erm... another far-sighted view from the top!

For me, the programme I was watching as an avid and committed weekly viewer in the early Seventies would be the same programme I would be working on by the late Seventies. Quite, quite bizarre!

On a Saturday lunch-time in early autumn, 1979, I nervously made my way into the formidable-looking BBC Television Centre in London's White City and set about finding the *Match of the Day* studio.

I was five days into my new career as an assistant producer in the world-famous BBC sports department and was about to spend my first afternoon of watching matches being played the length and breadth of the country, as they were beamed back to 'telly centre' to be edited down for transmission later that evening.

I was about to start work on *Match of the Day.* To be honest, I had to pinch myself. Here was I, football nut, Liverpool nut, telly nut, about to start working on my and many other people's favourite programme.

It was like a scene from *Jim'll Fix It* – which, in truth, it could have been, because that programme was being recorded in the same building as well!

"Get yourself some lunch in the canteen, it is a long day," said a helpful soul. So off I went up in the lifts to find the famous 'BBC canteen' and I wasn't disappointed.

As I queued up for my sausage roll, chips and beans (old habits die hard!) I spotted all sorts of people I am sure I recognised...

'I am sure he's the guy off...'

'Oh look, there's that girl who appears in...'

I was in my element – and still had an afternoon of football to come. I sat down to eat my lunch; there was no special sitting arrangement, when I was joined by my casual dining partners.

Hattie Jacques, the great *Carry On* star; Johnny Rotten – late of the celebrity jungle, but then in the heart of his Sex Pistols' revolution – and, finally, a guy suspiciously dressed up as a dark green and purple alien...

Nobody batted an eyelid but our 'alien' friend felt moved to explain he was on his meal-break from the *Dr Who* set and was due back on planet Skaro in twenty minutes – but he just had time for a couple of fried eggs!

Conversation between us was scarce but I was asked by Hattie which programme I worked on. "*Match of the Day*" I said nonchalantly, whilst my chest was bursting with pride.

Mind you, my Scouse sense of mischief nearly made me start my reply with a strangulated "Oh, Matron!"

I never looked back.

Liverpool's match was not one of the chosen games that day – despite having spent most of the decade as the programme's favourites – titles in 1973, 1976, 1977 and 1979 and an FA Cup win and two European Cup wins had meant the Merseyside club were big news – and people liked both their style of play and their propensity for goals.

Over the course of the season I had just joined up in, Liverpool would appear 14 times on the show in the league, FA Cup and Charity Shield and score no less than 38 goals.

But it was a crashing drive from Norwich City's Justin Fashanu against Liverpool that would win the BBC's famous Goal of the Season that year.

I quickly established myself as part of the *Match of the Day* production team which also doubled up as the midweek's *Sportsnight* team as well. People like Roger Moody, John Watts and Mike Moss were generous with both their time and their talent and I learned quickly. I struggled with some of the technical aspects of the job, but my editorial instincts were sharp and a lifetime's passion for sport, sports television and sports literature held me in good stead.

As did having a wonderful mentor in Mike Murphy, the editor of *Match of the Day*, who made me feel welcome and led from the front. A London boy, Mike nearly made the grade as a footballer at Fulham, worked with Jimmy Hill at ITV, and then followed Jimmy to the BBC. Mike was a one-off, a genuine hero of mine, who sadly died still a relatively young man.

On the final day of the 1979/80 league season, Liverpool's title clincher with Aston Villa was the 'main' match. The Reds duly won it 4-1 and my production job that evening was to make a closing sequence putting together all Liverpool's best moments from the season and set it to Gerry Marsden's 'You'll Never Walk Alone'.

I did it with super care and was as proud as punch as the closing titles sped through with my sequence taking centre stage. But there was a surprise awaiting me. As the names on the closing credits rolled through over the pictures a new name appeared on them for the first time... BRIAN BARWICK.

It was a quite surreal moment. You had to 'earn' your credit and your spurs in television in those days and having your name listed at the end of the programme for the first time was their way of saying – 'well done mate, you're in'.

In those days, the editing of the matches down from ninety minutes, to say, twenty, was a fine art – based on accurate logging of the action from the assistant producer and a video-tape editor's craft of mixing pictures and sound from one part of a half to something further down the track.

Strangely enough, it was more often the sound rather than the pictures that gave the game away, and not the commentary but the crowd's chants or songs that would seemingly stop in mid-flow! It was a real-life case of *'You're not singing anymore...'*

It was still a very clever system and one that everybody on the show took pride in. The VT editors for their seamless edit, and the production team for their cramming in as much action as possible in whatever time was allocated to each match.

On a midweek *Sportsnight* the pressure was heightened as the match edits went on air less than an hour after the end of the games.

This meant controlled panic in the bowels of Television Centre as spools, wires, buttons and leads were plugged in and pressed all over the place (you can sense that I was clearly au fait with all the technical jargon!) to get the match edits broken down into chunks and successfully on the air.

More often than not it was fine but there was one famous Wednesday night when both FA Cup semi-final replays – Liverpool v Arsenal and Everton v West Ham – went to extra-time and such was the heat, energy and activity needed to keep the programme on the air that one of the tapes simply melted on its machine as it was being played out to the nation!

All of this while a group of foreign broadcasters were being shown around the building and being introduced to the 'world famous' BBC Sports team!

For the 1980/81 season there was a seismic shift as part of a four-year agreement for ITV to alternate Saturday and Sundays between them on a seasonal basis.

By now I was trusted to edit the matches – the prime job – and quite often that meant watching and logging a Liverpool game being recorded in TV Centre on a Saturday afternoon – and editing it ready for transmission the following day.

It was at this point any personal bias for Liverpool was put on hold whilst I dealt with the issues of the professional challenge that faced me.

It became second nature. One was my job, the other my passion. And throughout my BBC, ITV and FA years I never crossed that line when it came to key decisions.

I was rarely challenged on the point but if so had my defence ready. And it was simple. Yes, I supported a football club, Liverpool, in fact and for all my life, but that early interest in the game had sent me confidently down a career path where the 'second nature knowledge' gained by such allegiance to the sport was a positive not a negative.

My role on *Match of the Day* became combined with being producer of *Football Focus* which meant all week my working life was in and around the game and a lot of the relationships I built up with clubs and their personnel stood me in good stead later in my career. I was also enjoying working with commentators like John Motson, Barry Davies and Alan Parry – as well as the presenters Bob Wilson and the irrepressible Jimmy Hill.

Jimmy was just an amazing character; not short on self-belief, but a whirlwind of innovation, opinion and personality and a man who had made a positive difference in the game. The abolition of the maximum wage for players, all-seater stadiums and three points for a win were three of his far-thinking ideas.

He was also a man who could turn a negative into a positive on the spin of a sixpence.

I was once walking around the perimeter track before a live game at Anfield. My companions were Des Lynam and Jimmy. The Kop suddenly spotted the unmistakable features of the former Fulham striker and hit him full-blast with a searing rendition of that popular favourite "*Jimmy Hill's a w****r, Jimmy Hill's a w****r*". Whilst Des and I kept our eyes firmly fixed on the track, Jimmy, his jaw-line jutting formidably forward, just responded to the crowd's observations by exclaiming: "That's fame for you!" and kept moving positively forward. Great man.

A new addition to the *Match of the Day* portfolio in the 1983/84 season was a series of live league matches. BBC and ITV were each given seven matches apiece and the BBC, with its key asset now back on Saturday evening, plumped for a Friday night as their live slot.

Not a complete success for the BBC, but Liverpool played their part. Ian Rush scored a hat-trick on an icy pitch at Aston Villa and a further two in an FA Cup Friday night demolition of Newcastle. Danny Wallace's overhead kick for Southampton against Liverpool on a live Friday night match also won him the BBC's Goal of the Season. On the more conventional Saturday night edition of the programme, Michael Robinson's hat-trick at Upton Park was captured on BBC cameras.

A four-year 'transfer' to *Grandstand* meant I was off the *Match of the Day* beat for a while but when I resumed my duties with the programme in 1988 I had risen to the rank of being its editor.

This was a great personal moment. From persuading my mum and dad to allow me to stay up and watch the show, I was now at its helm. My new role gave me licence to select the presentation and commentary team, choose the matches and create the running order, style and content for the shows. At the time, the BBC was in an arrangement with the FA for the FA Cup and England internationals, so it wasn't until the turn of the year that *Match of the Day – the Road to Wembley* really kicked in.

The whole series was completely over-shadowed by the sickening tragedy of the Hillsborough disaster, an event which led to 96 Liverpool supporters – football supporters – losing their lives. More about that later.

*　　*　　*　　*　　*

Alan Hansen was one of Liverpool's greatest players – and one of its most decorated. Eight League Championship medals, two FA Cup winners' medals, three Football League Cup winners' medals, and three European Cup winners' medals are clear proof of the talent and longevity of the Scotsman's playing career.

And, all of those medals were won with Liverpool in a spell at the club that lasted from April 1977 to February 1991.

He was an intelligent footballer, a defender who had the very 'touch and technique' and 'pace and power' he looks for in current players of today. In short, he was an outstanding footballer, an outstanding Liverpool footballer and for me in 1991, he was also a retiring footballer.

That interested me because just like a manager at a new club I was putting my stamp on how I wanted BBC football televised. We always had outstanding match directors, their work was world-renowned, but often the focus of attention was on the studio – and I wanted a new look.

Firstly, after years of great service, I moved Jimmy Hill from centre stage to inside forward, leaving his presentation chair free for Des Lynam to bring his style and savvy to the screen.

Des was the 'man' – an outstanding broadcaster who was at his best. We had just worked on BBC's coverage of Italia 90 together and felt we could carry that quality of coverage into our domestic coverage.

We needed some new blood and felt Alan Hansen may be able to provide it. He had done some initial work in the 'then' relative privacy of a very new broadcast player called SKY – and had done some work on the radio. I decided to offer him a role on BBC Television and Alan was persuaded to come on board.

And he has been part of the BBC football armoury for nearly 20 years.

I tried very hard in his early weeks to give him an insight into what I believed made a good television football pundit – not least because I feel it is often the case that television channels employ famous sports people without really explaining the rudiments of that particular job.

It doesn't naturally follow that a great sportsman makes a great broadcaster – not without some help and guidance. Of course, in time they develop their own style but some early instruction is essential.

Alan learnt quickly, and like all recently retired players found criticising his recent fellow professionals difficult at first but then, as time went on, found he became more comfortable and more distanced from the dressing room. And whilst it could never replace playing, the studio was to be Alan's new pitch.

He and Gary Lineker were the two new television 'faces' I introduced to BBC viewers. I'm delighted that Gary would go on to prove himself such a highly-accomplished frontman while Alan proved the first of a conveyor belt of ex-Liverpool players who have made football punditry and co-commentary their second successful career.

At the BBC, of course, Mark Lawrenson was re-united with his old playing partner Hansen; at ITV, Jim Beglin has built up a reputation as a fine co-commentator, Ian St John provided 'the Saint' in the brilliant 'Saint and Greavsie', John Barnes has straddled the channels, Kevin Keegan the same, and, of course, Jamie Redknapp and Phil Thompson are stars of Sky Sports output.

Add to those names, people like Jan Molby, Ray Clemence, Ian Rush, Alan Kennedy, Ronnie Whelan, David Fairclough, John Aldridge, and also Steve McMahon, now working as a pundit in the Far East, and you sense Liverpool players can talk as good a game as they used to play.

Oh, and then away from the footballing action, there's Bruce Grobbelaar whose cooking exploits on ITV's *Hell's Kitchen* made him an unexpected culinary hit!

The start of the Premier League in August 1992 set off a rocket under the game. The big television money from SKY made them the key new broadcast player. Overnight they became the new home of live Premier League football.

Meanwhile, Jonathan Martin, BBC's then Head of Sport and I worked hard to secure the Saturday evening highlights - which we did for a lengthy opening period of five years.

The man we were negotiating with at the Premier League was to become another important Liverpool Football Club figure - Rick Parry.

*   *   *   *   *

The first few seasons of the Premier League saw an important swing in power away from Liverpool and Arsenal to Manchester United.

Leeds United had actually clinched the final Football League Championship but Liverpool and Arsenal had shared the previous four - and Liverpool had won eleven of the last 20, indeed eight out of the last 14.

With a change of title - we now had the FA Premier League -

came a change in destination for the title, with United now the winners of 12 of the 19 Premier League titles.

At the helm at Old Trafford was another Scotsman, Alex Ferguson. Yet to be knighted, he had enjoyed huge success at Aberdeen, although Liverpool had beaten them home and away in a 1981 European Cup tie predictably billed 'The Battle of Britain'.

Ferguson brought some steely determination to the task of trying to dislodge Liverpool at the top of the tree. I think he made it his prime mission. He also quickly made the matches between Liverpool and Manchester United top priority – and now they are the biggest club game in the English game.

He also brought some animal cunning to his role at United, quickly establishing an 'us against the world' mentality. His fellow Scot, Kenny Dalglish, like many others, had previously employed a similar tactic to good effect at Anfield and another managerial luminary, Jose Mourinho is also well versed in the art of 'us against them'.

Ferguson often publicly claimed that his players were the subject of unfair criticism or misjudgements from all manner of people referees, administrators, opponents, opposing fans, the written press and, of course, the broadcasters.

Match of the Day came in for its share of that so-called 'hairdryer' treatment and Sir Alex made it known that he thought the programme, with Alan Hansen, front of house, Mark Lawrenson just starting out on his broadcast career and me, as editor of the programme, had a bit 'too much Liverpool' in its orientation.

As I have already pointed out, my personal allegiances would never affect my professional judgement and therefore I fought my corner furiously on this one. It became something of a recurring theme.

I remember one phone call between me and the Manchester United manager on a Monday morning that took the paint off my office walls so to speak. He was, it has to be said, a formidable opponent.

He made it clear that he felt the previous Saturday's *Match of the Day* programme had been unfair on United. I didn't think it had been, and said as much. When he raised the issue of me being a Liverpudlian, I said indeed I was, but added 'not professionally between 3pm and midnight on a Saturday.'

The conversation went on – about our backgrounds. I made the point that if you grew up in great cities like Glasgow or Liverpool, you had an allegiance to a football team either passed down to you or developed in the schoolyard. It was part of the DNA of those places and it was one of the reasons we were both in the professions we were in. Any perceived bias, either for Liverpool or against Manchester United in our coverage was of course, unfounded, I said.

Manchester United and Liverpool were top television 'draws' and, I said, I was always keen to headline the programme with their matches – and even more so if they had lost that day. That was news, whether those in charge at Anfield or Old Trafford liked it or not.

We agreed to disagree on most points and to get on with our lives but he did contact me later to put things right between us.

The discussion, however, had mysteriously slipped out into the papers and each prominent presenter, commentator, pundit and interviewer across the TV channels were asked in a straw-poll for their football allegiances – not unnaturally, most were based on their birthplace and childhood, some a little more esoteric and the matter was soon put to bed.

The irony of it all was on the particular day that Fergie and I had our liveliest exchange of views, I had received two letters of complaint. One from a Liverpudlian accusing the programme of being biased towards Manchester United and one from a United fan accusing it of being in Liverpool's camp.

I felt like answering their complaints by sending them each other's letter and then sending a copy of them both to Fergie!

A misplaced accusation of bias followed me to the *Sports Review of the Year* programme where Sir Alex let it be known that he felt that his players should have won the programme's team prize during my five-year tenure.

They certainly achieved good things in some of those years but it simply never happened, and as editor of the programme, with just one vote amongst others on the destination of that particular prize, I accepted the hit as part of the stuff that went with the job.

Fergie's relationship with the BBC has hit an all-time low in recent years, with his refusal to cooperate with post-match interviews, following his dismay at a *BBC3* programme on football business matters including those between him and his son Jason – then a football agent. I, for one, hope that the situation is resolved soon as his views on the game are important.

In truth, my own relationship with Sir Alex improved when I went to work with ITV, with whom he had built a very positive working regime prior to my arrival; and also when I was at the FA.

Sure, there was the regular pitch and toss of a season's football disciplinary issues which were dealt with in the FA's Governance department, but away from those, Sir Alex always provided a willing, experienced eye and ear on the domestic and international football scene – on and off field – whenever I was in conversation with him.

One thing is for certain, just as fellow Scot Kenny Dalglish and dyed-in-the-wool Scouser Jamie Carragher honestly reflected before playing and beating Manchester United last season, Ferguson has had a remarkable 25 years at Old Trafford and set the bar high for us in our ambition to wrestle back our M62 supremacy. But, as Jamie so rightly says, it is about time that we did something about it rather than expecting others to do it for us. It is time for us to wrestle back the initiative.

My time in charge of BBC's football coverage ended in 1995 – when I moved to the newly-created position of BBC Head of Sport (Production).

My place at the top of the BBC's football hierarchy was taken over by a good friend and an excellent colleague, Niall Sloane – ironically a long-time Manchester United fan.

Bias – what bias!

9

Just The Ticket

The 1970s would be an interesting decade for me... O-levels, A-levels, a university education, a move away from Liverpool and a move too at Anfield – from the Paddock to the Kop.

A decade of trophy after trophy for Liverpool; of five League championships, an FA Cup win, UEFA Cup and Super Cup success and, of course, two unforgettable European Cup wins.

But, of course, that was all ahead of us when in mid-June 1970, with Christie's 'Yellow River' ringing in our ears and the England defence of the World Cup coming to a sad end in Mexico, the new season's fixtures were released.

As always, that was quickly followed up by the free fixture card that would drop out of the *Liverpool Echo* newspaper a couple of days later. Nowadays, the immediate attention would be the dates of the Liverpool v Manchester United games. Back then, it was very much when the Merseyside derbies were being played.

The previous season's derbies had been contrasting affairs for the Reds. A thumping 3-0 win at Goodison was followed by a 2-0 home defeat in March, courtesy of goals from Joe Royle and Alan Whittle.

Those two Everton players would be on the scoresheet the next time the two sides met but the outcome would be very different.

Everton would go back to Anfield for the first derby of the season as champions, the classy midfield triumvirate of Ball, Kendall and Harvey being the engine room of a team that oozed confidence.

Liverpool were in transition, Everton were in a trophy hunt.

Then along came a game between the two teams that earned the distinction of being called 'The Derby of a Lifetime.'

That was the view of the *Liverpool Daily Post*. My own view? Well, in watching Liverpool for over 50 years, the game between the two Merseyside giants on November 21, 1970, is my favourite match of the lot. Without question, without debate.

And here's why...

The context of the match was that a young Liverpool side were about to face an Everton side that had recovered from a sluggish start to the season and were now climbing rapidly up the league. Liverpool were still, in fact, three places ahead of them but both sides were in mid-table.

Liverpool had recently laid out £110,000 for young Welsh centre-forward John Toshack, who had made his debut in a 0-0 draw with Coventry the week before and both teams had been making progress in Europe. Everton in the European Cup and Liverpool in the UEFA Cup. Catterick said his team needed the points, Shankly, not surprisingly, said that his young side were performing out of their skins.

As always with derby matches in those days, I, along with thousands of other fans, had queued up for hours (and hours) to get my priceless ticket for the match some weeks before.

And, as always, you would get to the ticket windows and find just two old blokes taking the money and distributing the precious bits of card.

Always odd things ticket queues. You spend three hours standing and conversing with people you've never met before, or since, and by the time that your brief acquaintance is over, you know the names of their sons and daughters, that the wedding is never going to happen, the dog has to go in for an operation, that you can get a good cheap suit at Blacklers and, whatever you do, never stay in the *Hotel San Juan* in Torremelinos.

In turn, I was able to tell them I had just taken my O-levels, with mediocre results, had spent a summer holiday on a canal boat and that, after many years of living happily in Eastham Close a decision had been taken to move 'up the hill' to a house near Childwall Fiveways.

A symbolic move for mum and dad – something they were justly proud of – but something of a pain in the ass for me because, even though we were only moving a couple of miles, all my childhood memories – happy ones – were housed in that small cul-de-sac we were leaving.

I got the hump actually and never went to see the new house until the first time I had to physically move into it. On a Friday morning in November I left to go to school from my old home and came back from school to my new one!

I got the back bedroom, brother David, the front one – and my parents got on with the business of settling into their new home. In fact it stayed our family home until my mum sadly died in 2007.

My second day in our new home threw up a conundrum. How do we get to the match? I had a new journey to plan – gone was the 6C and Football Special from Old Swan, now it was the 81 bus along Queens Drive and then a long walk up Priory Road.

And so, on Saturday November 21st, 1970, I set off on my new 'match route' to see a game that would stay in the memory forever.

To be fair, the game started poorly and got worse. At half-time, it was 0-0 and there was no expectation of what was to follow in the second 45 minutes.

The first goal of the game came in the 56th minute when Alan Whittle cleverly lobbed the ball over Ray Clemence from a position just outside the box. Seven minutes later, they doubled their lead when Joe Royle headed home from close range.

Everton in cruise control. A young Liverpool team on the rack.

Then captain Tommy Smith drew on his experience and his sheer will-to-win and drove Liverpool forward. A sublime cross-field ball set young Steve Heighway away down the wing.

A recent addition to the side, Heighway, a Warwick University graduate, went on one of his signature runs – leggy, direct and at pace – and hit a near-post shot which caught Everton goalkeeper Andy Rankin cold. Liverpool had a goal back.

It was no fluke Heighway would score the same goal against Bob Wilson in the Arsenal goal in the FA Cup final later that season.

Now just a goal adrift, Liverpool piled on the pressure and again Heighway was in the thick of the action, crossing the ball from the left with John Toshack rising above Brian Labone to head home his first Liverpool goal and, more critically, the equaliser.

2-2. Bedlam.

There have been many amazing occasions when the Kop have created a din to match anything the world over. For me, the minutes that followed Liverpool's two goal comeback on this afternoon were among the very best.

The whole ground was rocking – well, except that is for a slice of the Anfield Road End! The Kop's incessant *'Liverpool... Liverpool... Liverpool...'* must have broken the sound barrier.

Two goals in seven minutes astonishingly became three in 15 as an Alec Lindsay cross was flicked on by Toshack to master goal-poacher Chris Lawler. The Reds' quietest man set off the loudest roar for years as he blasted a shot past Rankin.

3-2. Hysteria.

There was no final twist to the story. We had witnessed a remarkable 21 minutes, played out to a wall of Red noise. Exhilarating.

It was just one of those moments of your life you can recount at a flick of a switch. Everton (champions, local rivals, two goals to the good) BEATEN by Liverpool (coltish, cavalier, three goals in 15 minutes). Amazing.

The trip home on the 81 bus was upbeat and then it was about finding a paper shop near our new home to buy the *Football Echo*. This was one edition that was going to be read, re-read and then stored for future enjoyment.

Years later I discussed that great match with one of its key game-changers, Steve Heighway, and he told me how close he was to actually missing the match.

Heighway was an unusual professional footballer. He had been born in Ireland and hadn't actually played the game until his early teens. Rugby was his sport until then.

He had studied Economics at Warwick University and was set for a career in teaching before a few games for Skelmersdale sent the scouts scurrying around to see him.

The first time we all saw him was as a winger playing in the Gerry Byrne testimonial. Indeed, such was his ambivalence towards the sport he had to ask his team-mates which end was the Kop!

He would go on to have a stellar career for Liverpool. But 'Big Bamber' as the press would coin him, after TV's *University Challenge* quiz-master Bamber Gascoigne, still had one unusual obstacle to beat.

Heighway had suffered with migraines as a boy which, for him, meant a splitting headache and temporary loss of sight. For the first, and indeed the only time in his 11-year Liverpool career he got an attack on the morning of that famous 1970 derby game at Anfield.

Shankly got him to lay down in a darkened room at the hotel they were in to prepare for the match, and Steve dropped sound asleep. On waking at lunch-time he had recovered and the headaches were all heading Everton's way!

The second league derby of the season was a dull goalless draw at Goodison but there was to be a third derby that season – an FA Cup semi-final.

The match was played at Old Trafford and I went with my dad and took up our places in the Stretford End.

Liverpool had managed only a 36-hour preparation for the big game having been delayed 24 hours completing a UEFA two-legged quarter-final win over German masters, Bayern Munich. Heighway and Brian Hall, another newcomer and fellow university graduate, were both rested from the European game.

Everton, meanwhile, had crashed out of the European Cup at the hands of unfancied Panathinaikos of Greece and Harry Catterick had returned from Athens and headed straight to his bed with 'flu. He would miss the semi-final.

Everton got their noses ahead early in the match, Alan Ball scoring from close range, and when Ian Callaghan had an instant equaliser rubbed out for handball, we began to get concerned. Fate then took a hand.

Fifty-one minutes in and Brian Labone had to leave the field with a thigh strain. With him went Everton's chances of staying ahead. Eight minutes later and Heighway drew three Everton defenders and then slid a pass to an in-form Alun Evans who swept the ball home.

It was also Evans himself who set up Liverpool's second and

winning goal – scored by an unlikely hero Brian Hall – his first ever goal for Liverpool! We went bonkers.

Brian Hall was born in Glasgow, raised in Preston and had studied mathematics at the University of Liverpool. Whilst there, he had signed as an amateur for Liverpool FC. On gaining his B.Sc. he was offered professional terms at Anfield and 'Little Bamber' was off and running.

I still see Brian at Anfield now. He returned to Liverpool in 1991 to head the club's public relations department and I regularly thank him for scoring that particular goal some 40 years on – and I think he's pleased I do!

The national press were united in their praise for yet another Liverpool comeback over their Merseyside rivals. "Liverpool, the young team which hasn't stopped for breath in this unforgettable season. Their second half revival-supreme would, I'm sure, have seen off any team in Britain." *Vince Wilson – Sunday Mirror.*

"The Reds surged on like a team inspired. Their fans helped. They packed the Stretford End creating a staggering noise and made it appear that Liverpool were back in front of their famous Kop." *James Mossop – Sunday Express*

"Whoever faces Liverpool at Wembley will have to reckon with the Kop. That could be quite a factor." *Geoffrey Green – The Times.*

As my dad and I left the game exultant, we were given one of those stray bits of information that regularly plague football followers. "Stoke have beaten Arsenal in the other semi," said a voice in the departing crowd – and our mood even heightened. Taking nothing for granted, an FA Cup final against Stoke City represented an easier match than against prospective Double-winners Arsenal.

So, on the way back to the car, we worked out how we would

beat Stoke..."Keep the ball away from Ritchie and Conroy... hope Banksy has an off-day ..." Then, as we started our journey back home, the car radio gave us the real truth. Stoke had led Arsenal late into injury-time until a last-gasp penalty from Peter Storey had squared things up.

Arsenal would win the replay at Villa Park and so the decade's first full season would see Liverpool back at Wembley against Arsenal – a repeat of the 1950 FA Cup final.

*   *   *   *   *

A cup final ticket...

For many decades the hunt for the elusive strip of card that gave you access to the big day at Wembley was the stuff of legend and myth.

The search started the moment the final whistle went at the semi-final and 'your' team was in the biggest domestic game of the year – indeed, an international event.

Everybody knew somebody who 'didn't deserve a ticket' but had one. Everybody knew somebody who would travel down to Wembley 'on spec' and everybody knew somebody who was prepared to swop or sell theirs. Or so the theory goes.

A game between two sides that could attract a crowd of 40,000 if a league encounter could comfortably attract five times that amount if billed as 'the FA Cup final'.

And so, in 1971, I was introduced to the dilemma: how do I get a cup final ticket? A little ironic given where I ultimately ended up!

But the search was genuine and the chances remote.

I wasn't a season ticket holder, I didn't have any friends in either high (or low!) places, and I didn't have any money, only my weekly pocket money, which would have just about the cost of the Cup final programme. However, I was determined to get to the final and I did... so here goes.

The story begins with me sitting on an aeroplane at Speke Airport about to go on my first-ever flight to my first-ever foreign destination. Along with a dozen or so school-mates I was setting off for Holland; Rotterdam to be exact, on an Easter football tour with my school, Quarry Bank.

A fantastic opportunity – four matches in seven days – including the big one against our age and ability equivalents at Feyenoord, the then European champions. Heady stuff.

My school football career had been fairly unspectacular; a committed, decent player who could play right-back or in the centre of defence. I also could try my hand up front if needs must. In the sixth form I vacillated between regular outings for the second XI and the occasional run in the first team at right back. In fact, in my final year at the school, I had all but clinched that slot in the senior team before severely twisting my ankle in a midweek game against the school's Old Boys team. Agony.

Of course, I tried to come back too quickly – as you do – and a dodgy Hopalong Cassidy performance against local hot rivals, De La Salle did for my already limited football ambitions.

I settled for a slot as captain of the second XI, with the occasional added bonus of having a maturing young winger called Steve Coppell playing ahead of me on the right wing. Steve would go on to play for Tranmere Rovers, Manchester United and England. I wouldn't.

I have kept in contact with Steve intermittently over the subsequent near 40 years – often invitees to the same football 'event'. It is always pleasing to see him and it was great to follow his career in the top-flight when he proved he was quite some player and subsequently quite some manager. Way out of my class!

Mind you, when his flat was flooded a few years ago, I was able to use my influence, as the then Chief Executive of the Football Association, to replace one of his prized England caps that had been damaged in the incident.

He came to FA headquarters at Soho Square to pick up the cap from me, and the rich irony of the moment was not lost on either of us. We chuckled about it and then went for a bit of lunch.

Mind you, I left Soho Square myself with an England cap, as part of my leaving gift when I left the FA. The coach, Fabio Capello, presented me with a commemorative England cap, which fortunately for England fans was for my services off the pitch rather than on it!

Anyway, a trip – a foreign trip – to play football was just the biscuit. Life came full circle two years ago when I joined teachers and other boys' parents on my son Joe's school football tour of Brazil.

Back in 1971, it was Europe and Holland, and friends like Michael Dagnall, Tony Endfield and Paul Sinclair were also on board – and like me were dreaming of being spotted and taken on by some great Dutch club. In our dreams!

Whilst we were having great fun in Holland pretending to be young superstars, Liverpool had announced the ticket plans for Wembley. And they didn't seem to include me...

I wasn't a shareholder, a stand season ticket holder, or indeed a Paddock or ground season ticket holder. I just went to every home match! Bar one...

Whilst in Holland (by the way, final score coming through... tick, tick, tick, Feyenoord 1... tick, tick, tick, Quarry Bank 1... Barwick heads off line in last minute) Liverpool were catching up their backlog with a Tuesday evening home game against Newcastle.

At that game, vouchers were given out with no information or promises. My brother David got his as he entered the Paddock and carefully put it in his pocket. He did spot that the serial number on the ticket ended with a '1' but thought little of it

A few days later, whilst Quarry Bank, having slightly 'over-celebrated' our marquee draw against Feyenoord, were getting thumped by a souped-up Excelsior side, it was announced at home that those people who attended the Newcastle match and had a voucher ending in the number '1' qualified for a £1 ground ticket for the final.

Quarry Bank school football party flew back into Speke Airport without the normal footballing fan-fare. There was no huge welcoming party, no media scrum, no airport press conference or, indeed, any open-top bus parked up ready to help us tour around the city. Ah, well... but had we had a seriously good time on and off the pitch.

Mum and dad picked me up and en route back to Childwall I posed the question they were dreading. In fact, I hit them with it within seconds of getting into the car.

"Have you had any luck finding me a ticket for the final?"

Mum spoke first. "Well, not really... no luck at all. David got a voucher that (her voice suddenly went all 'sotto voce') might have qualified for one but nothing else, no."

"Pardon?" I said.

"Your mum said David went to the Newcastle match and got a voucher that qualified him for a cup final ticket," said Dad in a very clipped fashion.

The car went quiet, and the conversation stopped stone dead. They both looked in the rear view mirror to see how that news had gone down. Well guess what... badly. Really bloody badly!

"What do you mean David got a voucher and a ticket? That voucher was supposed to be mine."

The front seats remained silent.

I reminded them of a pre-Holland tour agreement that I seemed to remember, but nobody else did (or was I mistaken?)

David was a little older than me, but had started going to football a little later than me. He has now been a season ticket holder at Anfield for the best part of 40 years or more. But in 1971, everything was up to play for.

What followed in the next couple of hours in our new posh home in leafy Childwall was the equivalent of the Battle of Little Big-Horn. Voices were raised... never fists... but voices... very loud voices.

I summed up my exciting trip to Holland in about 60 seconds. Flew there, drew with Feyenoord, flew home, and got on with the serious business of securing that precious ticket.

I put forward my case for it. Fan for 10 years, lived and breathed the club, scrapbooks, programmes, autographs, never missed a home game (bar one!). Oh, and that I would one day write about the damn issue in a best-selling book!

That was the least convincing part of my argument.

David's position, of course, was perfectly reasonable. He went to the matches on a regular basis, went to the Newcastle match, and got the voucher that got the ticket.

No decision was made for days. And Mrs Jackson, over at no.7, made the passing observation to my mum. "Things sounded a little strained at no.2 last night. Raised voices and that."

"Yes, cup final ticket argument... I wish they'd bloody lost to Everton, never mind win!"

"Yes, got the same problem in our house. What a nightmare."

I will never know the basis on which the decision was made. I'm not sure whether David was left all mum and dad's premium bonds in their will, was bought six driving lessons, allowed to actually ride that scrapheap called a motorbike he had bought or was finally allowed to go on holiday with his cousin Bill.

Whatever, when the whiffs of white smoke came out of the smokeless-zone chimney at no.2 Childwall Mount Road, I had won the argument. The ticket for the FA Cup final was mine. An uneasy truce fell around the house.

I wasn't particularly proud of myself but it wouldn't be the last time I would have an argument about cup final tickets... mind you it was probably the toughest.

*   *   *   *   *

The trip to Wembley was memorable. Ok, we didn't win the game and we didn't bring the trophy home but, for me, being at the great old stadium on the day of the FA Cup final was just the bees-knees.

I had actually been to Wembley twelve months before. The school had sent a coach-load of us down to see England play Northern Ireland in the home team's last game before defending their World Cup crown in Mexico.

In fact, on that night, we saw Emlyn Hughes set up a goal for Bobby Charlton on his 100th game for his country.

Three of us - me included - got lost on the way out of the stadium and spent over an hour trying to find the right coach to get us back to Liverpool.

When we had arrived from the north, in the middle of the afternoon, there had been about a dozen coaches parked outside the stadium - a doddle I thought - but when we came out, in the dark, there must have been about 500 of the bloody things. All pre-mobile phones and Blackberrys remember, so once lost, in trouble really. We just had to rely on gut instinct - and the compass out of one of the lads' pair of Wayfinders! When we found the right coach, we were greeted by stern looks from the teachers and whoops of ironic delight from our school-mates.

It was that painful memory I took with me as I stepped on to a Wembley Football Special at Lime Street early on the morning of May 7th. My dad had found a work colleague and his family who were going down on the same train as me to act as my chaperones. But once off the train at Wembley, we all agreed it was every man – and boy – for himself for the rest of the day.

My dad had told me (repeatedly!) not to lose my ticket. So had my mum (repeatedly!) David, strangely, didn't seem to care either way! Anyway, I put the ticket down the front of my trousers for safe-keeping. I worked on the theory if anybody managed to get it out of there they deserved to have it.

Mind you, the act of actually getting it out from that safe haven myself when eventually at the Wembley turnstile looked close to committing a criminal offence itself.

I did get a number of very strange looks as I shoved my hand down my trousers and rummaged around before proudly pulling out an envelope with a ticket inside it. "And that your Honour, is the case for the defence!"

Once in the ground and safely in my spot behind the goal at the Tunnel End, I drank in the sights and sounds of the FA Cup final. It was everything I hoped it would be.

Of course, as per tradition, the weather was red-hot, lovely bright sunshine matching the bright tunics of the marching band, which was closely followed by the community singing, before we let rip with a memorable pre-match rendition of 'You'll Never Walk Alone'.

The first 45 minutes of the game did not match the occasion and the heat was certainly telling on the players of both sides.

No goals. In truth, few chances.

The second half wasn't a bobby-dazzler either. Once again, no goals.

At the final whistle of normal time, I was reassured by a public address announcement that the Football Specials going back to Liverpool would wait in the railway station until the end of extra-time.

Self-evident, but if you are 16, on your own and just getting a little nervous it was like hearing the Gettysburg Address!

Liverpool took the lead early in the first period of extra-time – substitute Peter Thompson fed high-stepping Steve Heighway, who scored another one of his near-post goals. Arsenal goalkeeper Bob Wilson had left a gap and Heighway had found it and driven the ball through it.

I would mention that particular goal to Bob about every other week during the near 20 years I worked with him in broadcasting at both BBC and ITV! He did get a bit pissed off actually because he was a very good goalkeeper but hey... sorry Bob.

On the actual day at Wembley we all went completely mad as the ball hit the back of Arsenal's net. Mad. What Football Special? Who cares? We were ahead in extra-time in the Cup Final. Fantastic.

Then, in the middle of a raucous unified chorus of "*We love you Liverpool we do... we love you Liverpool we do... we love you Liverpool...*' THE SINGING STOPPED... INSTANTLY.

Arsenal had equalised. Whether it was George Graham or Eddie Kelly who scored it – the goal was scrappy – doesn't matter, it had rubbed out our advantage. Gutted.

Worse was to follow in the second period when John Radford cut in from the left, fed Charlie George who dramatically leathered the ball past Ray Clemence. 2-1. Game over.

In those days, the winners of the cup went up first. Arsenal had clinched the Double and joyously lifted their second trophy in a week. Of course, we all stayed to watch Liverpool captain, Tommy Smith and his team go up the 39 steps to the Royal Box and come back down with their runners-up medals. Shankly would have expected nothing more of us.

Then it was a mad scramble to get back to the station just outside the stadium and wait for your train – whichever one you had been allocated (although nobody did – and neither did I. When the first train rolled out of the station I was on it).

Four hours later I got off the train at Allerton Station, a few miles outside the Liverpool city centre and was delighted to see my mum and dad waiting there to meet me.

They looked concerned, expecting me to still be upset about the result of the game but in truth, just getting home safely had long been my only real ambition. At 16, London seems a very long way away from Liverpool and even longer when you are hungry, on your own – even in a crowd – and without a pair of Wayfinders on your feet to help you find your way around.

Mind you, I didn't tell my parents any of that!

Three years later I was back at Wembley, back at the FA Cup final, and this time I witnessed Liverpool completely outplay Newcastle United – Supermac and all.

My dad had got me a ticket; a friend gave me a lift there and back. It was a big day but in many ways a smaller adventure than three years before.

*   *   *   *   *

The star player and scorer of two goals that afternoon in 1974 at Wembley had actually also been an interested spectator for the Liverpool/Arsenal final three years previous.

Kevin Keegan, a young 21-year-old, had been bought by Shankly from Scunthorpe United a few days before the 1971 FA Cup final and his capture for the Anfield club would prove to be an absolute master-stroke.

What he lacked in height – he stood at just 5'8" – he made up for in sheer determination. He became the defining player of Shankly's new Liverpool and the catalyst for what followed under Shankly, and subsequently under the early years of Bob Paisley's reign as Liverpool manager.

I first saw Keegan play in a pre-season match at Tranmere Rovers and, as Butch Cassidy and the Sundance Kid so cutely coined the phrase, we all left Prenton Park with the same question on our lips. *"Who is that guy?"*

A fortnight later we knew, and so did the whole of the nation, as he scored within 12 minutes of his senior Liverpool debut against Nottingham Forest, in front of the Kop and the *Match of the Day* cameras.

Liverpool had a new star – the game had a new star – and in the fledging days of the commercialisation of the sport, companies had somebody to hang their hat, their coat, their jacket, their car, their hair products, their after-shave lotions and even their road safety messages on. Wherever Kevin Keegan was, he could 'splash it on'.

Keegan, articulate, media and fan friendly, became the football's first commercial superstar – but he could play as well.

For me, he was just somebody new and somebody to get very excited about. *Mr Perpetual Motion*, who took Liverpool close to the title in his very first season at Anfield.

He particularly built up a great working relationship with John Toshack and the combination of their skills proved difficult for opposition teams to manage. The following season, 1972/73, he and the rest of the Liverpool lads made no mistake in their pursuit of the league championship.

The most exciting game of that season was Liverpool's 4-3 home win over Birmingham. Played in torrential December rain, Birmingham led 2-0, then 3-1, but two goals from Alec Lindsay, one from Peter Cormack, a key player that season, and finally a Keegan/Toshack combination gave the Welshman a late chance to clinch victory for the Reds. Once a season an extraordinary game pops out of the fixture list and Liverpool v Birmingham was that game that season.

That famous win over Leeds at a buzzing Anfield with Cormack and Keegan himself the scorers all but clinched Liverpool the title over their nearest rivals.

Five days later, a goalless draw against Leicester City at Anfield actually confirmed the Reds' title success and gave Liverpool, and Shankly, their third Football League Championship in the space of ten seasons.

That wasn't all. Twelve days later, they would take a huge step towards realising another of Shankly's ambitions – conquering Europe. And his pocket dynamo, Kevin Keegan would be right at the heart of things again but not before an extraordinary false start.

Liverpool had reached the UEFA Cup final and were due to meet a German side, Borussia Moenchengladbach in the two-legged climax to the competition.

Two legs – well, three really, because the Reds' first attempt at hosting the first leg ended dramatically after just 27 minutes when Austrian referee, Erich Linemayr called a halt to proceedings as the pitch became water-logged through a bout of torrential rain. The Germans, a third of the way through a tricky away leg and the game still goalless, protested vehemently but Linemayr stuck to his guns and the game was re-scheduled for 24 hours later.

I went to both games, the abandoned one and the following night's reprise. But not everybody did – and, in fact, you could get in on the night of the re-played game for just 10p – much to the annoyance of people like me who had bought a full-price ticket for the previous night's game.

The Germans were furious, but for Bill Shankly, it had been an unlikely reprieve which he didn't waste. In the half hour that had been possible on the original night, he had spotted a perceived weakness in the air at the back of the German side.

He dropped Brian Hall and brought in John Toshack and the big Welshman had a big game, setting up chances for his team-mate Kevin Keegan to score twice. Larry Lloyd added a third and both teams missed penalties or rather Ray Clemence made a sensational spot-kick save from Heynckes. That would prove to be a vital save.

The second leg a fortnight later looked a formality but Borussia Moenchengladbach were having none of it. Just as Liverpool had been the vastly superior team at Anfield now it was the Germans' turn to be the dominant force on their home soil.

They played brilliantly and went in at half time two goals to the good, both scored by Heynckes and the second 45 minutes seemed to last a lifetime for the Liverpool players on the pitch, the Liverpool fans in the stadium, and the tens of thousands of us listening back home to the action as it unfolded on BBC Radio. We just made it.

If my memory serves me right, the team went around the city the night after winning their first European trophy – the League Championship trophy and the UEFA Cup both on show – as well as the European Light-Heavyweight Championship belt held aloft by Kirkby's very own boxing superstar, John Conteh, invited on the open-topped bus by fight-fan Shankly.

Conteh, a Liverpool fan, had beaten Olympic champion, Chris Finnegan two nights before and would later become a world champion. Liverpool, meanwhile, would enter a new era with a new manager who would make winning regularly in Europe just part of his under-stated managerial master-class.

10

Moving On

The Anfield transition from Shankly to Paisley was done seamlessly with 'continuity and stability' the buzz words coming out of the Liverpool boardroom.

"Why change something that has been tried and proved over the years for something which was untried?" This was the message to the fans from Liverpool chairman, John Smith.

Whether we, the fans, bought that prognosis at the time we certainly endorsed it in the years to come. The passing of the managerial mantle to the next in line in the Boot Room became an Anfield tradition, a way that delivered sustained success over the next couple of decades.

The early Seventies themselves had also been a period of change in my own life. Leaving school, joining my fellow students at the University of Liverpool before heading into the 'real' world as my dad, and every other dad, would, no doubt, call it.

That would ultimately lead me to leaving Liverpool and setting out on the professional and personal journey that has been so fulfilling.

Leaving school was a sad moment. I loved my time at Quarry

Bank, did reasonably well in my exams and recognised the quiet but caring leadership of its headmaster, Mr Pobjoy, as one of its huge assets.

Indeed, some 30-odd years later, on the day I started work in my new role as chief executive of the Football Association I received a hand-written letter from a now very elderly William Pobjoy.

Its contents were a good luck message and its sentiment one of support. I thought it was a lovely gesture and have kept it.

One of the big leaving events at Quarry Bank then was the annual Staff v Boys football match on the school field. It was a must attend, not least to see the beer guts and the white legs – and the teachers had them as well!

My leaving year was no different. Three hundred pupils, boys and girls, surrounded the touchline as the game was played. I had secured my berth at right back and we narrowly won a fiercely contested match, partially helped when I sent English teacher and demon winger Mr Prince almost into next term with a tackle Tommy Smith would have been proud of.

The teacher didn't just clear the touchline he was catapulted over the pupils on it. I was just glad I'd no more essays for him to mark otherwise I could have been in serious trouble!

A-Levels behind me – decent results – and in a late change of mind, I decided to go to my home town university, to study Economics, missing out probably on the 'whole' student experience derived from going somewhere further afield. But I still enjoyed my time at the University of Liverpool enormously.

I played football Wednesdays and Sundays and met people from all over the country, for the first time really. That in itself was new. I suddenly found people who supported other clubs. Neil followed Wolves, Pete's team was Coventry and Billy's Spurs.

It was a great spell. As well as football, I loved all elements of popular culture. Made a date every Saturday evening to watch Bruce Forsyth's brilliant hosting of the *Generation Game*; savoured the comic timing of Morecambe and Wise; the colour and froth of *Top of the Pops*; loved John Le Mesurier's gentle portrayal of Sergeant Wilson in *Dad's Army* – *"Do you think that's wise?"* – and never missed the magnificent police drama *The Sweeney*. Regan and Carter, John Thaw and Dennis Waterman, cleaning up the streets of London in their own inimitable style.

I still see re-runs of that show now on UK Gold, and apart from the wide lapels, pear-drop collars, kipper ties and flares, (but enough about my wardrobe) the programmes are still absolutely mustard.

Some years ago I was asked, through my television colleagues, to play for a charity team that the likes of Dennis turned out for. Our opponents that day? A former Liverpool 'greats' team!

We had a few guys from *Softly, Softly, When the Boat Comes In* and *Confessions of A...* and they had the likes of Ian St John, Willie Stevenson and Geoff Strong...

My job? To mark a certain Ian Callaghan. To be honest, Mr Prince was easier!

In fact, it got so embarrassing that deep in the second half of the game, Cally actually came up close to me and whispered where and how he was going to beat me when he next got the ball so I could spectacularly, for the first time that afternoon, whip it off him. Sure, a typically kind gesture from Liverpool's longest-serving player but even then, with me now breathing through my backside, I couldn't get close enough to him to execute the coup de grace.

In music, I was a keen collector; David Bowie, Rod Stewart, Elton John plus the gentler sounds of James Taylor, Carole King and Joni Mitchell; some Roy Wood-inspired Wizzard and Jeff Lynne's

Electric Light Orchestra, all favourites of mine at the time.

If Anfield was my prime venue for thrills and excitement, the Liverpool Empire briefly ran it close. Watching Bowie perform as his alter-ego Ziggy Stardust; seeing Elton belt out his hits whilst jumping on top of his piano Jerry-Lee Lewis style; watching Rod Stewart and the magnificent Faces party and parade and then seeing Paul McCartney's first concert in his home town since the break-up of the Beatles was just fantastic. And just because of the collecting bug inside me, I left every concert, with a tour T-shirt – one wear, one wash, one size smaller.

And, of course the tour programmes – four photographs and a welcome message – five quid. Ah well, one day on eBay...

The other music that absolutely sent me and millions of others soaring (no, not Mud, although I was and still am a dab-hand at Tiger Feet), was everything that came from Detroit, the home of Tamla Motown.

The Temptations, The Four Tops, Diana Ross and the Supremes, the Jackson Five, and my own particular musical hero, Stevie Wonder. Their music, his music, was just sensational, and still is when I put it on the car stereo.

Listening to them is one thing, meeting them is another and I have the former Liverpool captain and then Rangers manager Graeme Souness to thank for one of life's more unlikely events.

Souness would, in many people's eyes, blot his copy-book at Anfield but I choose to remember him as a great player, who would drive the team forward, never shirk a tackle, and score critical goals. An intelligent and strong player.

I remember his first Liverpool goal, a crashing volley against Manchester United at Anfield, as well as a stunning hat-trick against CSKA Sofia en route to the 1981 European Cup final and the match-winner against Everton which secured Liverpool a record fourth consecutive League Cup.

He had taken his talent to Italy and was now at Ibrox in his role as manager of Rangers. I was up there to interview him about a forthcoming game.

Before we settled down to have a conversation, he took me inside the stadium itself and I witnessed the extraordinary sight of a player, Mo Johnston, climbing into the boot of a car before being spirited out of Ibrox. Souness had bought Johnston, a Catholic and former Celtic player, from French club Nantes and was struggling to make his typically brave move stand up to the scrutiny of fans of both Rangers and Celtic. "Only way we can get him in and out at the moment," Souness said in a matter-of-fact way.

Now on the plane back from Glasgow, the seat next to me, and indeed several others on the aircraft, were empty right until just before it started its engines. Then a group of a dozen or so lively, boisterous black men and women came on board and filled all the vacant seats.

The vacant seat next to me was filled by a tall, big-framed, heavily-beaded man wearing dark glasses. It was Stevie Wonder.

I am rarely short of something to say but I did have to summon up all of my courage to start a conversation with my musical hero, and a guy I was due to see perform two days later at the Wembley Arena.

I couldn't let the opportunity slip, so my opening shot was "Good afternoon, Mr Wonder, I am the gentleman sitting next to you and believe you played in Glasgow last night."

Sometimes meeting your heroes can be a bitter let-down but not this hero, on this day. We engaged in conversation the whole flight (I'm sure he was thrilled!) and he closed proceedings by hoping I enjoyed his concert two days hence. Perfect.

These sort of bizarre coincidences do seem to follow me around but I will leave bumping into American rock legend Bruce Spring-steen in a Swedish hotel steam room three days before seeing him perform at Wembley for the next book.

Television, music and cinema. This was the era of some great popular and challenging movies. *The Godfather, Jaws, One Flew Over the Cuckoo's Nest, Clockwork Orange, The Exorcist* and the 'disaster' genre like *Towering Inferno* and the *Poseidon Adventure.* All were queued up for and enjoyed.

My football fix during this period was satisfied by my regular attendance at Anfield for Bob Paisley's early years, playing for my student team, Comecon (Commerce and Economics) and having an occasional turn-out for Quarry Bank Old Boys.

The fact that the latter played on a Saturday afternoon, combined with my own limited ability, meant my days with my school's sporting alma-mater was relatively short-lived, although I made some good friends there like Eddie Bentley and Dave Thornton, who I still enjoy bumping into occasionally.

Student football was a decent standard and our team was blessed with some good players. I drifted around the team – full-back, central defence or even the odd run-out at centre forward.

As well as playing – and beating – other university department sides, we also played our equivalent teams in other universities. In one such visit we very nearly came seriously a cropper.

We hadn't been particularly impressed with the vehicle the local coach firm had laid on to transport Comecon's football, hockey and darts team to Sheffield University for a set of friendly fixtures. And we were even less impressed on the return journey home, when, with 50 or so students just a trifle worse for wear after the traditional post-match hospitality, the coach actually caught fire.

What started as a smell of oil and smoke very quickly developed into a fast-moving fire that was heading from the front of the coach towards the back where, of course, we would all have made for when we got on the vehicle.

The ones nearest the front got through the fire before it really took hold and then the rest of us had to make a very speedy exit, without our belongings, through the emergency exit at the back, when we had finally managed to spring it open.

We all dropped onto the M6 dazed and confused and suddenly we were surrounded by police cars and police officers, guiding us out of the fast lane onto to the hard shoulder – and all of this in the pitch black just after midnight.

No less than a couple of minutes after we were all clear of the blazing coach it literally blew up, sending flames flying high into the night-time sky.

We were all ferried back to Liverpool in police vehicles, dazed but safe and then I made my way back home.

The following morning my mum said: "You got in late last night, where were you?" I flipped over the *Daily Express* onto its front page and said: "In that."

The paper's headline read 'Late-night coach blaze drama on M6.'

Just to complete a miserable 24 hours, Liverpool, winners of the FA Cup the previous season, went out to Ipswich Town in the fourth round of the following season's competition.

*   *   *   *   *

Steve Coppell's move from Tranmere Rovers to Manchester United, and his decision to finish his studies at Liverpool University meant he and we were the subject of some journalistic interest.

Indeed, when Steve, a Liverpool supporter, was due to play at Anfield for United against the Reds and those other university graduates, Heighway and Hall, both *Football Focus* and Granada's

Kick-Off programme turned up on the campus to preview the event. Steve rang around and we all bowled up, filled seats in the lecture rooms for him and were asked by reporters, Tony Gubba and Gerald Sinstadt, what type of bloke Steve was and so on.

Granada even sent a camera down to Cronton where Comecon played and filmed bits from the game including capturing one of my rare goals.

The following Friday we watched ourselves in glorious colour on Granada's *Kick-Off* and the following lunch-time saw brief glimpses of ourselves on BBC's *Football Focus*. Six years on from that broadcast, I would actually be the producer of *Football Focus*, going out filming with Tony on a regular basis and later would co-author a book with Gerald Sinstadt whilst working with him at the BBC. Spooky.

The actual game they previewed delivered the perfect result for me: a 3-1 win for Liverpool over Manchester United with Steve scoring United's only goal and at the Kop end.

Steve, of course, still a Liverpool fan today, would have a very successful career for club and country before injury cruelly cut his playing career short.

Stints in management followed, most notably at Reading and Crystal Palace, where he proudly brought his newly-promoted side to Anfield only to endure a humiliating 9-0 drubbing. Later that season he would be at the helm when his Eagles side would beat Liverpool 4-3 in extra-time of an FA Cup semi-final thriller.

Disappointed as I was that Liverpool hadn't reached the final themselves I was thrilled to bits for Stevie.

My final year as a student at the University of Liverpool coincided with Bob Paisley's first in charge at Anfield. The Reds just came up short, finishing runners-up behind Derby County. Early exits were also suffered in the two domestic cups – the FA Cup and League

Cup – and the European Cup Winners Cup, despite his debut in Europe heralding an 11-0 win over the Norwegians, Stromsgodset Drammen.

Phil Boersma scored two in that game and, in his best spell at the club, he also scored in the FA Charity Shield, a hat-trick in 37 minutes against Tottenham Hotspur and a truly fantastic goal at Anfield against Stoke City. That particular goal would be right up there with some of the greatest ever seen at Anfield but it wasn't captured on camera that day.

In the early part of the season, Boersma was teamed up front with Ray Kennedy, Arsenal's 1971 Double-winner who bizarrely was signed by Bill Shankly on the day he actually resigned from the club himself.

Kennedy started his Anfield career as a forward, but Paisley's canniness saw him move the strong man into the heart of the Liverpool midfield where his strength would help the Reds win the ball and carry it forward. He would also score vital goals for the club.

It was a season which would also see the introduction of two other future greats: Phil Neal, signed from Northampton Town and Terry McDermott, a Kirkby boy who had been up against Liverpool in the previous season's cup final. Paisley picked both of them to make their Liverpool league debuts in that most easy of games – the derby match at Goodison.

Neal, a relative unknown to Reds and Blues alike was able to pick up his boots from Anfield on the morning of the game and walk across Stanley Park to Goodison untroubled by fans of either side. He would go on to make 633 appearances for the Reds, scoring 60 goals.

McDermott, like Neal, would score for Liverpool in a European Cup final, win medals galore, and score a goal against Spurs which

Bob Paisley would describe as the best ever scored at Anfield. He would also be crowned Footballer of the Year in 1980.

Also saying 'hello' in the final league game of the season was a young local midfielder, Jimmy Case, and making his last league appearance for Liverpool was Alan Waddle, a lanky awkward-looking forward, whose brief Liverpool career for the Reds included a derby winner against Everton at Goodison and an appearance as a substitute in their European Cup semi-final against FC Zurich in 1977.

The year following my departure from the University of Liverpool saw me flirt briefly with furthering my studies at John Moores University, before settling down to get on the job hunt.

My preference was a career in journalism. I had always thought it would be a challenging yet fulfilling career but knew my chances were slim. I knew little of how to break into the business and knew nobody actually in it. Not a great combination.

I wrote letters everywhere and would stack the rejections behind the living room clock until I had so many it looked like time might fly... off the mantelpiece.

I took a clerk's job in Liverpool City Council, but felt it wasn't for me – a view I think they shared.

My job search did give me time to continue to watch Liverpool and play my football for a combination of Convocation (University Old Boys) and a pub team called the Storrsdale. The Storrsdale, a pub in the attractive district of Allerton, became a regular haunt of mine. Through it I met a great set of lads and we put together a football team and started playing friendlies.

My dad got us a football kit from an old police pal of his at the Liverpool County FA, Geoff Swinnerton. It was an old Liverpool away kit – white shirts, black shorts and red socks – and it did take a little gentle persuasion for some of the Evertonians in the team to actually wear it, but we got there somehow.

Anyway, it was fitting we played in the kit because the landlord of the Storrsdale was a gentleman called Norman Low, who had played for Liverpool before the Second World War.

Norman had done subsequent scouting for Liverpool and his pub was often a midweek stop-off point for Liverpool chairman John Smith to collect his thoughts.

Norman's wife Lil was actually the sister of the great Liverpool boxer Nel Tarleton who fought for the world title in a bout actually held on the pitch at Anfield in 1935. We looked to Norman for a bit of inspiration and advice, but having seen how we 'pre-fuelled' and then 're-fuelled' before and after our games, he didn't hold out much hope for us.

We would join a league in 1976 – the Kirkby Newtown Combination – and arrive like a coach-load of Lord Snootys to play some of the toughest and best teams in Merseyside football.

We did, however, have some very good footballers in our ranks and made a reasonable fist of our first season in the league.

By the time that was underway, Liverpool were both league champions and UEFA Cup holders, and I had landed a job in the profession of my choice.

The 1975/76 season was the campaign I made the big switch from the Paddock to the Kop. No small decision that. Changing your established spec at a ground takes some thinking about. Your eye-line on the game had been honed on where you regularly saw the action from and any change had to be carefully considered.

Many fans never budge from where they start watching their favourite team and, of course, get to know many like-minded souls around them. You all have your favourite players and always believe your spec wherever it is has the perfect view of whatever contentious decision is made on the day.

My two pals Andy and Ross are proper home and away Reds fans and have been for decades. Proper Liverpool fans. Indeed, Andy writes a weekly fan's column in the *Liverpool Daily Post* called Red Watch, where he intelligently positions his views on current Anfield activity.

They have two season tickets in the Kemlyn Road Stand and obviously spend most away visits behind the goal – up high or to the side. But it doesn't make any difference to them, they always believe that they have the perfect view of the 'killer' incident of the day and, if you argue from a different perspective or from a different view-point in the stadium, or, indeed, off the back of watching six replays on Sky, they will listen to your reasoning but still insist that what they saw was what actually happened. And good luck to them.

So, after over a decade in the Paddock it was time to become a regular standing on the Kop.

And, of course, it was great fun. Getting there early, one of the first in the ground, watching the crowd and the atmosphere build.

I decided to stand to the left of the goal halfway up. Well, at least that was the starting position. Throughout the game you were tossed this way and that, and sent up and down the mighty terrace, and only be re-united with your mates – and your shoes – at the end of the game.

The singing was excellent, the chants started in unison and the idea of a crowd 'sucking' the ball into the net felt real. Many times you felt the opposition buckle under the collective pressure of home team and home crowd. There was also the added attraction of watching the young lads in the Boys' Pen taking leave of their own spot – and their senses – by crawling along the girders at the top of the Kop roof to subsequently drop down into the world's most famous terrace. Anyway, I was now a Kopite, and would remain one for the next decade.

The 1975/76 season itself started in a way that didn't exude confidence. A 2-0 away defeat at QPR included a goal from Gerry Francis that would win BBC's Goal of the Season. Surprise title contenders QPR would take Liverpool all the way to the second half of Liverpool's last match of the season in their own pursuit of the title.

Paisley believed he had learnt the difference between being the boss and being the right-hand man during his first season in charge and was determined that his team would add consistency to their overall game. The domestic season went to the last match. Wolverhampton Wanderers v Liverpool, a must-win match for both teams. For Wolves it was to stay in the First Division, for Paisley's Liverpool it was to clinch their first championship since 1973.

On Wednesday, May 4, thousands of Liverpool fans made their way to Molineux . The M6 was chock-a-block. We were part of that hundred mile queue and despite giving ourselves plenty of time, just made it and managed to get a decent spec behind the net where all the goals would be scored.

Huyton-born Steve Kindon opened the scoring, a strong run and shot giving the home side an early first half lead which Liverpool couldn't pull back.

Back in London, a group of QPR players were watching pictures being beamed back to them from Molineux. Again, there was no live TV coverage of these games in those days.

At half-time they must have thought they were on the verge of their own piece of football history, but in a memorable second half, kicking towards Liverpool's massed ranks of support, three goals in the season's last 15 minutes gave Liverpool the win – and Paisley's first championship as manager.

And everybody there expected it to happen. Strangely it was tense, but not super-tense. Liverpool just got stronger the longer the game went on. We just knew it would be our night and the goals finally tumbled in.

First Keegan via Toshack, then Toshack via Keegan, and finally Kennedy with a third, giving Liverpool victory and sending the massive travelling support berserk. Even the Wolves fans accepted their lot – relegation – in good spirit.

It was a really special night for the Liverpool fans at the ground, the many locked outside, and the thousands on Merseyside and beyond. And I suppose the champagne was put back on ice in London, and the QPR players were forced to realise just how near, yet how far, they had come to landing an amazing prize.

After the match the scenes were memorable – and the journey back to Merseyside on a jam-packed M6 was one long motorway Conga. The traffic was at a standstill but we weren't.

One down, one to go; because Liverpool had also made their way to the final of the UEFA Cup again. Hibernian, Real Sociedad, Slask Wroclaw, Dynamo Dresden and finally mighty Barcelona had been put to the sword as Liverpool prepared to meet the Belgian league side in the two-legged final.

Their semi-final win over Johan Cruyff's Barcelona was a supreme triumph. A single goal from Toshack from a typical Keegan assist, gave Liverpool victory and set cushions flying at the Nou Camp. By the time the Spaniards arrived at Anfield for the second leg, their coach Hennes Weisweiler had been handed his notice and they had a new man in charge, Laureano Ruiz.

A tight game ended 1-1, Phil Thompson getting Liverpool's goal and Johan Cruyff, clearly acting almost as player-manager, had to accept the Reds had finally exacted revenge for the mauling at his Ajax hands ten years before.

The first leg of the final was actually before the vital Wolves league game and, at Anfield, the contest looked over before it had almost got underway. Bruges scored twice in the first twelve minutes. Two belting goals, the second a devastating volley from Cools. Both goals stunned the Kop, me included.

But it was one of those famous Anfield European nights when anything could happen – and did. On the hour Ray Kennedy pulled one back, two minutes later his shot came back off a post and Jimmy Case, on for Toshack, scrambled home a second.

Astonishingly, three minutes after that, Steve Heighway was pulled down in the box and Footballer of the Year Kevin Keegan stepped up to drill the ball home from the penalty spot.

Not Istanbul, but I can assure those of you not around at the time that the atmosphere in the ground, and on the Kop, immediately after that remarkable scoring sequence was absolutely electric. Sure, we still had a second leg to handle but we had witnessed a truly remarkable fightback.

Strangely, though, it was my 'second-best' football memory of that day. That afternoon I had been made a make-shift goalkeeper for my Comecon side in our university semi-final against a cracking team from the Law department. Against all the odds I had a blinder – a complete fluke – and we won 1-0.

Obviously small beer compared to events later that day at Anfield, of course, but still very special to me. We lost the university final heavily, I was back as an outfield player, and a certain Steve Coppell played in goal for us – four days after playing the 1976 FA Cup final. A unique double.

Liverpool, now English champions, went over to Belgium to face Bruges, now their country's champions and with a narrow lead from the first leg.

The game was tight but a Keegan goal three minutes after Bruges had opened the scoring, plus a mighty stern rear-guard action was enough to see the Reds home – and to be able to add the UEFA

Cup to the League Championship and the Central League title in what was Paisley's breakthrough season.

I made my way to Speke Airport the following day to welcome the team home. Season over – the next time Liverpool kicked a competitive ball in Europe I had also taken flight and moved away from my native city to pursue my own professional prize.

My pursuit of a career in journalism had led me to apply for a place on a graduate scheme at Westminster Press, a Fleet Street based Newspaper Group, which then owned dozens of provincial newspapers scattered the length and breadth of the country.

In life, I am a great believer in serendipity (mind you, I can barely spell it). It means that sometimes things are just meant to happen.

So, on the day I went down to London on the train for my interview, quaking with nerves, I arrived only to find that the person who was due to see me was sick and that to save me wasting my time the chairman of the company would see me during his lunch-hour.

Well, this was a mis-match if ever there was one; me, 22 and still in need of the odd rough edge to be rubbed off, in front of an experienced publishing professional – and a toff to boot.

The meeting went splendidly. And against all the odds we hit it off. I told him I was desperate to have a go at being a journalist and he listened with kindly interest and said they would be in touch in due course.

I walked back out into a hot summer's afternoon in Fleet Street, humming the *What The Papers Say* theme and hoping that in a few weeks, as promised, I would hear from the company and that my career would be off and running. And I did – and it was.

In late August 1976, I set off with my parents to make the move to my new home – Barrow-in-Furness – birthplace of Reds' star Emlyn Hughes and home to the *North-Western Evening Mail*.

I would spend three happy and informative years there learning the rudiments of journalism – shorthand, typing, deadlines, story-shaping, interviewing techniques, telephone manner.

It was all new to me but I found it fascinating and was hungry to learn. For me it was the right way to get into the trade, working with a great set of colleagues and I found that every day threw up a new and interesting challenge.

And, of course, every evening I could read my pearls of wisdom in the evening paper – and the following night have my fish and chips wrapped up in them!

11

Flat Caps and Red Caps

On a damp Saturday in May 1983, Liverpool prepared for their final home league game of the season. It was against Aston Villa, still, then, the reigning European champions.

As often was the case at Anfield in that spell, home games in May invariably meant prize-giving time.

Liverpool had won the championship the previous season, and had done so again, so they just had to take the beautiful trophy out of its display cabinet, have it re-presented, paraded around the ground for the fans and then put back where it belonged.

To be fair, this was the sixth time in eight years Liverpool had been crowned champions of England – the SIXTH time in eight years. And that phenomenal achievement was led by the man who was celebrating his 44th consecutive year at the club that week. That man was Bob Paisley.

A more unassuming person it would be difficult to meet but North-Easterner Bob, born in Hetton-le-Hole, would have been entitled to shout from the highest rooftops given the scale of his success during his nine year reign as the manager of Liverpool.

Six titles, three League Cups, five Charity Shields, one UEFA Cup, one Super Cup and, of course, THREE European Cups.

The man who had replaced the 'irreplaceable' Bill Shankly had taken the club on to even greater things and all of it with the air of a man just going about his every day business.

He had a quiet dignified authority, an encyclopaedic knowledge of the game, and a huge trust in his players and staff. "I'll let the team do the talking for me," he would say.

And they did match after match, season after season. However, this season, 1982/83 was to mark the end of his illustrious time in the managerial hotseat at Anfield.

Upon his retirement he was elected to the board and later worked as an advisor to Kenny Dalglish, but this day in May he selected an Anfield team for the last time and took the bows from a grateful set of Liverpool supporters.

Sportsnight, BBC's flagship midweek sports magazine show asked reporter Alan Parry and myself to shadow Bob during his final emotional week and prepare a 30-minute film for the following Wednesday. We thought it might be a challenge.

Bob was such a humble character, an introvert, a doer not a talker, but we needn't have worried. Firstly, he gave us fantastic access to both his professional and family life and secondly, former team-mates, his current and former players, and local dignitaries queued up to have their best wishes filmed for posterity. He was a very popular man.

He was also a man who never lost his roots; beautifully illustrated on that match day when he forsook all the pre-match champagne and rich buffet of meats, fish and desserts, for something much, much simpler.

As hundreds of guests enjoyed football's newly-fangled corporate hospitality, we filmed a faithful old Anfield retainer carefully carrying an old wooden tray on which was a bowl of vegetable soup and two Cornish pasties.

On a journey he had made many times, the make-do waiter turned right at the bottom of a corridor and headed towards the door marked 'Manager'.

Inside the small neat office was Bob, dressed in his trademark cardigan, working out his line-up for the afternoon's match.

These were unique images. Bob carefully and neatly putting pen to paper and a lifetime's experience to good use, before writing out in long-hand his choice for the Reds' latest test. His team –
Grobbelaar, Neal, Kennedy, Thompson, Lawrenson, Dalglish, Lee, Hodgson, Souness, Johnston and Fairclough.

Job done – he put his pen down and set about his simple lunch. Mind you, as Alan Parry put it so neatly in his commentary, it must have been a big day – pasties? He normally only had pies!

It made a wonderful opening sequence to the film; in a single image we felt we had managed to capture the essence of the man. Not for him the great hullabaloo, but the simple down-to-earth pleasures of life. It set the tone for the film, in which time and again people paid tribute to an ordinary man with an extraordinary talent in his chosen field.

On the way to the ground that Saturday, Bob had popped into the Liverpool Supporters' Club and thanked the fans gathered there for their loyalty and support. His gracious words were tinged with sadness and a shaft of wit.

"Obviously it is a big day for me, my last day... but at least I know that. There'll be managers working today who don't know it is yet!" His audience roared and his face lit up with joy.

Earlier in the week we had seen a similar expression of happiness as he played with his grandchildren in the lounge of his family home, repeatedly sending them down a toy slide and winding the wall clock back to the hour so the cuckoo would come out and surprise his audience of tiny tots. He so enjoyed their wonderment at it all.

On the walls of his lounge were any number of certificates, plates and mementos of his football achievements – but here in his lovely Woolton home, he was grandad, dad or just Bob, Jessie's husband.

Jessie told us they had been married since 1946. On a train journey from his barracks, soldier Bob had accidentally dropped his great-coat on her pack of sandwiches (that old trick, Bob!). They got talking and were together from that moment hence. As they sat in the garden enjoying the warm spring evening sunshine, the film showed them gently reminiscing about their early lives together.

Jessie told us: "Life has changed all around us but we've not changed as people. I remember when Bob got £10 a week in the winter and £8 in the summer and we thought we were doing nicely then. It's all changed now, of course, but he hasn't, Bob hasn't."

"Yes, that's right. Jessie still gets the same house-keeping – 30 bob!" Bob quipped and the couple chuckled happily.

Bob and Jessie had three children, brothers Robert and Graham and daughter, Christine. Robert and Graham, like me, had both been pupils at Quarry Bank and later played their weekend football for Quarry Bank Old Boys. One of their Quarry Bank School team-mates was Dave Saunders, son of another member of the Liverpool footballing brains-trust, Tom Saunders.

The Paisleys were a close-knit family and one that enjoyed each other's company. Sport was always on their agenda. Bob himself was an excellent cricketer and he had a lifelong love of horse-racing.

Bob later took some time out to tell us what he had thought about his time in the Liverpool hotseat – and his decision to take the job.

"All I wanted to do was to check with the staff and check their reaction to me taking the job – but they were all for us, and that. Anyway we all needed a job!"

Later in the documentary, his assistant and ultimately the man who succeeded him in the Anfield hotseat, Joe Fagan added his own thoughts.

"When Bob took the job, he didn't know how he was going to handle it – because Bill had such a strong personality and character and Bob was different. But Bob did brilliantly, getting the right players, setting them and the staff up right – and six titles in eight years... well, it is unbelievable really."

I once sat with Paisley on the Paddock wall at Anfield watching a private pre-season kick-about between members of his squad. We were up on Merseyside to get an interview with his new goalkeeper, Bruce Grobbelaar and defensive recruit Mark Lawrenson. It was a beautiful August morning a few days before the start of the season and I was a privileged spectator.

There must have been only about a dozen of us rattling around the newly spick and span stadium – with that unmistakable smell of freshly mown grass – and a new season in the air.

Bob sat down with me and reporter, Alan Parry, and gently commented on what was happening on the pitch. He watched things with a deeply experienced eye. He spotted things we didn't... obviously. One thing I do clearly remember is how well he thought Mark Lawrenson would fit into the side and sure enough a few days later the former Preston and Brighton man made his debut for Liverpool and became a hugely significant player for many seasons to come.

Paisley understood players, what made them tick and how they could best be used on the field.

And indeed, even though he was just days away from finishing in his role as Liverpool manager, our cameras captured his final Liverpool signing, full-back Jim Beglin from Shamrock Rovers.

Beglin, now an accomplished broadcaster, would be a member of the Double-winning side before a serious injury curtailed his career.

We followed Bob on his short journey from Anfield to Melwood and as he went about his work, we went about ours, the camera crew and myself finding ourselves on the roof of a 17-storey block of flats just outside the training ground perimeter.

From that remarkable vantage point, and with a huge lens, our cameraman was able to gently zoom in from the wide expanse of Melwood with its training area, pitches, sweat-box and dressing rooms to a single person on the edge of the action – watching Liverpool's players going through their paces.

It was Paisley, his eagle eye not missing a trick as the players prepared for the following day's game. As he stood there, he was joined by his assistant Joe Fagan. In many ways the camera captured the passing of the managerial mantle from one footballing sage to another.

On match-day itself we were accorded some other insights to the 'Liverpool Way.'

In rare access to the 'inner sanctum' – the Liverpool dressing room – the *Sportsnight* cameras were able to witness the players' final preparations for the forthcoming afternoon's action.

Phil Thompson stretching his thin frame from side to side; Sammy Lee having a damaged ankle bandaged by Joe Fagan; captain Graeme Souness in small talk with long-serving backroom boy, Reuben Bennett and Alan Hansen reading the matchday programme.

Coach Ronnie Moran was checking over the Villa line-up and

working out who would play where, and how the Reds could exploit their weaknesses and guard against their strengths.

Bob Paisley finally entered the dressing room and quietly gave me the nod that our camera crew would have to make themselves scarce. Then he went around the players, a word here and a word there.

He sought out his star striker, Kenny Dalglish, standing by a treatment table and in a typically understated manner congratulated the Scotsman for being chosen the Football Writers' Footballer of the Year. Dalglish's response was similarly understated. No big deal. Just two men secure of their place in football history. Then it was out onto the pitch to collect the championship trophy – again.

Captain Souness received the trophy and handed it straight to Paisley – mirroring the gesture the players had made earlier in the season when they beat Manchester United in the Milk Cup final at Wembley.

On that occasion, they had persuaded him to lead them up the 39 steps and collect the trophy on their behalf. He was reluctant then but later spoke of his genuine pride at the players' gesture. The team even persuaded him to take off his mac and famous flat cap before heading up the steps in a pristine new suit and Liverpool FC tie.

Again in May they wanted him to do the same. Only this time at Anfield. They wanted him to take the plaudits from his home crowd. The fans went wild, and the Kop sang his praises, then as his players got ready to start the game he disappeared down the tunnel with the trophy nestled in his hands – for the last time.

As he handed it over to an assistant, he was entitled to say: "Put it back in its usual place," but that wouldn't have been Bob. Such a modest individual. Anyway there was another match to win.

At the end of the game, a 1-1 draw, we watched as the Liverpool players celebrated their title win in the dressing room and Bob Paisley stood quietly by, no doubt contemplating the end of a distinguished personal era.

"People may think I'm not laughing all the time but I'm laughing inside. I've certainly enjoyed it. And in my own way, I get a lot of pleasure from it."

We later retired to the Boot Room, and filmed tales of Bob from Fagan, Moran and Evans.

Liverpool's Boot Room has always had mythical status in football and would be where the coaching staff would host the visiting manager and his coaching staff. Whatever the result and whatever controversy a game had thrown up, all would be forgotten in that special room – as a glass or two of something special was taken on board. It became the most famous room in football. And it was a thrill to capture some fly-on-the-wall footage from within this remarkable footballing think-tank.

I recently mentioned the Boot Room to an old friend, former Southampton manager, Lawrie McMenemy. He said he only won once in eight visits to Anfield – and often thought the only thing you would get out of an away trip there was a nice post-match welcome from the lads in the Boot Room.

He said he went in there after one particular game wearing an expensive new coat. The Liverpool coaching staff watched with amusement as he tried to find an upturned beer keg, they doubled up as seats, that wasn't dusty and dirty.

And then he was offered a drink.

He said each different football boot box had a different bottle in it. Whisky in one, red wine in another, white wine in another and so on... and the wine, like the welcome, he said, was always terrific.

On Bob Paisley's last day, we filmed him coming into the Boot

Room with a beautiful silver service – teapot, sugar bowl and cups. With an embarrassed chuckle he addressed his mickey-taking colleagues: "A present from the Villa for me – I think I'll leave it here with you guys – a bit of class for the Boot Room!"

We turned the camera off and quietly made our exit leaving Bob and his closest football mates to discuss in private the previous ninety minutes, nine years, or whatever came up.

Mind you, Bob was the ultimate 'bit of class' for the Boot Room – and they knew it.

*　*　*　*　*

Twelve months earlier Bob had gone through the same routine when Liverpool clinched the league title with a stunning home win over Tottenham Hotspur. As memorable as the victory was, the ovation accorded former Liverpool great, Ray Clemence, now a Spurs player, as he ran towards the Kop before the start of the second half topped it.

Later that summer Clemence would be part of an England squad that went to the World Cup in Spain.

As part of the build-up to the tournament, England played Scotland at Hampden Park in a 'Centenary' international. I was at the game for the BBC and after England's 1-0 win jumped a lift back to Liverpool with Phil Neal, Phil Thompson and Scotland's Graeme Souness.

Their post-mortem on the game lasted a few minutes and a few miles as we drove on the motorway out of Scotland and then their thoughts turned to the summer – and the World Cup ahead of them.

Souness would be joined in Spain by Liverpool team-mates Alan Hansen and Kenny Dalglish in the Scotland squad, whilst the two

Phils would have Terry McDermott alongside them for their first foray into World Cup finals football.

And I was able to throw in my twopenneth as well as I, too, was off to Spain and the World Cup – and, I knew my team, the BBC, would be there from the beginning to the end.

Originally carded to work as a producer with the England team, I was disappointed when at the last moment I was switched to be with Northern Ireland instead.

Disappointed because the routine was that you stayed at the World Cup as long as 'your' team did – and Northern Ireland were not fancied to come through a group including Yugoslavia, Honduras and hosts, Spain.

Anyway, off to Valencia I went to meet up with my reporter for the trip – David Icke. Yes, the self-same David Icke who has subsequently gone on to become, well how can I put this delicately, pretty extreme in his views on how the world has been run so far – and by whom – and how it will all end 'a week on Tuesday' – give or take a century or two.

Oh, and also how he believes in the positive energy of the colour turquoise.

And it would seem he has followers everywhere.

When I knew him he was a football reporter. Mind you, I knew David was special when he walked across the swimming pool to meet me as I arrived at our Spanish hotel. He was extraordinary.

In the middle of the night I would hear him bashing away at the typewriter keys in his room next to mine.

"What were you writing last night?" I would say to him at breakfast.

"The script for today's film," he replied.

"But we haven't shot it yet. Not a single frame of it. We don't know what it will be about yet."

"The words will fit," he would say with great portent.

On reflection, I think I was possibly at the birth of David's ability to look into the future – albeit 24 hours at a time in this case.

What neither of us could have predicted – well, me anyway – was that Northern Ireland would become one of the stories of the tournament.

Two draws against Yugoslavia and Honduras meant they went into the final group game still in contention to qualify for the next stage. But the plucky Irish had to overcome the obstacle of beating hosts Spain in front of fanatical fans in Valencia's famous Estadio Mestalla. And they did.

The Spain of 1982 was not the Spain of 2010 and Northern Ireland, via a Gerry Armstrong goal, did for them. It was a huge turn-up – Northern Ireland had won the group, and Spain, whistled off the pitch, squeaked through in second place. It was the story of the tournament so far.

I was on the touchline as the game ended, and my instructions were fired to me from BBC's base in Madrid. "Get Billy Bingham (Northern Ireland's manager) and Gerry Armstrong... get them before ITV. And make sure we can see you."

The last part of that command explains why if you watch the official FIFA film of the 1982 tournament, 'G'Ole!' you see a BBC producer in a bright red cap (of course) in a fast-moving media scrum racing on the pitch in pursuit of the celebrating Northern Ireland team.

And, in close attendance is my ITV counterpart, a woman called Pat Pearson. I think it was a close run thing – and we probably ended up with one 'target' each.

Anyway, our tussle for the first post-match interview is enshrined in that movie, much to the mickey-taking delight of my two sons who watched the film being re-run on ESPN last Christmas. I think

I was behind the sofa at the time.

Northern Ireland ultimately exited the tournament at the next stage, as did unbeaten England – but the BBC asked me to stay on until the end of the tournament. Brilliant.

One of my travelling companions by this stage of the competition was Sir Bobby Charlton, or plain Bobby, as he was then. He was good company.

I remember one evening he knocked on my hotel bedroom door and said the Rolling Stones management had got in touch with him and asked whether he wanted to go and see the world famous band who were due to play in Atletico Madrid's Estadio Vicente Calderon that night.

"Do you fancy it?" he said.

"Absolutely" was my reply.

Which is how I found myself with one of English football's most iconic figures picking up tickets and back-stage passes for an unforgettable evening of music from The Stones.

The following morning I remember writing a postcard to my mum and dad which started. 'Things going well. Working hard but enjoying it. Went to see the Rolling Stones last night with Bobby Charlton.' I didn't send it.

We both went to that epic semi-final between West Germany and France on a stifling- hot night in Seville – and then I was delighted to be given a ticket for the final itself by my BBC bosses, Bob Abrahams and Alec Weeks.

And they told me to just to enjoy the match and, indeed, the whole experience of being at the World Cup final.

I did. And some.

Italy beat Germany 3-1 in the magnificent Bernabeu Stadium and, in a final twist to my first memorable professional trip to a World Cup, I ended up that evening in the same hotel as the celebrating

Italian team and coaching staff.

To have some well-deserved privacy they finally forced closed the doors of their post-match party to a mixture of both a persistent press pack and the hoards of frenzied Italian fans. In the attendant scramble, however, I found myself on the 'inside' of the room not the outside.

And so, for ten minutes or so got to know what it's like to win the World Cup – mingling with the likes of Bearzot, Rossi, Tardelli and Zoff – before being asked, red cap and all, to make myself scarce.

12

Euro Stars and
Euro Scars

I have never been a committed home and away Reds supporter –
and freely admit it. Reasons? Well, during my 50 years supporting
the club, they have ranged from age, cost, distance, work, official
role and, well, just life – in no particular order.

I absolutely commend those that are 'full-time supporters' and
am sometimes envious of the moment each summer when the
fixtures are published and people can start planning their journeys up and down the motorways and railways of the country for
the next ten months.

That is not to say I haven't travelled thousands of miles down
the years to see my team play – and not just in the latter years as a
so-called pampered VIP. Far from it.

On a train journey recently, to Liverpool ironically, I killed the
time by going through all the league tables – including the Blue
Square Premier – working out how many clubs (and away grounds)
I had visited in following Liverpool 'on the road'.

I got to around 40 clubs and over 50 grounds – some of them
many times over, straddling the north, south, east and west of the
country.

Saturday 3pm kick-offs (remember them?), Saturday lunchtimes and early evenings, Sunday lunchtimes and late afternoons, Monday, Tuesday, Wednesday, Thursday evenings – even Friday evenings in the '80s, Boxing Day, New Year's Day, Good Friday and Easter Monday... I, like you, have done them all.

Invariably by car, quite often with mates, Andy and Ross, up and down the M6 in my Liverpool days – up the M1 from London – or, indeed, across London itself since settling down in the south. Here's (a probably incomplete) list of clubs I have visited on my Liverpool travels down the years:

Arsenal, Aston Villa, Barnsley, Birmingham, Blackburn, Bolton, Brentford, Brighton, Charlton, Chelsea, Coventry, Crystal Palace, Derby County, Everton, Fulham, Ipswich Town, Leeds United, Leicester City, Luton Town, Manchester City, Manchester United, Millwall, Newcastle United, Norwich City, Oxford United, Portsmouth, QPR, Reading, Sheffield United, Southampton, Stoke City, Sunderland, Tottenham Hotspur, Tranmere Rovers, Watford, West Brom, West Ham, Wigan Athletic, Wimbledon and Wolves.

Of course, you could probably add another 20 clubs to the list that I have visited on none 'Liverpool' days whilst carrying out my broadcasting and football duties.

These days, living in London, some of LFC's away games are easier to get to than some others. That said, the Reds' home games are now away games, if you get my drift.

Times too numerous to mention have I turned the key in the front door around or shortly after 2am having left Anfield 'bang on the final whistle' of a midweek game. But you have to be there don't you?

Following Liverpool also guarantees an opportunity to see the world. I think I have chalked up watching the Reds in around 15 countries and am always in awe of the fans that go 'everywhere'. With Liverpool that guarantees some interesting passport stamps and some exotic duty free.

For me, though, the stamps that record trips to Rome (twice), Paris, Brussels, Istanbul, Athens, with a day trip to London thrown in, bear witness to my attendance at some of Liverpool's landmark occasions.

* * * * *

May 23, 1977 – 6pm, Lime Street Station. My brother David and I were dropped off by dad ahead of the longest train journey we were ever likely to make.

As the ticket said – *'Rome and Back'*. The two of us, plus a few of our mates were setting off on one of the most memorable journeys of our lives. To the 'Eternal City' to watch Liverpool make their long-awaited debut in *the* club game – the European Cup final.

From the moment David Fairclough had scored that vital late winner against St Etienne in the quarter-finals, it had looked nailed on that Liverpool would make the final itself. And they did.

A kind draw in the semi-final had paired them with FC Zurich of Switzerland who put up little real opposition – and so it was all guns blazing to Rome. I had booked annual leave for the week of the final months before and then had to explain to my girlfriend of the time that I would be spending it with a group of blokes at a football match – in Italy! Not the easiest sell but needs must – and so we were ready for the off.

My memory doesn't stretch to why a train against a plane but I'm sure cost and availability played their part. I'm also not sure whether a match ticket was part of the package. Anyway, as the train pulled out of the station, there was a fantastic roar from those on it – and those waving it away.

Our train was just one of a number that left Lime Street that night and in truth the engines could have probably run on the pure adrenalin of the passengers on board.

The combined sense of anticipation and excitement was simply tremendous. Everybody was decked out in red and white and sharing the same sense of belief that they were going to Rome to see Liverpool win the European Cup. This was a real adventure.

Sure, we had all been at Wembley for the FA Cup final on the previous Saturday and seen us narrowly lose to arch-rivals Manchester United, but many people, me included, saw that game as a precursor to aiming for a greater prize in Italy.

Of course, it would have been great to have added the FA Cup to a league title won with something to spare. But it didn't happen – and we had quickly moved on.

The 'Essential Information to be Read by All Passengers' told us that Rome 'is a long way from Liverpool.' Thanks for that. And that you should ensure you take 'sufficient money or refreshments to last the full journey in both directions'.

This wasn't a bad bit of advice – what they didn't tell us was the trains wouldn't stop on the way back and there would be nothing to spend your money on. Anyway I am getting ahead of myself.

Our travel companions on the trip included Pete and Alan 'Alby' Roberts – two guys who could have gone on *Mastermind* with 'Having Fun' as their specialist subject. Also with us was Pete 'Cob' Webb – a 'gentleman builder' who had decided to bring his Union Jack flag with him – plus flagpole.

We settled into the journey – and despite the advice given us, we had eaten all our sandwiches by Crewe. In fact, I had polished mine off by Runcorn!

This would have consequences for the rest of the journey – and the return trip – when the hunger pangs really kicked in.

As the train flashed through the English countryside, the conversation was all about how we would win the game in the Stadio Olimpico and what we would do to celebrate the achievement in Rome.

Pete and Alby, as always, were full of lively anecdotes – the rest of us a receptive audience. Then, as Pete got to his feet to exaggerate a point, the train came to a sudden halt and he crashed forwards into a light fitting. Blood everywhere. Deep cut on his upper arm. From just having us in stitches, Pete suddenly needed some of his own – and quickly.

We pulled into London (I think) and said our farewells to Pete. He headed off for hospital and a morning return to Lime Street. The rest of us pressed on to Dover Harbour and the ferry.

The ferry crossing behind us, we had a couple of hours to kill in Ostend during which breakfast was taken. We then settled into our new train that would take us across Europe to Italy. The route had been affected by a French industrial dispute and we were diverted through Germany.

The journey passed peacefully and a little sleep was even taken (our compartment, was next to those of the travelling stewards – and therefore amongst the best, a fact that became a thing of some envy and intrigue from our fellow passengers. In truth we had just been quick off the mark when boarding the train).

We arrived in Rome about 6am Wednesday morning and were given our instructions for the return journey – basically, be here after the game or be left in Rome – and the day was ours to enjoy.

It started with a real bonus. A phone call home from Alby had established that Pete, having been patched up, had caught a later train out of Ostend and was also heading into Rome.

A meeting point was established – a message which would be

passed on to him – if Pete was able to make a phone call.

It is something that we all take for granted these days, an ability to keep in contact. But before mobile phones, BlackBerrys, iPhones and such-like, you had to depend on a phone booth, the right change, and fingers, rather than lines, crossed. It was not easy.

A beautiful warm morning awaited us in Rome and we didn't waste it.

One of the world's greatest cities and a 'must-see' destination point for world travellers, we set about visiting its great landmarks – the Coliseum, the Pantheon and the Trevi Fountain.

It is reckoned that over 25,000 Liverpool fans were in Rome that day, and I reckon all of them went to see the Trevi Fountain and many of them dipped their feet in the water to cool down. It was a fantastic day.

The afternoon was spent on St Peter's Square in Vatican City – fittingly, the first miracle of the day had already happened as we bumped into Pete, complete with heavy bandage and a whole new 'travel' story to add to his future repertoire and our group was back to its original numbers.

It was a day to cram as much sight-seeing in before making our way to the stadium.

Next stop – St Peter's Basilica, and as we entered the porch of the famous cathedral, a Scouse voice chimed out: "Are you members?" We looked up and recognised a doorman from one of the Liverpool city-centre night clubs we regularly spent our Fridays nights in. I suppose once a doorman always a doorman.

Finally it was time to have a spot of late lunch and a large glass of white wine. We found a spot and settled in for a couple of hours. The mood and the food were fantastic. We just knew this was going to be a day we would remember for many years to come.

Cob's flag, which in truth had been a pain to transport around suddenly took centre stage. My brother, David was minding it for him when a passer-by, decked out in Liverpool colours asked if he could borrow it. Yes, said David perfectly reasonably – and our new friend picked up the flagpole, and took it around the corner of the restaurant.

Next thing we knew, there was a heated argument between said friend and an Italian waiter, with the flagpole being used as a medieval lance. Not helpful.

Brief international incident; flag and flagpole ultimately lowered, and David, though totally innocent, the subject of a decent slab of emotional Italian rhetoric from the restaurant manager – and now his eight waiters!

Bill paid quickly. Move on.

When we reached the stadium it was absolutely buzzing. The five of us found a point to meet after the game, wished the Reds well and went our separate ways – our tickets being spread around the ground. Inside the stadium itself it became quickly apparent the Liverpool fans seemed to outnumber the German supporters of Borussia Moenchengladbach four-to-one.

The colour, noise, vibrancy and sheer chutzpah of the Liverpool supporters was just tremendous.

When the team came out to prepare for the final I think their collective breath must have been taken away.

If Wembley had now become Anfield South, the Olympic Stadium in Rome had become *Anfield Further South*.

The game itself has been well documented many times. Stunning opening from Terry McDermott, Case mistake, Simonsen equalising, critical Clemence save from Stielike, an unlikely Tommy Smith headed goal, then Keegan outstripping Berti Vogts and penalty converted by Phil Neal. Job done.

As Emlyn Hughes lifted the huge beautiful trophy, the stadium, or the vast majority of it, went berserk. This was the pinnacle for the Reds. Twelve years on from the disappointment of losing against Italian giants Inter Milan, in a dubious semi-final, they had gone one better in Rome.

During the second half of the game there had been an announcement to tell all of those supporters travelling back to England on the special trains to report immediately after the game to a particular station. This was not what had been expected – it had been thought we would be able to spend a couple of hours celebrating before making our way to the station to get the train.

Anyway, our group met up – still high on the game – and made our way via a trolley bus to the assigned station.

Soon we were on board, and equally quickly we were rolling out of Rome, leaving the scene of our greatest triumph behind us.

We settled into a compartment. Our group of five companions had become six, as we seemed to have inherited an old gentleman, who was short of a bit of comradeship and a bit of safety and security. He was very welcome to be with us.

He was also to become a critical player in the return journey, because no sooner were we rattling down the track than we were informed that we would not be stopping very often, and not at all in Germany – which is a big country.

It seems as though our beating a German team in the final had made the natives restless and overnight some of the more boisterous had become train-spotters. Germany, however, is a big country and the thought of travelling through it without stopping did raise some alarm bells. Whilst we all wanted to get back home to Liverpool as soon as possible and join in the mass celebrations there, it did seem important to us to stop reasonably often so we could pick up some grub. We were starving.

Nothing doing and the train exited Italy and headed non-stop towards Germany. It was at this point, we a) regretted having eaten all our sandwiches by Crewe on the outward journey and b) discovered that our new friend was a veteran of many a long journey who hadn't eaten all his provisions on the way to Rome, had plenty left for the return hike – and was our new best mate!

Let's call him Harry. Thirty four years on from the event his name totally escapes me.

Harry even had parcels of food marked 'Thursday' and 'Friday'. This was an organised man – and a godsend. Over the next 24 hours, we helped him rattle through 'Thursday' and also polished off 'Friday'. To be honest, we were disappointed he didn't have 'Saturday' and 'Sunday' sorted out for us as well...

In between a bite of Harry's chicken legs and quiche, we all tried to get some sleep. Really difficult, very uncomfortable and only manageable in short bursts. The train itself was roaring along, jam-packed with tired and hungry men, women, and children.

Eventually the guard on the train had got the message from so many people he arranged to stop at the next station for a comfort and café break – ten minutes.

As we pulled in to the station, and piled off the train, another engine pulled into the platform opposite – complete with a series of dining cars, coupled together – and full to the brim of German diners tucking into lunch.

What happened next belonged in a *Carry On* movie, for just seconds before our train set off on the next stage of its journey, we looked at the dining cars on the opposite track – and saw a brief swarm of our fellow-travellers race through the German dining compartments and emerge to great cheers with hams, chickens, sausages, all types of vegetables – and even a choice of dessert! The odd diner was even left minus a sausage – mid-bite.

Now I absolutely abhor violence, and there wasn't any - instead there was a sense of Robin Hood and his Merry Men about the whole split-second escapade.

The rest of the journey passed without incident, it was just interminable. We all wanted to get home in time to go to Anfield to be at Tommy Smith's testimonial match - perfect timing for Smithy - but our train eventually pulled back in to Lime Street about 7pm on Friday evening - nearly 40 hours after setting off from Italy. But what a story to tell.

So it was quickly home, a shower, a change of clothes, a bite to eat and then off to the pub to bore everybody rigid with our tales of derring-do! Marvellous.

*   *   *   *   *

Now if I was asked to name my top twenty Liverpool matches, it is not unreasonable to expect all of The Reds' European Cup final wins to be comfortably spread throughout the list - a bit like you'd expect at least five Beatles songs to be in any list of the all-time top twenty singles.

Well, for me the 1978 European Cup final between Liverpool and Bruges would not make it. Why? Dull game won by a special Dalglish goal. Dullish opposition. And, after the adventures of the previous year, Lime Street to Rome, a dull journey - from Liverpool to Wembley.

No cut arms, no Trevi Fountain, no Harry and his food parcels and no problems. Boring. What a match at Wembley against Belgian opposition did guarantee was that just about every Liverpool fan who wanted to be there - was.

The ground was just a mass of red and white - of Liverpool songs and Liverpool chants - and sure enough, Anfield South witnessed the latest lifting of the cup 'with the big ears', as it was known. Once again, Emlyn Hughes lifted it over his head to the sound of a Scouse-filled Wembley sending its joy skyward.

Terrific. Then it was back on the train and home. All in the space of 12 hours. Us 'Marco Polos' who had gone on the big adventure the previous year felt a little short-changed by the experience but, hey, we were European champions again – so get over it!

*   *   *   *   *

Three years later we were off on our travels again, this time Paris – and a final in the famous Parc des Princes against those legends of European football, the great Real Madrid. Surprisingly, only 48,360 attended the game and two of those souls were me and Andy.

Now both living in south-west London, indeed sharing a house with another Liverpool mate, Greg, and a Manchester United fan, Kevin, Andy and I were now long-distance Reds fans – with the opportunity to see the team in action, restricted by work (I worked Saturdays) and play (Andy played football on Saturdays). Still if we could see them – we did.

If not, no worries as I was supplied with all the latest Merseyside football news by a parcel delivered every Tuesday morning by the postman. Sent by my dear old mum, it would contain the previous weekend's *Football Echo*, Monday morning's *Liverpool Daily Post* and a packet of *Maynards Wine Gums*. The parcel arrived without fail every week – and each one was straddled by what seemed to be a complete roll of sellotape.

Despite some gentle suggestions to my mum that the amount of sellotape seemed a trifle excessive, it rarely seemed to change, so every Tuesday evening was spent trying to extricate the papers and sweets from their wrapping without tearing them to pieces.

And then gently picking off bits of sellotape from the end of my fingers.

The Echo souvenir paper *Allez Les Rouges* had arrived from mum a couple of days before Andy and I set off for Heathrow and a short flight to Paris.

We went out on Tuesday afternoon, enjoyed a bit of sight-seeing on Tuesday night and Wednesday daytime before setting off in good time for the final.

The game itself was disappointing but won with a cracking goal by Alan Kennedy. Over 20 years later, Kennedy would provide the cabaret for Andy's 50th birthday party – held appropriately at Anfield. After the game in 1981, we met up with all our old mates from Liverpool – veterans of Rome '77 and had a great night of celebration.

*   *   *   *   *

If 1977's trip to Rome had been an adventure of one type, the repeat journey there in 1984, would also be incident-packed but with a personally sad ending.

Liverpool had made the final beating Odense, Atletico Bilbao, Benfica and Dinamo Bucharest on route – and were now going to play Roma – in Rome! It did seem remarkable that arrangements couldn't be fluid enough to change the venue, once perhaps the semi-finalists had been known, some ten weeks before the final itself. That would have guaranteed the match would not be played on the actual home ground on one of the teams actually in the final. But no, nothing doing, so it was Roma v Liverpool in Rome.

My travel companion for this final was my wife, Gerry. Yes, since Liverpool's last appearance in the final in 1981, I had got myself married.

I had met Gerry at the BBC. She was a very talented film editor, who, at that time, had been seconded to the Corporation's sports department.

A very bright, attractive lady, with a great passion for life, Gerry had made sense of my occasional wayward direction and production of short films for *Football Focus* – by turning the day's rushes into very acceptable pieces of television.

We got along great, and one thing led to another, and so in October 1982, we were married in a church near her parent's home of Newbury. Gerry's parents, of Irish descent, had moved there from their home in Catford, London when Gerry was a young girl.

Gerry was, and still is, a huge fan of keeping fit. She loved doing her aerobic classes, way before anybody came up with the name, and still to this day does daily physical jerks to keep looking great.

Whilst neither set of in-laws predicted the marriage would last – they didn't think we had known each other long enough – next year we will celebrate our 30th wedding anniversary and will share those special moments with our pride and joy – two sons, Jack, 21, and Joe, 20.

Gerry's contribution to any perceived success I may have had in my working life is total. She has provided the security, strength, stability and savvy to allow me on both our behalves to take risks. And been ready to pick up the pieces if things have got difficult. My beautiful rock.

One thing that has kept us sane, as well, is that we don't share the same interests. We are in the 'opposites attract' column and that meant, when we first met, football, for her, was work not pleasure, and her knowledge of the game was limited to what she needed to know.

Thirty years on that's still pretty much where we stand.

She accepted early on in our relationship that I was already wedded – to football. But she has managed to walk the line of dignified indifference to the ups and downs of the sport, especially useful during my period as the CEO of the FA.

Despite the regular furore in that job, when our family door was shut, we were a normal family like everybody else. She made sure of that.

Anyway, that was all years ahead of us when we made our way to Rome with friends for the 1984 final.

The previous weekend I had made a significant professional stride forward, editing my first *Grandstand*, keeping the programme on track and on time.

A few years later it would be second nature but not back then. A phone-call, prior to the show, from David Coleman wishing me luck was much appreciated. After all, I had spent the last 20 years of my life watching and listening to the great man.

The show went well, but later that day another phone call knocked my spirits. It was from my mother telling me that my dad was in hospital back in Liverpool with a chest infection. This was complete news to me – and completely new to me as well. I had never had either parent be in hospital before and was obviously keen to know what was what.

I was told he had admitted himself a couple of days before, after feeling unwell. He had made my mum promise not to tell me prior to my doing *Grandstand* that day.

It seemed he was making good progress, and obviously in good hands. We discussed me coming up to see him and mum suggested I come up at the back end of the week.

The following day, May Bank Holiday Monday, it was announced that Eric Morecambe had died suddenly, just two weeks after that other comic giant, Tommy Cooper, had also suffered a fatal heart attack. Both were big favourites of my dad.

We arrived in Rome – and met up with friends, old and new. As well as watching the game, Alan Parry and I had been given the job of getting some post-match reaction to the game from the Liverpool camp. It was ITV's turn to cover the final but BBC's *Sportsnight* would carry a report on the game and then broadcast some post-match interviews with the team.

The only way to get that message to the players was to get close to them. So Alan and I went down to the tunnel area before the game, and using our passes and know-how, got in amongst the Liverpool players. So much amongst them, that when they went out onto the pitch, an hour before the kick-off to check out its condition, and its surroundings, we were with them.

Indeed, Alan and I were also out there inspecting the pitch – and you could sense one or two of the Italian security guards were thinking, 'Hey, have you seen those two – we have nothing to beat.'

Message having been delivered we watched the game from the stands and saw Liverpool overcome home advantage and win an epic penalty shoot-out which saw Bruce Grobbelaar immortalised for his 'wobbly' legs and Alan Kennedy for his winning penalty – the second time he had made the decisive strike to win the European Cup for Liverpool.

For Joe Fagan, the Liverpool manager, it had been a remarkable debut season in the job – a treble – League, League Cup and, now, the European Cup.

We did our interviews, and learnt Souness had played his last game for Liverpool. He was heading for Italy and a new career with Sampdoria.

Our travel companions, including Gerry, had set off ahead of us for the hotel where the club was staying. We'd also been given the same information and so Alan and I, an hour or so behind them, also started to make our way to the hotel.

Not before we had been chased down a now deserted road by some Italian fans – they were probably annoyed we hadn't actually played for the Reds and given Roma a better chance of victory.

We actually took shelter briefly in a fire station before a taxi was organised to get us to the hotel. Thankfully the local brigade weren't called out to a fire while we were there.

What followed was a long night; it seemed, like the previous time Liverpool had won in Rome, that everybody knew where they were staying and just made their way there.

The following day we made our way wearily home, satisfied but making plans for a swift trip up to Liverpool to see my dad the following day.

We got home about 9pm – and the phone went ten minutes later. It was my brother, David, telling us the terrible news that my dad had died unexpectedly earlier that evening.

It would seem he had suffered from a pulmonary embolism – a blood clot – which had ended his life.

It was shattering news.

The result, the match, the Cup now meant little or nothing.

Earlier that day, my dad had said to my mum. "I hope Gerry and Brian get home safely from Rome."

A typically considerate thought.

We did – but not in time.

*　*　*　*　*

A fortnight before Liverpool's fateful night at the Heysel Stadium in 1985, I boarded a train at Waterloo Station to take me to Southampton and our second-last game of the season. I went down to the buffet car to buy a sandwich and beer and bumped into Liverpool chairman, Sir John Smith and chief executive, Peter Robinson. We started chatting and I asked them whether they were looking forward to the game in Brussels.

Neither man greeted the thought with huge enthusiasm, which, of course, surprised me. This, after all, was Liverpool's fifth European Cup final. Opponents would be Italian giants, Juventus. It would be another chance to build on the legendary European reputation of the Reds.

"The stadium isn't up to the match – too old and not safe," said Robinson to me.

He was one of the most experienced administrators in European football at the time. He continued: "We have told UEFA all this, but nothing has happened." His foreboding, shared by Smith, would prove to be hugely insightful.

A fortnight later we were all in Brussels for the latest adventure following Liverpool's fortunes abroad. But this time, the match, the performance, the result simply didn't matter because of what preceded it.

I travelled over to the game with mates, Andy and Ross, and we were in the ground in good time. Our tickets were for the side of the pitch at the same end, but opposite where the fateful incidents happened.

What was clear was that this was no 'modern' stadium and did not seem a fitting venue for such a major occasion.

I'm not sure that we were conscious of the severity of what happened before the game – a gang of supporters charging another set by chasing them across a terrace was sadly part of the reality of watching football during this era.

The tag 'hooliganism' had attached itself to the game – and it was a stigma that took years to go away.

Once again, without the benefit of modern communications, we were broadly in the dark about why the game's kick-off seemed to be being delayed and, of course, what had been the tragic consequences of the pre-match charge of Liverpool supporters through a flimsy fence - little more than chicken wire, to attack rival Italian fans in blocks Y and Z.

The consequence of that charge was the deaths of 39 people - all but eight of them Italian - and over 400 people injured after a wall collapsed.

The crumbling stadium, the inadequate reactions of the Belgian police force and the inaction of UEFA ahead of the final all contributed to this awful situation - but so did the actions of those Liverpool fans in charging other people waiting for the match to get underway.

Slowly, but surely, information was being filtered to us by incoming spectators - 'injuries, possible deaths' soon became 'fatalities, possibly as many as twenty' and so on.

Given my professional background, I treated such unconfirmed reports with caution, but I did sense that a major incident had taken place and one that would have serious consequences in due course. The atmosphere inside the stadium had become very tense indeed.

The news of potential fatalities of their own supporters quickly inflamed the Juventus fans and their mood turned dangerous and dark.

It was a very difficult situation.

By the time the game actually began, some hour and a half after the scheduled kick-off time, it had become clear that people had died in the reckless charge - and although there was a football match taking place in front of me I had absolutely no interest in it.

Given my future role, in being the lead executive at major football events at Wembley, Cardiff, Anfield, Villa Park, Old Trafford and such-like I have asked myself the question about whether I would have supported the actual playing of that match in that circumstance.

The honest answer is I'm just not sure. The decision was taken to play the game by way of trying to manage and police further potential violence – the atmosphere in the stadium was beyond tense. And probably to buy the authorities some more time to work out how to handle the rest of the evening, both in and around the stadium, and in Brussels itself.

This was UEFA's, and the Belgian authorities' way of dealing with the immediate on-night issue, the aftermath of the dreadful pre-match incident. Of course, more prescient action, long before the night of the game, may well have prevented it happening at all.

Certainly I, along with many others, felt totally detached from the game being played out in front of us and, in truth, thought it slightly grotesque and totally meaningless.

For the record, Juventus won it, the future UEFA President Michel Platini scoring from the penalty spot. I think the right team won the game.

For Liverpool, and English football, our reputation was dragged through the mud, again.

Liverpool were banned indefinitely from European competition, as were our English counterparts, including a brilliant Everton side who had just qualified for the following season's European Cup. In the event, the general ban lasted five years, with Liverpool serving a further season of exclusion.

Some fans were brought to justice – 14 in all – but only after a tortuous legal process. Police and football officials from Belgium and UEFA were also brought to book.

For those of us there, it was a deeply disturbing situation, and as we left Brussels, we all felt tainted by the reckless acts of the few. These were deeply troubling times for English football.

13

The Collecting Bug

It seems to me that people either are collectors of stuff – or aren't. One man's treasured memento is another's piece of trash. And I don't think there is much middle ground.

There are those who feel having a little piece of personal or public history around them is a necessary part of living a rounded life, whilst others are too busy getting on with their own 'three score and ten' to reflect back in any major way.

Neither is right, neither is wrong. But I know which camp I am in. Whether by accident or design, I am an enthusiastic collector.

In the interests of brevity and not boring some of you, I will keep the list of what I collect fairly short.

Over the years, as well as a lifelong affection for Liverpool FC and football in general, I have also enjoyed listening to, watching, reading about and, indeed, meeting some of the great British comedy stars of the past 50 years.

Certainly, my childhood holidays to places like Bournemouth and Scarborough meant I saw first-hand the comic skill and timing of the greats like Tommy Cooper, Morecambe and Wise, Norman Wisdom and the incomparable Ken Dodd as they bashed out their summer seasons. Each artiste spared the time to sign me an auto-graph and thus started a collection of books, photos, tapes, scripts, and such-like of all the great comedy names.

That collection runs into dozens of books – biographies and autobiographies – with that brilliant, if troubled, British comic genius, Tony Hancock, sharing top-billing with the many tomes written on Eric and Ernie.

All the *Carry On* team seem to have been subject to literary examination; Sid James, Kenneth Williams, Hattie Jacques and Barbara Windsor, as have many of the *Dad's Army* stars. Books on Will Hay, Terry Thomas, Leslie Phillips, Spike Milligan and Peter Sellers also feature on my shelves. And many more.

Signed photos of Hollywood comic greats Laurel and Hardy, Charlie Chaplin, Bob Hope, Phil Silvers and the Marx Brothers also adorn the walls.

Anyway, they make up part of my collecting bug as do books, programmes, photos and autographs from the great world heavy-weight boxing champions of the past – Muhammad Ali, Joe Frazier, Floyd Patterson, Sonny Liston and Joe Louis, for example.

My research on Joe Louis unearthed the fact that the 'Brown Bomber' actually signed for Liverpool FC as part of a war-time pub-licity stunt when he was travelling through Britain with his fellow American soldiers.

Louis-Carroll, what a fantasy knock-out front line that would have been!

Music – LPs, DVDs, concert programmes and so on... my wife Gerry reckons I have Stevie Wonder's Greatest Hits about seven times over in seven different forms (guilty as charged).

All things World Cup 1966; add things like favourite shoes, ties, suits and so on and you get the picture. Gerry would, of course, add another... DUST!

Point being, I am a collector and my lifelong affection for LFC has meant they haven't been ignored in my quest to live in the present surrounded by elements of their past.

Indeed, my collection of Liverpool memorabilia has steadily grown since keeping safe (probably without much aforethought) the programme from my first Liverpool home game, Liverpool v Leyton Orient in October, 1961.

Since that time I have managed, without subscriptions and the like, to collect every home match programme from then until now and, indeed, have mopped up others from a few seasons before that too.

Either through my own attendance at a game, or through my brother David or mate Andy, or via the Liverpool Programme Collectors Club I have gathered up well over 1,000 consecutive issues and still, by hook or crook, retain a 100 per cent hit rate.

I am also down to single figures in needing a few programmes to complete having every away programme since the Reds made it back into the top division in 1962.

Add FA Cup finals and semi-finals, their League Cup equivalents, FA Charity and Community Shields, European finals and earlier ties, World Club Championships, friendlies and such, and you get the sense that I am a serious committed collector – whatever tag follows because of it.

And, of course, the vast majority of this collecting was done before the arrival of eBay and with it, a global market place for items connected to such a famous brand. I have done it largely for fun.

As well as programmes I have a very large collection of books on the club – individual player autobiographies, some sketchily written, some like those in recent years of Steven Gerrard and Jamie Carragher hugely readable. Club histories by the ton – each trying to find a new way to bring the famous matches and stories to life again.

End of season annuals, glossy magazines and 'special' newspapers previewing or reviewing a major occasion or anniversary. Match tickets, autographs going back pre-war, bubble gum cards, scrapbooks, photographs – you name it I have it.

Stored neatly as I put it, gathering the D-word as Gerry would. I do personally draw the line on the purchasing of players' medals that sometime come on the market because of their owners passing away or falling on tough times. Whatever, I still see them as very personal tokens for those who won them; an achievement earned that, for me, cannot be bought.

Through my 'collecting bug 'I have been able to compile a comprehensive selection of items that track the famous history of the Anfield club.

Over the years I have picked up some both remarkable and unremarkable items that, in their own way, are as important pieces of social history as anything that others would deem to be a little more culturally 'significant'.

So, I thought I would just lift the lid on some unusual or special items – or some particularly special to me – that also have their own interesting story to tell.

Liverpool v Rotherham Town
September 1st, 1892, matchday programme

Liverpool's first ever game at Anfield was a friendly against Midland League side Rotherham Town. The kick-off 5.30, the same time Everton were scheduled to play against Bolton Wanderers at their new ground, Goodison Park.

Although the Liverpool directors tried to engage in a bit of

Victorian 'hype' – 10,000 turned out at Goodison and a fraction at that number came to see the birth of the new Liverpool team at Anfield. Turning out in their unusual blue-and-white-quartered shirts, the Merseyside team won 7-1. Admission to the ground was three pence and the programme, I have on my office desk in front of me, cost just one penny. It cost me just a little bit more than that when I bought it over 15 years ago.

For your penny, you got the team line-ups, a portrait of, and a tribute to, 'our esteemed president' Mr John Houlding, a lengthy explanation of how offside works (no change there, then), a guide that admission prices for Lancashire League matches would actually be four pence, and that the next match, against Higher Walton would kick-off at 3.15.

There were adverts for Ellinger & Bouldings 'Splendid Stock of Boots and Shoes', for Boydell Bros. 'Leading Tailors' and for Salt Regal – a morning "pick-me-up". This effervescing antiseptic salt seemed to clear up anything and everything – 'flatulence, nausea, giddiness, heartburn, acidity, palpitations, headaches, indigestion, feverishness, irritations of the skin, weariness' – and perhaps, most notably – problems from errors of 'diet, eating and drinking!' Ah, finally got to the point. A little bit of social history and, in many ways, something of an historical document.

Liverpool AFC – Bye-Laws for Players
– small card, circa early 1900s

When Liverpool brought Tom Watson, the secretary of Sunderland's 'Team of all Talents' to Anfield in August 1896, it was a statement of intent. His Wearside team had won a hat-trick of league championships and his reputation as a strict disciplinarian preceded him to Merseyside.

Liverpool's new secretary-manager Watson, at the prompting of club's driving force, 'Honest John' McKenna, went to Stoke to sign Scotsman, Alex Raisbeck, Liverpool's first real star. He wouldn't have been home-sick at Anfield though, as there were another 13 Scotsmen on the books – courtesy of McKenna.

Watson's commitment ultimately paid off with a first league championship win for Liverpool in 1901, another in 1906 and the club's first appearance in the FA Cup final in 1914.

A great character, Watson sadly died in 1915 after 19 years at the helm for Liverpool, Alex Raisbeck amongst his coffin bearers.

My memento of his time in office is a small red-backed card, the size of a playing card that listed out what Watson expected of his players.

They had to 'attend the ground every Tuesday, Wednesday and Thursday morning at 10.30 till 12.30 and afternoons from 3pm till 5 o'clock.

The match committee would pick the team, and 'no smoking in a saloon (!) previous to a match will be allowed. Every week the Trainer shall report to the Committee a record of players at training.'

Interestingly, the rules card made the point that 'the Captains of the respective teams shall have FULL control on the field of play'. An initiative I tried to introduce – or re-introduce, it would seem, during my time at the FA some 100 years later!

The 1914 FA Cup final
Liverpool v Burnley – a match-card

A few years ago I obtained a frail 'match-card' for Liverpool's first FA Cup final in 1914. The 'Official Match Card' for the 'Final Tie' as it called the annual climax to the season, cost one penny.

It informed us that Liverpool would play in scarlet jerseys and white knickers!

The match against Burnley at Crystal Palace attracted a crowd of nearly 73,000 – although it seemed many more attended – and, amongst them one very special guest, King George V, the first reigning monarch to attend the final. He sported a red rose to acknowledge both teams came from Lancashire.

The Liverpool players, supported by 20,000 fans, actually arrived at the Crystal Palace in a fleet of taxis. The roads around were clogged (I know, nothing changes).

The game itself was a tight affair and won by a single Burnley goal scored by Bert Freeman. Liverpool would have to wait 51 years to lift that special trophy.

A contract between Liverpool Football Club and William Chalmers – signed September 6, 1923

Yes, I managed to obtain a contract between the Reds and winger, Bill Chalmers who subsequently went on to make just two league appearances for the Anfield club.

His terms in this contract in 1923 reflect the seismic change that has taken place in the fortunes – both personal and playing – of today's top stars.

Enshrined in this document are Chalmers' weekly wage – £5.00 a week and the fact he received a further £10.00 for signing on. Different times.

The co-signatory on the contract was one Matt McQueen, the secretary-manager of the club.

McQueen played for Liverpool in the first season 1892/83, lived in Kemlyn Road, Anfield and was responsible for signing South African Gordon Hodgson, a future record goalscorer for the Reds.

Souvenir of the opening of the Spion Kop

This ribbon-bound booklet, issued on Saturday, August 25th, 1928 explained the opening of the Spion Kop New Stand would take place shortly before the kick-off of their opening game of the season against Bury.

Fittingly, it would be conducted by Liverpool forefather, and now President of the Football League, John McKenna. This 12-page booklet outlined with great pride that it was the first roofed-in Kop in the country, two-thirds of its possible spectators could see the game without 'a single intervening stanchion', and that 36,000 cubic feet of concrete had been used in the building of the new stand. Also, it proclaimed that if all the steps on the Spion Kop were 'strung out in a line, that line would be longer the length of the Liverpool docks'.

Of course, what the ceremonial brochure couldn't tell us was what the club had just built and was opening that day, would become the most famous football terrace in the world.

Liverpool 1936/37 – a set of autographs

Autograph collecting has always been one of the key 'connections' fans make with their heroes – either in a book, on a photo, on a shirt or on the occasional bare torso. Collecting signatures are part of the history of football, sport, entertainment and public life in general.

These days players often put their squad number alongside a faster-than-the-speed-of-light squiggle – back in the more prosaic days of the 1930s, the players would sign their names in a descending line, starting with the goalkeeper – and at the bottom of the list would be room for the manager.

I have lots of sets of this type of signature structure, the one in front of me now is from 1936/37 and starts at the top of the page with goalkeeper Alf Hobson.

He was a rarity in that he signed both his names.

It would seem the norm then was for the more formal initial of first name then the family name – marking the austerity of the time.

Alf Hobson was followed down the page, in a strict straight line by: J.Harley, R.E.Savage, Bradshaw, McDougall, B.Nieuwenhuys, Eastham, F.Howe, John Balmer, and Alf Hanson. Bringing up the rear at the bottom of the page was trainer Chas Wilson.

Amongst those signatures were some famous Reds whose names will sound familiar to some.

There was Tom 'Tiny' Bradshaw, who was actually tall hence his nickname, and played nearly 300 games for the club; Berry Nieuwenhuys, 'Nivvy' was recruited from South African football and played both pre and post-war for the Reds, and John 'Jack' Balmer, a clever forward who made his Reds debut in 1935 and played his final game in 1952 – 17 years later.

Balmer, with his distinctive bald head, was a favourite with the Anfield crowd.

He captained the club and became famous by becoming the first player to score hat-tricks in three consecutive league games in 1946/47.

His three against Portsmouth at Anfield were followed by four at Derby and then another three against Arsenal back at Anfield.

It meant he had hit the back of the net 10 times without another Liverpool player scoring in between.

He was also my mum and dad's favourite player of that era and they often used to regale us with stories of his goalscoring and entertainment value.

Menu from Queen Mary for farewell dinner – Liverpool's tour of the America and Canada May/June 1953

Liverpool FC made regular post-season tours to the United States and Canada. One in 1946 helped them steer their way to the title the following year, and they had subsequent tours in 1948, 1953 and 1964.

In 1953, they set off on board Queen Mary and enjoyed a rich fare of dining as they left English shores. The menu shows about 20 potential starters, from smoked salmon and capers through to Poireaux a la Grecque (no, me neither!) Main courses – sirloin of beef, braised York Ham, Squab Chicken en Cocotte or Roast Stuffed Vermont Turkey were amongst other mouth-watering dishes. For dessert, well, try Soufflé aux Liqueurs, Bombe Caprice or Fraises Romanoff.

I hope there was a gym on board for the players to burn off all that exotic grub! Anyway, the menu, signed by all the players on the trip including Bob Paisley, Billy Liddell, a young Ronnie Moran and captain Phil Taylor, is a wonderful collectors' item.

As indeed are the programmes I obtained from the matches on that tour, including the one between the Chicago All-Stars and 'Liverpool of England', as the Reds were colourfully billed in the USA. Nothing much of detail in the programme itself, other than a young lady's name and Chicago address hurriedly scribbled in pencil on its back page. The mind boggles...

Liverpool's promotion to Division One 1961/62 – programmes and souvenir paper

Having collected every Liverpool home programme for the past 50 years I suppose I could pick any season to represent that element of my hobby. So I have plumped for the first year – and Liverpool's last year in the Second Division.

The first programme of the season displayed urgency – desperation even – to get the Reds back in the division they felt they belonged.

In 'The Chairman's Message', T.V. Williams wrote: 'Despite what you may have read elsewhere from ill-informed critics, you can take it from me, with all the force of emphasis of which I am capable, that the directors of Liverpool Football Club are as keenly anxious to get the team back into the top flight of football as the most fervent supporter on the Spion Kop.'

Opponents in the opening home match were Sunderland, with a certain Brian Clough leading their line. Liverpool won that game 3-0 and went on to convincingly secure promotion.

The message 'From the Boardroom' in the last programme of the season, against Charlton Athletic was suitably more measured. 'The Championship having been won and our aim of promotion to the premier sphere achieved, we would like to pay tribute to our manager, staff and players for the great efforts they have made to realise this ambition.'

Of course, promotion meant a demand for a souvenir paper and I remember going up to the top shops to get mine. Quite impressive, *Salute to Liverpool FC* cost one shilling, had a colour photograph of captain Ron Yeats on the cover, and messages of congratulations inside from the footballing fraternity – Alf Ramsey, Harry Catterick and Albert Stubbins included, plus local politicians like Bessie Braddock and famous comedians like Arthur Askey and Ted Ray.

The paper also had a 'full colour presentation art plate' – a colour photo to you and me, of the team, staff and directors.

In truth, it captures a wonderful sense of the football hierarchy of the time – there are 30 people on the photograph and only 15 of them are footballers.

If you rightly excuse Bill Shankly and trainers Bob Paisley and Joe Fagan, both wearing rather sinister white 'medical' coats, you are left with a few other club officials and on the front row – with seemingly no embarrassment, no fewer than nine directors centre stage.

Behind them at the top of the photograph is that famous large red sign 'LIVERPOOL FOOTBALL CLUB' that adorned the front of the Main Stand roof. I wonder what became of that piece of history when the stand was modernised.

The 1965 FA Cup final – Liverpool v Leeds United – autographed match programme and songsheet

Although I have various copies of the programme from the day Liverpool finally won the FA Cup on May 1, 1965, my favourite is one I picked up at an auction a few years ago.

What makes this one different is that on the programme's cover are a series of autographs that reflect over 50 years of trying to lift that famous trophy.

For, as well as players who actually starred in that day's great win like captain Ron Yeats, goalkeeper Tommy Lawrence, and winning goalscorer, Ian St John, there were signatures from those who had tried and failed in 1950 – the likes of goalkeeper Cyril Sidlow, full-backs Ray Lambert and Eddie Spicer and centre-backs Bill Jones and Laurie Hughes – and very specially, a former player had signed himself 'Kenny Campbell Liverpool FC 1914'.

Campbell had played for Liverpool in the 1914 final and now was rightly representing that group of players along with those of the finals of 1950 and 1965. A small piece of history.

Of course, in those days, taking part in the pre-match community singing was part of the 'Cup Final afternoon' – and my song-sheet from the day tells me that the crowd would be invited by conductor, Frank Rea and the Band of the Royal Marines to join together in singing up to eleven (!) songs including – and reflecting both sides' geographical status – 'She's a Lassie from Lancashire', 'On Ilkley Moor Baht 'At', as well as standards, 'John Brown's Body', 'Let Me Call You Sweetheart' and, of course the cup final hymn itself 'Abide With Me'. One concession to the band, and the city of the moment, was the inclusion of the Beatles' She Loves You'. I hope everybody was singing!

The Official History of Liverpool FC – Platinum Performance Award presented to BBC Video, 1988

During my first 10 years with the BBC I became aware of the sheer volume and quality of the Corporation's sporting archive.

Having been covering sport from the fledgling pre-war days, to key advances in the '50s, through to its maturity and widespread appeal in the '60s, '70s and '80s , the BBC had a simply unrivalled library of films and video tape capturing the country's greatest sporting moments – and the generation-defining highlights of its great stars.

I often used the self-same pictures to bring an interview or a film story to life as I did my spin as a member of the BBC Sport production team. With the onset of domestic video tape recorders came a chance to exploit that amazing archive and show it to a whole new audience. I was first in the queue when the film library doors were finally flung open.

I knew the project I wanted to do – and BBC Enterprises decided to back me. My idea was to create a 90 minute video tracking the history of Britain's most successful football club.

So, in early 1987 I began to gather up the best BBC footage from the previous 50 years, augment it with some marvellous Pathe News films, add some appropriate interviews reflecting all the different eras – lay down a haunting music track and then have the whole thing brilliantly narrated by John Motson.

Motty and I did many of these tapes together subsequently – including *Liverpool in Europe, The Kop* and *Liverpool – The Official Centenary.* We also did a three-tape box-set tracking the *History of Match of the Day,* which still seems to be on sale today. I occasionally get the odd royalty payment from the BBC via an overseas sale in somewhere like the Philippines or Burkina Faso.

But *The Official History of Liverpool FC* was the first – and possibly our best effort. Its first screening was in the Executive Suite at Anfield on Thursday, September 17, 1987. A buffet lunch was then served!

It quickly went on general sale and was a smash-hit. In fact it was heading for the Christmas no.1 slot in the video charts before being pipped at the post by Andy Pandy, Bill and Ben, and, of course, The Woodentops.

It would seem another enterprising group in the BBC hierarchy had realised the market in nostalgia and made a tape glorifying the days of *Watch with Mother.* They would go to make another smash-hit sequel.

Anyway, we had enjoyed our pre-Christmas moment top of the pile and in June the following year we were awarded a 'platinum disc' comprising the video's cover-shot of Kenny Dalglish for sales worth £300,000.

In 1995, John and I were awarded another 'disc' each for topping a million unit sales in football videos.

It all seems like a lifetime ago and I'm sure they'll look a bit ancient now, but as well as the sheer fun of it, there was lots of hard work, long hours involved, and to this day, I cannot bear to watch certain famous Liverpool goals on television, having seen them literally thousands of times whilst producing our best-selling videos. Still I'm sure it's the same for Andy Pandy, Little Weed and Spotty Dog!

The Royal visit to Anfield, May 1993
– invitation and ticket

In late March, 1993, I took a telephone call in my BBC office from Liverpool's Chief Executive Peter Robinson. I always found PBR, as he was tagged, unerringly polite – and also unerringly brief on the phone. I had often found I was holding a conversation with myself five minutes into a call with PBR. He had quietly moved on to the next one!

Anyway, on this particular day he was a mite mysterious. "Are you free on Friday, May 28th? Can you be at the club at lunch-time? Fully suited and booted?"

Of course, I said yes, and allowed myself a momentary thought that despite a lifetime's average performances for Rudston Road Primary, Quarry Bank School, University's Comecon and Convocation, the Storrsdale Sunday League side and even the Tuesday six-a-sides with my mates at the BBC and despite the fact I was knocking on 39 years of age, that Liverpool had finally discovered me. I would be signing on the dotted line in May and then giving England international Rob Jones a run for his money for the right-back berth at Anfield.

"Would you like to meet Her Majesty the Queen?" "Pardon?" I said, almost expecting him to say 'Well you started it!'

Anyway, to my delight, Peter Robinson was inviting me to represent the BBC on the day the Queen and the Duke of

Sven and David Beckham aren't letting me in on the joke as we prepare to board the plane for the 2006 World Cup

Above: With Fabio Capello... we didn't compare notes on ties!

Left: Steve McClaren's first day at the FA... it got tougher

And you are? With the legendary David Beckham, of course

Welcoming 'my team' to 'my club' – England play Uruguay at Anfield

Sitting pretty...
Controller of ITV
Sport, with the
channel's 2001
trophy haul

Never off duty...
facing up to the
press as the voice
of the FA

Amongst friends... with Des Lynam, Stephanie Moore and the late, great Sir Bobby Robson

I hadn't won the 1992 BBC Sports Personality of the Year trophy – but was just off to polish it...

Outside the Bernabeu on World Cup final day. Spain '82 was a great adventure

About to be tackled by 'Crazy Horse' at the unveiling of Emlyn's statue in 2008

Places you go... people you meet. From top left (clockwise): With Gabby Logan, a top person and presenter; former neighbour and comedian Les Dennis; with David Jason at Silverstone; with Anne Robinson – the weakest link was my jacket; with Ray Winstone and Prime Minister Gordon Brown

Above: With Mum and David in later years. Below: My very own first team – with sons Joe, Jack and wife Gerry plus one well-behaved dog Bertie... and 'Bite Yer Legs' Barney!

Above: Copacabana Beach, 2009.
Anything Pele can do...

Left: At Anfield, going to the match
- it never loses its appeal

Below: Proud to be Professor Barwick
- back at my old university

Edinburgh were due to visit Anfield as part of a wider visit to Merseyside.

And so, on May 28 1993, I turned up at Anfield for a unique occasion, along with over 15,000 members of the public. During the Royal couple's visit they seemed visibly moved by the warmth of the reception they received. They saw handicapped children demonstrate their football skill on the Anfield pitch, visited the Hillsborough Memorial outside the Shankly Gates and listened intently to a rousing version of 'You'll Never Walk Alone'.

On her arrival, the Queen, accompanied by chairman, David Moores, had been introduced to some of the playing legends of the club, past and present; current manager Graeme Souness and former holders of that post, as well as other notable Anfield individuals.

Paul Docherty, ITV's chosen representative and I were also placed in the receiving line and were delighted when the Queen stopped to have a brief conversation with us – reflecting on how much football meant to the city of Liverpool. Then, she was away and gone, and we were left with some nice memories of a good day.

And so in my collection of 'stuff' is the card inviting me for lunch for the royal visit, the programme of events and the ticket that gave me a front row seat for the activities taking place on the pitch that day.

England v Uruguay, Anfield March 1, 2006 – All Areas Pass

A very proud day for me as my professional and personal lives collided in a very significant way. This was the period when the England senior team took the show 'on the road' whilst Wembley Stadium was being re-built.

The team went all over the country for seven years as they made their way through a combination of home European Championship, World Cup qualifiers and prestige friendlies.

And now they were at Anfield to meet the South American stars of Uruguay – and, as the Chief Executive of the Football Association, I was the person ultimately responsible for the smooth-running of the occasion.

Of course, I was blessed to have great staff to help me – but if there was one football ground in the country I knew my way around it was this one.

Anyway, armed with my all areas pass, I went about my pre-match duties both inside and outside the stadium.

There was an extra intrigue about the game as it was the first since we had announced that the FA and their coach, Sven-Goran Eriksson, would be parting company after the World Cup finals in Germany later that year.

I sat down for the pre-match dinner and made sure a good friend, Greg Sorrell, got the pleasure of sitting next to Sir Bobby Charlton on our table. Later Greg sat next to me as the match got underway.

I always tried to share some of the 'perks' of the job with my best and oldest mates – people who I felt I should look after just that bit more specially for the short period I was at the helm of the Football Association. That night it was Greg's turn.

Then I was on the Anfield pitch to meet the teams and then back in the stand to watch the action unfold.

A cracking game transpired. Uruguay took a first half lead before England equalised with a goal that had tinges of Liverpool past and present about it.

Substitute Jamie Carragher fed future Red, Joe Cole, whose pin-point cross was headed firmly into the net by the then Liverpool striker Peter Crouch. The winner, almost with the last kick of the game came from Joe Cole himself.

Post-match conversations done, our Uruguayan colleagues off home safely I slipped off with Greg for a pint at my old local then popped in to see my old mum.

Perfect night.

14

The Darkest Day

After Bob Paisley departed, Liverpool would never be the same again. The years that followed ensured that in more ways than one. The club dealt with the consequences of events at the Heysel Stadium in 1985 as positively as they could.

Denied European football, their new player manager Kenny Dalglish had won the domestic Double in his first season in charge, and in 1987/88, with the likes of the brilliant John Barnes, Peter Beardsley and Scouser John Aldridge added to the squad they had romped home to another championship, playing some remarkable football, and then with another Double in the offing, fell to a classic FA Cup upset when losing to Wimbledon's so-called Crazy Gang in the final itself.

On route to that final, the Reds had played and beaten Brian Clough's Nottingham Forest in the FA Cup semi-final. Twelve months on, the same competition threw up the same semi-final pairing at the same venue.

Saturday, April 15th, 1989 started as many did for me at this time – watch *Football Focus,* take check calls from on-site directors or commentators and make my way into BBC Television Centre,

Wood Lane, White City to put together that evening's edition of *Match of the Day*. I had been the editor of *Match of the Day: The Road to Wembley* since the start of the season and the programme was building momentum towards the FA Cup final itself in May.

No live coverage at the time, we had cameras at both the semi-finals, Liverpool v Nottingham Forest at Hillsborough and Everton v Norwich City at Villa Park.

On that particular Saturday, the programme's presenter, Des Lynam and his side-kick and expert pundit Jimmy Hill had requested my permission to attend one of the semi-finals in person before returning to front the show later that evening.

As we were only dealing with two games I said it was fine for them to be on-site and they plumped for the Liverpool game. I, meanwhile, was settling down in the viewing rooms at Television Centre ready to watch the games and decide the shape of the programme's running order.

As was often the case I was joined in the viewing room by visitors. That was quite a common occurrence if somebody in the football industry couldn't get to their game for whatever reason. We were also a favourite place for passing celebrities in the BBC corridors who found our famous little room on the second floor – Room 2143.

That day I was joined by two notable people, the late Sir Brian Wolfson, the then chairman and chief executive of Wembley Stadium, and Jarvis Astaire, another key player at Wembley and somebody I did regular business with in the sport of professional boxing. He was a famous promoter, along with partner Mickey Duff. They had provided boxing for the BBC for years. Both men were very welcome. Sir Brian was a Scouser and a big Liverpudlian.

My brother, David, had gone to the match – but only when he had managed to get a ticket for the West Stand – the seating area above the fateful Leppings Lane terracing. A seasoned football follower he had stood in the Leppings Lane End the previous year and felt crushed – very crushed.

Indeed, so had many Liverpudlians that year and when Liverpool and Nottingham Forest were matched up in the semi-finals of the FA Cup and Hillsborough chosen as the venue, Peter Robinson, a man of great experience, had asked the authorities to swop the two sets of supporters around, with Liverpool getting the larger facility – their Kop End. His plea fell on deaf ears.

My visitors were experienced stadium people and both Sir Brian and Jarvis started to take an extra level of interest in the pictures being beamed back to London from Hillsborough.

"That can't be right," said Sir Brian, "the middle of the terrace is full and the sides are still almost empty." As soon as he said it, I looked at the pictures and the same thought struck me.

The match got underway but it became clear there was a lot of crowd agitation behind Bruce Grobbelaar's goal at the Leppings Lane End of the ground.

At six minutes past three, a police officer ran on the pitch to tell the referee, Ray Lewis, to take the players off the field.

The scenes that followed were simply horrifying to witness as people spilled onto the pitch to escape the crushing that was taking place. Fans helped fans – lifting them up into the stand above, and people were climbing – or attempting to climb out of the terrible situation behind and around them – and also to help ease the crushing.

Advertising hoardings were being ripped up and used as emergency stretchers for the injured. It was unlike anything we had seen before.

Back in London, I alerted my BBC colleagues who were live on air with *Grandstand* – normally the flow of information we would send them would be goals scored and goalscorers from the afternoon's games. This time my message to the studio gallery was that there was a very serious problem at Hillsborough and they needed to be across it. *Grandstand* had already spotted it and went live to the pictures as they were carefully and sensitively directed by highly experienced producer, John Shrewsbury. He had produced the previous 10 FA Cup finals, and had gone to produce a major FA Cup semi-final, now he was producing something totally different.

Live television was something I'd learnt to respect. I'd done thousands of hours of live programming, and you often think you had all the answers – but then something would happen which would find folly in that confidence. This was one of those days.

I think I offered *Grandstand* either Sir Brian or Jarvis as studio guests, given their undoubted expertise, but the programme's producers stayed on the pictures and the first-hand commentary from Hillsborough.

I got in touch with Des Lynam and said 'Stay as long you need to get a true picture of events – and then you and Jimmy Hill set off down the motorway because *Match of the Day* is staying in the schedule but it will be a very different programme than it's been before.'

Throughout the evening we were getting a much clearer picture all the time about the sheer depth of the disaster – the scale of the human tragedy involved.

From a professional perspective we were in a strong position – in truth, stronger than our BBC colleagues in News. Des Lynam was a first-class broadcast journalist and had seen the tragic events unravel first-hand whilst I was from Liverpool itself and had an inherent understanding of the depth of the sorrow that would be felt not just in my home town but throughout the world.

And so we went on air with a very different edition of *Match of the Day* from the one we had set out to do.

We made an apology, but really none needed for not showing Everton's 1-0 win over Norwich City and simply concentrated on the events of Hillsborough.

The programme was reduced to 30 minutes, and really it was a minute-by-minute eye witness account from Des on what he had seen – backed up with the pictures we had available. We built up a profile of the afternoon and the balance of the programme, my job, was critical.

We then went live to a darkened Hillsborough where John Shrewsbury was still delivering pictures to news organisations around the world. People were beginning to arrive with flowers and Shrewsbury was able to set up a two-way interview with new FA Chief Executive, Graham Kelly. I respected him for doing it – we had spent a lot of the evening trying to reach the then Minister for Sport, Colin Moynihan without success.

Des and Jimmy swopped their thoughts and the programme drew to a close.

It was a very emotional programme for me personally to do given my background and leanings – and it was the only *Match of the Day* ever transmitted without any football in it.

And it was a programme we had to get right – and I feel we did. It was contemporaneous, honest and authoritative... and to a man, we all wished we hadn't had to make it.

I became the 'point-man' for the BBC over the next few days, the person a news programme could ring to supply them with a phone number, an expert or a constructive suggestion.

As always I was astonished how thin the callers' knowledge of the subject was – and it made me wonder if that was the same in every story the news crews stumbled on.

I travelled up to Liverpool and Anfield on the Tuesday of the following week – personally, because I felt drawn to go back home, but also because I felt professionally it was important for a BBC executive to go and express first-hand our condolences.

By then the Kop, and the pitch, was awash with flowers. I laid mine, amongst the hundreds, thousands of others. I then spent a little time with Peter Robinson and Kenny Dalglish in the club's inner sanctum and watched with real admiration as the players and their wives and girlfriends quietly spoke to shocked and distraught relatives of those who had died or were injured in Sheffield the previous Saturday. I then left the club to its grieving and private thoughts.

I was back in Liverpool several times over the next fortnight before going up on Friday week to help in the television preparations for the following day's Hillsborough Memorial Service at Liverpool Cathedral.

I went to the rehearsal of the service on the Friday evening. The following day there would be a packed cathedral. The night before there was probably no more a couple of dozen of us there.

There was a walk-through of the service and Kenny Dalglish got up and rehearsed his bible reading. The service was due to end with a blessing followed by a profound silence.

On the day this silence would finally be broken by a single chorister singing 'You'll Never Walk Alone.'

As they rehearsed this sequence on the Friday evening, the sound of this young chorister singing – a lone beautiful voice in such a magnificent setting reduced the small impromptu congregation to tears. And as he finished his refrain, the magnificent Liverpool Cathedral organ drew in all its musical breath and then poured out the song's melody again.

Its sheer power and majesty filled the building, the song's message never more significant. It was a deeply emotional few minutes – and, for me indeed, the moment the whole enormity of what had gone before actually hit home.

The following day the organ's power would be matched by the sound of a thousand voices singing in unity and strength, a gesture of togetherness and support.

*   *   *   *   *

Eventually it was deemed time to resume playing football again. A Hillsborough Memorial Match at Celtic Park provided some wonderful images as the whole crowd sang a heart-felt rendition of 'You'll Never Walk Alone'. Then, fittingly, the first competitive game was against Everton, a club and a set of fans who had handled themselves so sensitively and had been so supportive during the immediate difficult post-Hillsborough period.

The FA Cup semi-final against Nottingham Forest was replayed – but at Old Trafford on Sunday May 7 with a 1pm kick-off and a restricted capacity. In a change of policy the game was broadcast live on television, so we went up to cover it. Liverpool came out victorious and so set up another all-Merseyside FA Cup final.

On May 20, Liverpool and Everton met at Wembley and the Reds won a closely fought final 3-2 after extra-time. It was a fantastic football match, played in a great 'Merseyside' atmosphere, and probably, I would suggest, with a fitting outcome.

That night, we ended our *Match of the Day* programme with a moving musical sequence of pictures – both Red and Blue – to the tune of 'Ferry Cross the Mersey' – a song that had been released to raise money for the Disaster Fund.

As the last beat of the music played out on the air, the phone rang in the studio gallery; it was Bill Kenwright, now Everton chairman then Everton director. He was ringing to say we had 'caught' the atmosphere of the occasion – and the spirit of Merseyside in those difficult times perfectly in our closing titles. I appreciated the call.

Six days later, I was present at Anfield to witness the most extraordinary end to a league season there may ever be – Liverpool had picked up maximum points in four 'catch-up' matches and went into the final game of the season three points clear of their chief rivals Arsenal, and knowing that the Gunners needed nothing less than a 2-0 win to wrest the title – and the Double – away from Liverpool.

It looked an impossible task and Liverpool contained them in the first half. The second half just began to look a strain for the Liverpool players – their eighth game in 23 days. Alan Smith scored and now the Londoners needed one more goal for unlikely glory.

In a remarkable finish, Michael Thomas, then of Arsenal, hit the vital goal with literally seconds of the match – and the season – to spare. They had done it just in the nick of time.

Once again Anfield dealt with losing out on this close thing with great dignity.

They applauded the new champions and many people believed, like me, that as disappointing as it was, the lessons of the previous few weeks had given us a true perspective...

Football is football – but life is life.

15

Missing The Boat

After two decades of domestic supremacy and exciting European conquests, the 1990s proved to be a big let-down for the Reds and their followers – including me.

The previous decade had delivered six championships, two European Cups, two FA Cups and four League Cups – the club was now ordering Brasso by the crate.

But all that was about to end. When Peter Beardsley's goal clinched victory over Tottenham and with it Liverpool's 18th title success in May 1990, we all thought the next one was just 12 months away. We'd all got terribly complacent about it if truth be told.

In fact, 21 years on we are still waiting to win it again. That, by any measure, is disappointing. Especially when it is combined with arch-rivals Manchester United's step-change in fortune.

For Liverpudlians this has been a hit and miss period. Huge highs – Istanbul – and several lows. Remember the 1996 FA Cup final and those white suits?

You can argue that it is just the pitch and toss of sport. Teams dominate, then lapse, then maybe dominate again or that there are fundamental reasons for the swing in supremacy.

Either way 'our' Reds suddenly found ourselves watching 'their' Reds lifting the league trophy and with the regularity we had previously enjoyed. And it was a new league trophy because it was a whole new league – the FA Premier League – and, with it, a whole new ball game.

Rupert Murdoch had come along, and with the help of the big clubs, Liverpool included, had given his new subscription service, SKY Television, the launch-pad to dominate the sports broadcast landscape by purchasing the rights to cover the Premier League games exclusively live. Indeed, as was often the case, Liverpool were broadcast history-makers when they featured in SKY's first live Premier League match away at Nottingham Forest.

Twenty years on SKY are still doing it – and, in that time, the game has moved from being a domestic passion to a global phenomenon – from a Saturday afternoon habit to an any day of the week commitment.

The top players have become 'A-list' celebrities, and very rich. They have also been drawn from all over the world, and the clubs themselves have built new stadiums and been subject to foreign take-overs – for good and ill.

I have two boys, Jack and Joe, and neither has seen 'their' team win the title – Jack's Liverpool and Joe's Aston Villa (it's a long story). It has been the era of Manchester United, Chelsea, Arsenal... with a bit of Dalglish's Blackburn Rovers thrown in.

Anyway, as Liverpudlians we entered the '90s expecting more of the same and it didn't happen. Dalglish left, Souness arrived – but the honours all but dried up.

I did expect Souness to continue the trophy-winning trend. He was almost on automatic-winning-pilot at Rangers but I think he felt he needed to change things around at Anfield and probably did too much too quickly.

The 1992 FA Cup final victory over Sunderland was his best moment, but he watched the game on the trainer's bench wrapped in a blanket, under orders to stay calm, having just recovered from critical heart surgery and his own published 'inside story' lost him some support and respect amongst the Reds followers. I briefly touched base with him at the team hotel on the night before the final – and the strain of his major operation, his 'controversial' story and the big match ahead was clearly etched on his face.

I, personally, have always found him to be a decent guy to deal with – an intelligent, forthright individual – both as player and subsequently as manager.

Ian Rush scored in that final, a record fifth goal in FA Cup finals, and he was also captain when the team, inspired by a brilliant Steve McManaman double, won the League Cup three years later. His last appearance for Liverpool – as a substitute, his 660th in all – was indeed in the Reds' dreadful 1996 FA Cup final display against Manchester United.

Rush is rightly a legend at the club, the all-time record goalscorer, with 346 goals – and a player who was an absolute master of his craft.

I often sit next to Rushie now at games at Anfield and his genuine love for his old club is unabated. None of this old pro stuff – sit rooted to the spot when somebody scores and *the game was better in my day* – if Liverpool score he is up there with the rest of us. Without fail. He 'kicks every ball' and has a knack of also 'playing' the game in his head, so when Liverpool are on the attack, he is suddenly leaning into you, making a 'back' for himself, then he will spring back into his seat, and sell you the 'dummy'. You find yourself spinning in the wrong direction!

He also gives you a running master-class commentary on where the Reds' strikers should be running – and when and why.

Rushie is a terrific guy, fun to be around and, without doubt, Liverpool Football Club's best-ever striker amongst some very tough competition. I must have watched him play for Liverpool hundreds of times and, as he bore down on goal, I always felt we were just 30 seconds away from the game re-starting from the centre-spot. Goal scored.

He made a habit of scoring in cup finals – and against Everton. He scored 25 goals against the Goodison men in his time – which must have seriously peed off his Welsh team-mates, Kevin Ratcliffe and Neville Southall.

In fact, even when he was winding his career down at Newcastle he nicked a winning goal in an FA Cup tie at Everton.

He was a 'dead-eye Dick' striker for me. He converted chances, timed his runs, used his head both physically and figuratively, and played each game and his whole career to a finish. That career straddled 16 years at Anfield, with a year's sabbatical in Italy at Juventus. From being a shy youngster, he ended his time at Liverpool having captained the club.

Another player who straddled the two decades was John Barnes. He was signed in 1987 along with Peter Beardsley and John Aldridge, two other Anfield stars. Barnes became a genuine all-time great of the club.

His fantastic ball skills, close control, dribbling and goal threat made him a folk-hero on the Kop but also a target for opposing fans – some of whom hit him with the racist taunts that infected the game at this time. He rose above them.

One of football's classiest acts, I first met him when, as a young Watford player, he was preparing for the 1984 FA Cup final against Everton.

He invited us to his tiny flat to film him watching tapes of his and my hero Pele. The son of a diplomat, Jamaican-born Barnes talked enthusiastically about the Brazilian star, and played his football with a similar style and rhythm. Indeed, it was his stand-out goal for England against Brazil in Rio later that summer that got people really interested in him. I also saw him score a terrific goal against the Reds at Vicarage Road. Anfield scouts, no doubt, took note.

Once at Anfield he quickly became a fans' favourite. I remember him scoring a brilliant double against QPR in his opening season, running from deep and bamboozling defenders before stroking the ball in the net. The trend was set.

He was still gracing the team 10 years later. His early days saw him attack from wide; his latter time at Anfield would see him tucked inside feeding the prolific Robbie Fowler. He also could score goals - outdoing even Ian Rush in one season - his strike against Everton in Dalglish's final match in charge in 1991 was particularly remarkable.

His love of contemporary music also led him to create the famous/infamous (delete as appropriate!) Anfield Rap prior to the 1988 FA Cup final - and latterly sing up front on New Order's 'World in Motion' before Italia 90. Both were massive hits.

When I went to work at ITV in the late '90s, John had already established himself as a pundit with interesting things to say. I kept him in that role through and beyond the 2002 World Cup. A good 'tourist', John was always a popular member of the team and I enjoyed his company immensely.

*　　*　　*　　*　　*

The Nineties themselves were a period of decline for Liverpool - and we all knew it. In truth, there were some players wearing the famous Red shirt who simply wouldn't have passed muster in the preceding years.

Having finished as runners-up in 1990/91 the Reds followed it up with a run of 6th, 8th, 8th, 3rd, 4th 3rd, 4th and 3rd – a clear sign that we had become more contenders than champions.

I think the club had also missed the boat in fully exploiting their commercial possibilities. Liverpool's sensible maxim of 'doing our talking on the field' now needed a similar approach off it to keep abreast of developments in the commercialisation of the game. Things were moving fast.

Liverpool were still the 'stand-out' name in English football the world over, but the tide was turning – and we didn't seem as well equipped as others to manage and fully exploit that commercial onslaught.

Roy Evans followed Souness into the manager's job – a son of the Boot Room he was Liverpool through and through, and I found him a decent guy to deal with – and I joined him on his first foray into Europe – the opening round of the UEFA Cup in the far-flung footballing outpost of Vladikavkaz.

One of the issues with no longer being a shoe-in as champions of England was that the club missed out on the growing revenues attached to the commercially-attractive Champions League. This became a genuine problem over time. Just as Liverpool's domestic ascendancy slipped, the financial rewards from playing – and succeeding – in Europe's top football competition went absolutely through the roof. This was to put some financial clear water between our rivals and ourselves for several seasons.

UEFA's 'second' competition also had the habit of sending you into some weird and wonderful footballing back-waters, unlike its senior equivalent.

The journey over to the city of Vladikavkaz, home of almost one million people, a thousand miles from Moscow, proved an interesting one. I had bought the broadcast rights to show the game on the BBC and travelled with Liverpool's players and officials over to Russia.

Our Aeroflot flight was short on creature comforts but we did seem to attract some unlikely company as we came in to land – four armed helicopters surrounded the plane.

Not your normal welcome but I was later told that it was a way of the North Ossetia Republican security forces receiving our plane as a 'friendly' visitor. Vladikavkaz was next door to Georgia and 'war-torn Chechnya'.

As was my custom on overseas trips, when the players went to train at the stadium on the eve of the game, I would follow their convoy and check out the television facilities and meet my broadcast colleagues from the host country.

Well, when I arrived at Spartak's ground I found no television trucks, no cameras, no microphones, no wires, no cables and, slightly worryingly, nobody.

A brief search of the facilities sent me scurrying back to the hotel and a phone line to London. "Listen, I may be over-reacting slightly here but on the basis there is no scanner, no cameras, no microphones, no wires, no cables and nobody from the local television station to be found – I'd have a 'Miss Marple' up your sleeve for *BBC2* tomorrow afternoon!"

I went to the ground some five hours before kick-off on the day of the match and still there was nothing to give me comfort. Back on to London: "Actually, have a couple of 'Miss Marples' on standby – still no sign of the local TV guys."

Just over an hour before the game, with me just a little frantic (i.e. going bonkers) a rickety old TV van turned up – carrying just three cameras and a length of old cable. Now, I am no technical expert, as those who worked with me would testify, but even I knew that to rig in an outside broadcast in under an hour was pushing it – by at least a couple of hours.

I went into the old scanner van and with over-exaggerated relief thanked my Ossetian TV colleague for bothering to show up and offered him my traditional gift of a bottle of whisky.

I had been taught this trick by one of my great mentors at the BBC, Bob Abrahams. "It's an act of friendship" he would say. "And then they'll go the extra yard for you".

The Ossetian recipient of my gift took the bottle gratefully, opened it and took a very large swig from it. I was straight back on the phone to London. "The scanner van, cameras, cables and direc-tor are all here now – and given what I've just seen I recommend you get another Miss Marple out of the library."

Eventually, the game and its coverage got underway, and as I sat back to relax and follow the match I had to take an urgent call from BBC's London studios: "We are getting the pictures – lots of reds and greens."

"Good," I said, "the pitch is green, and the shirts are red."

"Not here they're not" came the reply "the shirts are green and the pitch is red!"

And, so the afternoon went on, loss of pictures, loss of sound, loss of pictures and sound, loss of temper, loss of hair... you know, that sort of thing. In fact, we could have done with Miss Marple in Vladikavkaz to sort out the bloody mystery of the missing television programme. A final whistle has never sounded sweeter. I heard myself muttering 'never again' as I stumbled out of the commentary booth.

I went down to the scanner van after the broadcast had finished to 'thank' the director for his efforts. He smiled, burped, and then ceremonially handed back... a half empty bottle of whisky!

Over on ITV the following night was the latest batch of matches in the UEFA Champions League – a revamped European Cup with untold commercial riches attached to it. All spick and span, cutely marketed, multi-camera coverage, standard kick-off times and I caught myself thinking 'Now that would be fun to work on.'

Although the '90s didn't deliver a batch-load of trophies, or the financial riches of the Champions League, there were some thumping good games at Anfield.

In January 1994 Liverpool shared a remarkable 3-3 draw against Manchester United. Trailing 3-0 in the first half, a double from Nigel Clough and a late equaliser from Razor Ruddock took the roof off the stadium. It was a tremendous match and I managed to get a special late-night slot for it on *BBC1* the following night given the huge reaction to it.

The end of the season saw the final game at Anfield with the Kop as a standing terrace. On Saturday, April 30, 1994, Liverpool played hosts to visitors, Norwich City and a set of Liverpool legends were also there to show their respect to the iconic Kop.

I was there to watch Albert Stubbins, Billy Liddell, Cally and Smithy, Phil Thompson and Steve Heighway, amongst others, come on the pitch and wave to the famous terrace. The crowd roared back in return.

The loudest cheers were reserved for Kenny Dalglish and Joe Fagan, who escorted Nessie Shankly and Jessie Paisley onto the pitch. It was a family occasion and the club printed a special edition of the matchday programme to mark it.

Included were contributions from all sorts of people with their own memories of the Kop, and I am delighted, my own special thoughts were sought for that publication.

The game itself ended as a 1-0 defeat – Jeremy Goss firing home the last goal at the Kop end – but it didn't spoil the occasion.

Some thought the end of the Kop as it was would change the atmosphere forever but it all became clear very quickly that wouldn't be the case. Liverpool fans, quite rightly now all-seated, could still spot a classic when one came along.

Such a game – often defined as the best Premiership match – was Liverpool v Newcastle United on April 3, 1996. It was an absolute corker.

Newcastle came to Anfield with their fading title challenge exasperating manager, Kevin Keegan.

Robbie Fowler put Liverpool ahead; Ferdinand equalised. Ginola got a second for the Magpies; Fowler got his second in the 55th minute... only for Asprilla to nudge Newcastle ahead once again. Stan Collymore, who had a hit and (mainly) miss career at Anfield, got it right that night – a 68th minute leveller then an injury time winner set up by John Barnes. Anfield went completely potty. It was an *'I was there'* night.

Amazingly, when the teams met the following season it again ended up 4-3 to Liverpool, Newcastle pulling back a 3-0 half-time deficit only for Robbie Fowler to pop up with a sensational winner.

Robbie Fowler had been a revelation as a Liverpool striker. He was two-footed, but his left was his best. He could also head a ball, and knew instinctively where the goal was. I couldn't believe our luck when just as Rushie was bringing his Anfield career to a close, Fowler, an absolute natural, was there to replace him.

He and his mate, Steve McManaman, brought a new burst of energy to the club. Both match-winners, both gifted, both typical Scousers – full of life, full of mischief.

I really enjoyed watching them strut their stuff and they were charm personified to me when I introduced my two young sons to them on a flight back down to London after a game at Anfield.

Astonishingly, another truly gifted goalscorer was also about to make his Liverpool first-team entry – 17-year-old Michael Owen made a late substitute's appearance away against Wimbledon in May 1997.

I had been told a lot about this guy by club officials but this was my first look at him in the flesh.

His impact was instant. He scored within 10 minutes of coming onto the field at Selhurst Park, beating a defender for pace and beating the keeper with conviction.

We lost the game but had unveiled another star.

Fowler and Owen – now that was going to be fun.

And, within 12 months, one of them was going play a huge part in one of the most memorable evenings of my entire television career at my new broadcast home... ITV.

16

The Big Switch

Leaving the BBC after working there for some 18 years was a decision I didn't take lightly – but I did take quickly.

By 1997, I had risen through the ranks of BBC Sport to the rank of Head of Sport (Production), the BBC having created an internal system – and internal havoc – in creating both a production and broadcast division. My opposite number in the broadcast division was Jonathan Martin, who I, and almost everybody else, still considered to be the boss.

I really had enjoyed my stint as editor of *Match of the Day*, *Sportsnight*, Olympics, World Cups and *Sports Review of the Years* but had stepped out of programme-making and into senior BBC management.

I then had a chance to run for Controller of *BBC1* in 1997 and got mighty close to landing that iconic broadcast post – I believe I made the final two. But I didn't get it, took it on the chin and just resumed my existing duties, but others elsewhere felt I might be unsettled and ready for a change.

One man with that thought, was David Liddiment, a brilliant programme-maker and now broadcast supremo at ITV.

He was creating his new commissioning team and had my name pencilled in against the Controller of Sport post.

He was persuasive, both philosophically and financially, and added a second element to a potential new career at ITV.

He wanted me to run the channel's sports output – but also to launch ITV2 – the commercial giant's first new channel since 1955. He said it would go to air inside 12 months and he wanted me to shape and craft it. The combination of the two roles was the clincher for me. That, and my desire to test my skills in a commercial broadcasting environment.

From initial conversation with Liddiment to decision was a fortnight and I shook hands on the deal after a memorable Chinese banquet and several bottles of white wine. I may have regretted the final bottle (or two) the following morning, but I never regretted the decision to move to ITV.

I think that my leaving of the BBC was a genuine shock to the organisation and to the UK broadcasting 'village' as a whole. I think I was considered to be a BBC 'lifer' by the industry.

My BBC contemporaries treated the decision in two distinctly different ways. Half thought it was the right move at the right time, and half thought I was disloyal. What I knew was that I had loved the experience of working for BBC Sport and its tremendous team. I had worked the proverbial '25 hours a day, eight days a week, 53 weeks a year' for over 18 years. I had also received a terrific education in the art of television – and seen the world.

I had been to World Cups, Olympic Games (both Summer and Winter), Commonwealth Games, World Heavyweight Championship fights, European Football Championships, Wimbledon, the Grand National, Formula One Grand Prix, the Open Golf Championship. I'd met sporting icons past and present – Pele, Muhammad Ali, Carl Lewis, Bob Beamon and even Red Rum!

I'd worked with some of the Corporation's finest presenters: Des Lynam, David Coleman, Harry Carpenter, Steve Rider and some of the BBC's finest commentators – Peter O'Sullevan, Bill McLaren, Peter Alliss and, of course that great footballing duo, Messrs' Motson and Davies.

I'd enjoyed it all – indeed it had been an absolute privilege to be part of it all but now it was time to move on.

But not before I had made one call. When I got the job at the BBC in London in 1979, my parents were ecstatic. Now I had to phone my mother to tell her I was leaving the Beeb to join ITV. She was disappointed but trusted my judgement and became a loyal viewer of ITV for the next seven years! I also asked my assistant Marianne to join me at ITV. A big decision for her but with typical loyalty she said yes without hesitation.

As is the custom in these situations, once it was known I was leaving the BBC I was asked to vacate the organisation pretty damn pronto. I fully understood the reasons why, but as I scooped up my belongings into a black bin bag and slipped quietly away I did think it lacked a little bit of class on the Corporation's part.

I wouldn't be the first or the last person to jump between British broadcasters. Indeed, the last three Director-Generals were recruited from outside the BBC. So will the next one probably.

Anyway, slip away I did, but not before I bumped into the BBC newsreader and presenter Jill Dando on the way out of the building. News and sports people tended to know each other because of the similar nature of their business.

Jill expressed her disappointment at my leaving the BBC and wished me well. Sentiments I returned. How sad that within 18 months, I, like many millions of others, would be deeply shocked and saddened by her tragic untimely death.

At ITV, I had joined an organisation that was about to go into a growth spurt – and top-class sport was part of the mix. Champions League Football, Formula One Motor Racing and the Rugby World Cup were three top-class mainstays and in 1998 they were supplemented with the World Cup in France.

I had to sit outside the meetings that split the match schedule between my old and new employers but with the likes of wily Jeff Farmer, a tremendous ally, and the clear-thinking of ITV lawyer and future FA colleague Simon Johnson we got a good split of World Cup games. Jeff and Simon subsequently became my two contract buddies when we went out to get or retain sports broadcast contracts – the 'cabal', as our ITV colleagues affectionately dubbed us, had a good strike rate too.

The World Cup was the first event where my television skills would be matched against my former employers. The BBC had traditionally trounced ITV when the channels had simultaneously transmitted games – and I had enjoyed my share of that reflected glory. Now I was likely to be on the receiving end of it. However, the tournament threw up a freak result which gave us at ITV a remarkable opportunity.

England had been expected to easily win their group but slipped up against Romania and had to settle for second place – and an unexpected and huge test against Argentina. The game would be played in peak-time on a Tuesday evening. In the event it was a classic and watched by the biggest television audience on either channel that year – a whopping 23.8 million. Simply massive.

You'll remember the game. Beckham's sending-off, Campbell's disallowed goal, 2-2 after extra-time, England beaten on penalties and that goal from Liverpool's 18-year-old Michael Owen.

His famous run and cross shot was simply sensational and changed his life overnight. For Liverpool and England fans it was a fantastic moment. The goal was that good.

He was already building a reputation but that goal against Argentina sent it soaring. There would be other games and goals – the 2001 FA Cup final for instance – but at that time, at least, Liverpool fans were chuffed to call Michael Owen one of their own.

Of course, BBC beat ITV on the head-to-head in the final but the England/Argentina game gave ITV not only the best audience figure of the year but that was followed by England against Colombia as the second highest – also on ITV.

The opening title music for ITV's World Cup coverage – now a keenly anticipated decision – was a collaboration between a Liverpool band Apollo 440 and that master of the 'rock event with lasers' Jean-Michel Jarre. I checked out the other day how many albums the charismatic Frenchman had sold in his career and found out it was a cool 80 million.

Impressive eh... but that didn't stop my ITV colleague Rick Waumsley and me going to the recording studios and telling JMJ how we wanted him to re-mix his platinum hit 'Rendez-Vous' for our titles. He was charm personified as Rick, who fancies himself as a bit of musician, asked him in what key he would be playing the tune – and then when I, musically challenged, resorted to drawing a line on a piece of paper heading upwards to signify I wanted the piece to end in an upbeat flourish.

Jean-Michel looked at the scrap of paper – then at me – shook his head and seemed a little puzzled, so I resorted to using my schoolboy French. That proved less than valuable as Jean-Michel didn't know where the railway station was.

Back at his synthesiser – and with the smile of a man who had now seen and heard everything, JMJ hit the keyboards and delivered the theme perfectly – with, of course, an upbeat flourish at the end. And he dramatically swept his hand upwards as he did it, then nodded through the studio glass waving an imaginary piece of paper.

The song went to number 12 in the charts and I put a lot of that down to its rather special finale. I also die with embarrassment at the thought of having told a master of his trade how to do his business. I am expecting a laser across our house at any time.

I have to declare that I was also responsible for ITV's lowest audience figure of the year too. Virtually nobody was able to watch *ITV2* on its launch night in December 1998 but launch it we did – via Vinnie Jones and Billie Piper setting off a firework display across the Thames. I am delighted to say that *ITV2* is now a well-established award-winning channel.

My time at ITV was highly enjoyable. I learnt a new set of skills, understanding how commercial television worked. Having spent all my previous experience at a licence-funded organisation I had to adjust to a new business model where the programmes had to make back, and more, than had been invested in them.

David Liddiment had put together his 'A' team – people like Steve Anderson, ex-BBC, who headed ITV's news and current affairs arm.

Kirkby-born Steve, a full-on Liverpudlian, and I would put the world to rights every Monday morning depending on the previous weekend's football results. Serious stuff over, he would then go back to plotting the week's agenda in the world of politics, royalty, industrial disputes and international affairs.

Nick Elliott, ITV's brilliant drama commissioner, would each week at our programme review meeting, explain to us why whatever he had commissioned for the previous week's television, had either succeeded or failed.

It was like dipping into a regular master-class. I loved it.

The channel's Controller of Entertainment was an incredibly

talented if highly-charged lady called Claudia Rosencrantz. She had the office opposite mine. She had no interest in television sport but knew what worked and what didn't, whilst I had a long-standing regard for the small screen's light-entertainment genre.

The end of our corridor was always busy. I would watch as celebrities like Bruce Forsyth, Michael Barrymore, Barry Humphries and a young up and coming duo called Ant and Dec went in and out of her office. She, in turn, watched as my on-screen talent team and also famous sports stars hoping for a break into television, went in and out of mine. We were always intrigued by each other's guests.

I did ask her one day who the smart-looking chap sitting in her office had been. She said: "He's a guy called Simon Cowell, he's an executive in the music business and I think he's about to be a big star."

"How come?" I said.

"Because I'm going to commission an entertainment series about finding new pop talent and part of the trick of it will be making the judging panel the centre of the show. The stars of it actually – and Simon could become the biggest."

"Judges as the stars eh... can't see it myself," I said.

Ah well, stick to what you know!

*   *   *   *   *

I was a contented man leaving Paris the day after the 1998 World Cup final. ITV had done a good job on the tournament but there was somebody happier heading to England.

Gerard Houllier, who had coached the French team in the early '90s, had subsequently helped as part of the technical team behind World Cup winners, France.

Now, five days after celebrating the great French victory, he was to take up his new challenge as on July 17 it was announced he was the new joint manager of Liverpool Football Club.

He was appointed to work alongside the existing manager, Roy Evans. But would it work? It sounded like one almighty fudge from the outside, whatever the internal merits of the move.

Indeed, I had a pre-season meeting with Peter Robinson regarding broadcast rights to their European games and I couldn't leave without exploring the rationale behind the decision and asking the question on every Liverpool fan's lips. "Yes, but who picks the team?"

By November, we knew the answer. Houllier. Evans, an original cast member of the Boot Room, had resigned. A hugely popular Anfield man, Evans felt the two-header wasn't working and knew it had to be him to stand aside.

Ronnie Moran, another huge Liverpool figure also stood down at the same time. A very influential member of the back-room staff, Moran had led the team out at the 1992 FA Cup final.

The club, guided by Tom Saunders, realised they needed to maintain a 'Liverpool' presence in the managerial team and the name of Phil Thompson entered the frame.

Acrimoniously sacked by Souness, Thompson would prove to be a vital and positive new member of staff. A Scouser, a big Liverpool FC man and a successful ex-player, Thompson had assets that Houllier lacked and a new managerial duo was formed.

After settling in, Houllier started to shape his 'own' team – Steve McManaman had chosen a new and successful life in Spain with Real Madrid; Paul Ince, Jason McAteer, Phil Babb and David James among others were not to the Frenchman's liking and were also off on their travels. Over the next 18 months in came the likes of Finnish defender, Sami Hyypia, a simply inspirational signing;

goalkeeper, Sander Westerveld, Germans Dietmar Hamann and Markus Babbel, the Swiss defender Stephane Henchoz and Czech midfielder Vladimir Smicer plus the experienced old Scot Gary McAllister and a barrel of a man, Emile Heskey from Leicester City.

And then, of course, there were a couple of Academy boys. Local lads forcing their way into Houllier's reckoning – Steven Gerrard and Jamie Carragher.

The last two names have rightly ended up as legends of the club – genuine Anfield heroes. Indeed, in my 50 years watching the Reds, Steven Gerrard, has come closer than anybody to knocking King Kenny off his perch as Liverpool's best-ever player – and, of course, he still has time to do it.

It has been fun to be there to see Steven and Jamie play out their whole careers as Liverpool players – and I'm pleased I saw both their first team debuts.

And sure, Gerrard has been tempted to leave Anfield on a couple of occasions but, in these days of rich overseas owners, high finance, astronomical wages and super-busy agents, I am pleased such overtures were ultimately resisted, because one-club loyalty has become almost an obsolete tour of duty in professional football and because of that we may never see the likes of two such highly-gifted players committing themselves so completely to the cause of Liverpool Football Club in the future. They are a couple of one-offs that have become the perfect pair for Liverpool. When they kiss the badge they mean it... and the fans believe it.

Gerrard and Carragher have also given the team a 'Scouse-ness' that is reassuring to the Liverpool fans. Yes, it is terrific to play home and host to some of the world's best footballers but the club, for many generations, has also been built on local footballing talent, local heroes and local passion – and that to my mind must never be lost. It is what makes the club stand out.

I have had the pleasure of spending some time with both players, invariably when they were away on England duty, and have found both of them to be decent people to be around. Inquisitive, intelligent and informed. And different. Carragher outgoing, Gerrard more of an introvert.

Critically, they are still turning in performance after performance for the club (and country, in Gerrard's case) and this, in a season just past, when the crowd has responded very positively to the introduction – some by design, some by necessity – of a new crop of young Liverpool players. Some English, some British, some foreign and some Scouse. Terrific.

Mind you, they will have to blow-torch the shirts off the backs of Gerrard and Carragher – they intend playing forever. Indeed, it will be strange to see a regular Liverpool team without those two Red bravehearts.

Of course, Gerrard and Carragher were at the start of their Liverpool careers when the club embarked on the 2000/2001 campaign that proved to be Houllier's special time at the club.

In February 2001, the Reds clinched their first trophy for six years – the Worthington Cup – when they kept their nerve in a penalty shoot-out win over Birmingham City in Cardiff's Millennium Stadium.

Indeed, it was a young Jamie Carragher who scored Liverpool's final penalty – and it was another Scouser, Robbie Fowler who scored a terrific left-foot volley in the normal time and one of the shoot-out penalties and then lifted the trophy itself as stand-in captain along with the injured Jamie Redknapp. He was also voted Man of the Match.

One down – two to go. The second trophy on offer was the FA Cup. Cardiff again, opponents Arsenal. I set off for this final in my guise as ITV's Controller of Sport. I was staying at the Celtic Manor on the eve of the game and my dinner guest that evening was ITV's football presenter... Des Lynam!

Yes, in one of my more unlikely exploits I had managed, along with ITV's Director of Programmes, David Liddiment, to persuade the best sports broadcaster of his generation to move from his long-established home at BBC to join me at ITV.

It was the biggest 'talent' transfer story in television for years. Des was television's best presenter and BBC's biggest star and so his signing for ITV was big, big news.

David Liddiment and I had plotted this little escapade during our train journey to the south coast for a meeting at Des's home there.

I had immensely enjoyed working with Des at the BBC. We were considered a 'team' and I loved the idea of hooking up with him again and for Liddiment's part, he was keen to have a channel of stars. Des became a target for us.

I had actually worked with Des at the BBC since 1980, originally on a regular Friday evening segment, *Sportswide*, into the hugely popular nightly-show *Nationwide*.

The programme proved a tough testing ground for both of us. One week I was responsible for the programme 'falling' off the air in spectacular fashion nearly giving Des, a highly accomplished radio broadcaster but still TV rookie, a heart attack in the bargain as they cut back to him in the studio unexpectedly to hold the fort.

A couple of weeks later, I left him high and dry again when I got delayed in heavy Friday night London traffic with the programme's main guest, US boxing legend, Marvin Hagler.

We then subsequently got lost in the labyrinthial corridors of BBC's Lime Grove trying to find the *Nationwide* studio.

I arrived with a rather exasperated fighter and his mouthy American manager, just in time to hear Des bidding the viewers a fond fare-well – and apologising for Hagler's apparent no-show.

Des was charming about it. Hagler, over in London to challenge for the world middleweight crown, was, shall we say, a little less sanguine about it all. And I still feel I was partially responsible for the tough-as-teak fighting machine making such short work of our British world champion Alan Minter the following night. I had definitely got him angry!

Des and I worked well together.

He was a quite brilliant television presenter and I felt editorially on top of my game. We both felt we knew 'our' audience.

And we had some unexpected successes as well. Between us, with generous help from his elegant partner, Rose, we came up with the idea of using the iconic Italian tenor, Luciano Pavarotti's rendition of 'Nessun Dorma' as the theme music for BBC's cover-age of Italia 90. It just brilliantly fitted the bill – and the opening title sequence became an award-winner.

It proved a fantastic choice. I knew we were on to something three days into televising the event when I heard our milkman whistling the distinctive tune and then making a stab at singing the climactic end notes in his own version of Italian.

The aria (as us experts call it) was a worldwide phenom-enon, Pavarotti's fame widened and four years later on the eve of the 1994 World Cup final, Des and I were both invited to the Three Tenors Concert at the Los Angeles Dodgers Stadium. Terry Venables and his wife joined us.

To say our tickets were decent is slightly under-selling it as we were spirited beyond a galaxy of Hollywood A-listers – Dustin Hoffman, Walter Matthau, Tom Cruise, Whoopi Goldberg and Arnold Schwarzenegger, and settled into our seats a few rows behind three of the evening's chief guests, a guy called Frank Sinatra and his mates, Gene Kelly and Bob Hope.

Des, David and I had a convivial meeting and discussed the possibility of a move to ITV.

The offer of presenting top-class live football, including the multi-starred UEFA Champions League, and a lucrative contract, meant Des had some serious thinking to do.

On the train back to London, Liddiment asked me, given my knowledge of how Des ticked, how I felt the meeting had gone. I told him I felt it had gone well – but would know more later in the day. "How do you mean?" asked David.

"If Des phones me tonight I think we're on... if he doesn't phone then he doesn't fancy it," I countered.

That night, ironically, I was out at dinner with Bob Shennan, the new BBC Head of Sport, to discuss mutual broadcasting business. Bob is a good guy, and a big Liverpudlian, and we laugh about that dinner now – but I'm sure at the time he felt let down when the 'Lynam' news came out.

When I got home after dinner with Bob, my wife Gerry asked how our evening had gone, and then in passing, said: "Oh, by the way, Des phoned half an hour ago – can you phone him back in the morning." Bingo!

I was about to start jury service, and Des about to start a holiday, and so we were both 'out of the way'. Negotiations were carried out quickly and quietly.

Three weeks later we unveiled Des at a press conference as ITV's new top sports presenter. It was front and back page news. TV's equivalent of signing Andy Carroll, I suppose.

Anyway, Des was at the ITV helm for the channel's coverage of the 2001 cup final – and watched a game played out in absolutely sweltering conditions. I know I have never felt so hot or uncomfortable at a football match, the sun being directly in our faces. It was boiling and at half-time, a lady came over to me and offered me her sun protection lotion and a bottle of water. I must have looked hot.

Anyway, hot off the field, and hot on it; Arsenal that is, not Liverpool. This was a day when the Gunners overwhelmed us but couldn't finish the job off. Time after time they broke through but somehow the game stayed even.

Finally, midway through the second half, Freddie Ljungberg got Arsenal ahead. They went for the kill but couldn't get a second. And lived to regret it.

This was 'the Michael Owen Final'. As the game reached its closing stages, the diminutive striker came into his own. He had arrived at the final in a hot streak of goalscoring form – and, on this steaming hot day in Cardiff, he conjured up two more out of nowhere to single-handedly win Liverpool the match.

His first, with the assistance of substitute Robbie Fowler, was a shot low in the corner from a cross from McAllister; the second featured a magnificent run and chase before placing the ball past Seaman. It was a goal worthy of winning any game or cup final. He received the European Footballer of the Year Award at the end of 2001.

Owen's subsequent moves to Real Madrid, Newcastle United and, more controversially, Manchester United, have seemed to cast him adrift from the affections of supporters at Anfield. He will be in nobody's top ten. The fans quite reasonably exercise their right to decide who will or won't be given legendary status and so it should be. But make no mistake, for a critical short spell, Owen made the difference in some big Liverpool matches – and that shouldn't be forgotten.

Unlike folk hero Robbie Fowler, who was revered in two spells at the club, Owen chose to leave the Reds which set him aside and certainly his ultimate choice of club was always going to be controversial. I just have a view that for a short space of time, even shorter when you consider their respective injuries, in Robbie Fowler and Michael Owen, Liverpool were simply blessed with having two of the greatest strikers in world football and we had BOTH of them at the same time. We should enjoy that fact. In 2001, one had won us the Worthington Cup final and the other, the FA Cup final.

The third final that spring was the UEFA Cup final. This match was to be staged in Dortmund and the opponents were the unfancied Spanish club side, Deportivo Alaves.

The game was thought to be an easy one for Liverpool, but what transpired was a nine-goal thriller. Liverpool steamed ahead, 20-year-old Steven Gerrard getting a goal after Babbel had got the first. The Spaniards got one back, but McAllister scored a penalty to restore the Reds' two-goal advantage going into half-time.

The Spaniards hit back. 3-2, 3-3. Robbie Fowler came on and scored a magnificent goal, Liverpool's fourth and surely the winner. But no. Jordi Cruyff emulated his watching famous father by scoring against Liverpool with a late, late equaliser. Extra-time, and Golden Goal time, delivered by a Spaniard FOR Liverpool – an own goal by Alaves' Delfi Geli.

It had been stunning entertainment in front of a huge Reds following in Germany and I spent the rest of the evening re-living old LFC glories over a beer or two with Paul Tyrrell, then my colleague at ITV, now Liverpool FC's Head of Press and Ian Ayre, a big Reds fan who is now the club's highly accomplished managing director.

Three days later, Liverpool got a fourth big prize – qualification for the UEFA Champions League. They went to Charlton Athletic and hammered them 4-0. Fowler got two goals and Owen nicked another.

I was at a wedding that afternoon but had found out the latest score on the way into the church and the final score on the way out of the church when the service ended. Hallelujah.

At the start of the next season an unprecedented fourth and fifth trophies followed for Houllier's men – an FA Charity Shield win over Manchester United followed by a UEFA Super Cup triumph over Germany's Bayern Munich.

The Reds' Premier League campaign began at home against Tottenham Hotspur – and, once again, the Reds were chosen to break new broadcasting ground, being the first match shown on a new Saturday early evening football programme on ITV called *The Premiership*.

Yes, the previous year I had headed up ITV's team in the negotiations with the Premier League for Saturday night highlights. We were obviously taking on an established monster in BBC and *Match of the Day*, but a combination of a hugely competitive bid and a different ambition for the programme – an early evening slot – won us the day. In fact, I'd had a sense we would win the rights the previous evening when I pulled up in my car at the traffic lights heading into my London home.

Alongside me drew up a car with a certain Greg Dyke in the back seat – he was BBC's DG by then and we were close neighbours. He didn't see me – but I watched him feverishly rattling instructions down his mobile phone.

For all I know he may have been ordering his Chinese take-away but I allowed myself the thought that we had the Beeb on the run and went to bed that evening a little bit more confident of success.

We did get awarded the rights the following day, a big news story,

Des and now *Match of the Day* had left the BBC. Greg went on the attack – we had overpaid he said. Probably true actually, but the BBC all but matched that financial figure three years later!

The decision was announced to the world in the midst of Euro 2000, with ITV again giving a good showing against their traditional rivals in a tournament stretched across Holland and Belgium. One reason for that was we had some strength and experience in our pundits line-up that included three former England managers; Glenn Hoddle, Terry Venables and the wonderful Bobby Robson.

When the day's work was done we had plenty of great social evenings, including a memorable one in a small bar outside Amsterdam, when Bobby, always inquisitive, was asking Terry about an edition of the *Stars in Their Eyes* programme, the Cockney crooner had just appeared on.

"I was Anthony Newley on it, Bob."

"Never," said Bobby wide-eyed. "Go on give us a bit of the song."

Terry, as good as gold, gave us the briefest of renditions of 'What Kind of Fool Am I.'

"Wow, not bad," said Bobby.

Seeing an opportunity, I prompted: "If you went on the show who would you be Bobby?"

"Jimmy Durante," came Bobby's instant left of field reply and without a hint of hesitation or a 'Tonight Matthew, I am going to be…' the great man then started singing that marvellous song 'Make Someone Happy'. Such an appropriate sentiment from Bobby.

At this point, our third former England boss, Glenn Hoddle, joined us in the bar, got up to speed with what we were discussing and not to be outdone, declared he would have been David Bowie on the show and then hit us with a bit of the Bowie/Queen classic 'Under Pressure.'

With the England managers' alumni belting out their songs, some

England fans then casually wandered into the bar and, having been spotted, our would-be star vocalists returned swiftly to discussing the virtues of 4-3-3 and other such football stuff. If only those fans had been there five minutes earlier...

Anyway, ITV had the rights and a programme title. *The Premiership* had U2 bashing out the theme tune and had a new slot – Saturday night, seven o'clock. That was ambitious, actually an hour later than what we would have liked, but we felt there was a young audience out there who weren't around to watch football highlights later in the evening.

We tested the market – and football. I remember asking Lord Alan Sugar – he was plain Alan then – whether he thought it was a good idea. He didn't knock it but told us his 'good lady' was in charge of the TV controller in his house early on a Saturday evening – and he thought that was the case nationwide.

Des Lynam presented the programme with lively-minded Terry Venables and the hugely personable Ally McCoist in the studio and fledging broadcaster Andy Townsend out on the road in the infamous Tactics Truck.

This particular venture was not a resounding success and the truck was off the road by programme three!

Thankfully, Andy's new broadcast career survived that early bang on the bumper. The new on-air time was a challenge for the production team but they made it. What the programme did suffer from was a shortage of actual programme time and also seven consecutive Saturdays which if they had constituted a week would have been the sunniest since records began! Nightmare.

By late October, ITV's advertising boys – and one of the channel's big stars, Cilla Black – were demanding a return to what they and the ITV audience knew best and were familiar with.

The Premiership was moved back to the old *Match of the Day* slot and we took the publicity hit. *Cilla 1 Des 0* comes to mind.

Once we had dusted ourselves down we went on to develop a programme that I thought editorially matched its hugely-respected opposite number at the BBC. It also helped bring through new young presenters like Gabby Logan – now an established television talent – and it was blessed with a strong commentary team of Clive Tyldesley, Peter Drury and Jon Champion. I genuinely believe that *The Premiership* was a decent watch – as indeed does Des. Anyway, it is all subjective stuff.

And just like room 2143 at the BBC, the ITV boys had a room where we watched all the games coming into the building. Every Saturday afternoon, we would all be glued to the monitors, have a go in the sweep, be treated to cream cakes and sweets – and be helpless with laughter at Ally's latest antics both north and south of the border. He had even starred in a football film with Hollywood star, Robert Duvall – late of *The Godfather*.

For Ally, it was two movies rolled into one – his first and his last! Duvall managed to somehow survive the experience and keep his career on track. Ally, of course, has since taken up the managerial reins at Rangers.

ITV Sport enjoyed other successes with its UEFA Champions League coverage which had been part of the channel's output since its inception in 1992; Formula One – it was fun doing business with motorsport ring-master Bernie Ecclestone, a one-off – and its Rugby World Cup coverage.

Motor racing and Rugby Union weren't naturally my thing – but as crucial parts of our portfolio I made it my business to get to know them well. And quickly.

I remember shortly after starting at ITV, heading out of our offices one Thursday evening before the Easter bank holiday, armed with a small suitcase.

"Going anywhere nice?" said the lady on reception. "Well, yes Buenos Aires to work actually – and I am going out tonight – see you back here at work on Tuesday morning." And so off I went to watch the Argentinian Grand Prix. There and back inside three days, eager to get up to speed with a sport I wasn't totally across.

I enjoyed working with the two F1 turbo talents, Murray Walker and Martin Brundle enormously. Despite being long in the tooth, and already hugely popular, Murray wanted to know how to improve his performance and I helped him, whilst Martin was starting to build up his formidable reputation as a pundit and just needed steering, so to speak, on how to get the best from his know-how. The likes of Neil Duncanson, who ran the channel's F1 coverage and I, were able to help him.

Rights negotiations were done with Bernie Ecclestone at his offices in Knightsbridge and were always fascinating experiences. You left each meeting thinking – 'now how did that actually go?' And you were never sure.

One thing I did learn from Bernie was the art of client management. If ever I had cause to ring his office, he would return the call within the hour if he was busy or not.

The acquisition of the 2003 Rugby World Cup broadcast rights was a close run thing between the BBC and ourselves – and we won. It proved to be a big win as England's rugby team became front-page news when they were crowned world champions in astonishing style in Australia.

I was in Sydney for the final, with my ITV colleague Jeff Farmer, and despite us both being dyed-in-the-wool football men, there is no doubt as Jonny Wilkinson's vital kick sailed between the posts to secure England their historic victory over hosts Australia, we both knew we were witnessing something truly, truly memorable. And something enjoyed by over 14 million viewers.

On a run of good form, we even went out and secured the Varsity Boat Race – a bit off limits for ITV – and then I watched with pride as our talented production crew went out and won a BAFTA for their coverage of the event. When trying to secure the Boat Race rights I had to sit in front of a set of committee members and explain why the organisers should move from their traditional broadcasting home, the British Broadcasting Corporation.

"Are you going to do anything different?" said one po-faced, ultra-cautious committee member.

"Oh, yes." I said. "I want to put a third boat in the race."

I think oxygen was being administered to the aghast committee man when I chanced my luck a bit further and explained I was also going to take the race around all the other rivers in England. Two more committee men hit the floor. At this point I had to explain I was just joking to lighten the mood somewhat. Still got the contract though.

Not everything worked. ITV had built a formidable reputation in broadcasting live big-time boxing – but the sport was migrating to subscription television by the time I got there. We tried to stay in it but began to lose confidence. Not least when, on one evening, we transmitted a fight live on a Saturday night from St George's Hall in Liverpool. During the main contest one of the wooden planks forming part of the ring floor snapped underneath the canvas, and for a brief moment we made sporting history as both boxers had to adapt to having to fight the contest UPHILL.

More seriously, ITV, as a company, had to take the reflected hit from the swift demise of its side-business ITV Digital in 2002, something that went down very badly with the football business and the Football League in particular, who were short-changed by the broadcasters' undistinguished exit.

*   *   *   *   *

At Liverpool, Gerard Houllier's fantastic run of trophy-lifting in 2001 was brought into sharp perspective when he suffered serious heart problems during the half-time interval in their home game against Leeds United.

In his absence, Phil Thompson took over as Houllier's stand-in and did brilliantly. I think that caretaker period was really important for Phil because it put behind him the troubles he had endured in his earlier coaching period at Liverpool. As Houllier's stand-in he stepped up to the plate and delivered in a mature, classy style.

I was at Anfield on the evening Houllier was re-introduced to the crowd. Gerard emerged from the tunnel to a huge ovation and a warm embrace from Roma manager Capello and the Reds, inspired by the occasion, went on to record a famous 2-0 win.

The rest of the Frenchman's reign was one of clipped success. Runners-up in 2002 and a League Cup final win over Manchester United the following year but some signings like those of El-Hadji Diouf and Salif Diao didn't cut the mustard and there seemed a missed opportunity in not retaining Nicolas Anelka.

Given Manchester United and Arsenal's dominance, it made Houllier's exit from Anfield sadly inevitable. A student of the facts and figures, his interpretation of the same became a little selective and so, as football works, he was shown the door in the summer of 2004. He remains to this day a huge advocate of Liverpool Football Club and his time spent at the club is fondly remembered.

So a new era was about to descend on Liverpool Football Club in the guise of wily Spaniard Rafa Benitez, coach of La Liga's over-achieving Valencia – and also sporting life at ITV was also about to change as the commercial television giants were in the hunt for a new Controller of Sport.

Their existing one – Brian Barwick – was off to Soho Square... and a huge job at the Football Association.

17

Life on The Square

I don't know how often *you* get in a taxi, the driver turns around, asks you where you want to be taken, has a quick glance in his rear-view mirror, then another double-take, before hitting you with "It was a poisoned chalice, wasn't it, mate?"

An unlikely phrase to spill from the lips of a guy, no doubt, clued up on the local 'knowledge' but not probably on the history of chalices – poisoned or otherwise.

Anyway, I get it – still – about once a fortnight from cabbies. And then there's the postman, the milkman, the lads in the pub and the keep-fit freaks in the gym. "Poisoned chalice, Brian, better off out of it." The poisoned chalice they are referring to, of course, is the position of Chief Executive of the Football Association. A job I left three years ago.

It was a position I'd actually started on January 31, 2005 and stepped down from (now there's a euphemism) on August 20, 2008. I'd spent over three and half years in the role and would spend a further four months on the payroll. Gold watch territory in that job. And do you know what? I rather enjoyed myself.

I found the job to be exciting, testing, exasperating, challenging, enthralling, frustrating, impossible and rewarding – and invariably all on the same afternoon.

'Impossible to turn down and impossible to do' one guy recently told me.

Well, perhaps, and sure the job was full of surprises, not all of them pleasant, but as a person for whom football had been a life-long passion the idea of helping the game, however briefly, was a risk, and a professional diversion, worth taking.

When I joined my new colleagues at the Football Association, the circumstances of my predecessor's departure – the Palios/Eriks-son/Alam saga – meant the public interest in the organisation was more Albert Square than Soho Square – immense, intense and a little intrusive. But that was what I had signed up for, so my view was just get on with it.

Indeed, even on the day of my final interview for the job, I had been tracked by the ubiquitous SKY Sports News cameras and was actually asked that classic football question *"How do you feel?"* as I slipped out of Soho Square after being grilled by the FA board. Pretty good, it seemed, as later that day I was offered the chalice... sorry, job.

I haggled over the money and the length of contract – but as the FA had already announced my appointment I was in a rather strong position! Anyway, I wanted it. For me, it was an opportunity of a lifetime.

As my wife Gerry and I drove home that evening my elevation to one of football's top jobs was the main item on a *BBC Radio 4* news bulletin. "Enjoy this moment," I said. "It may be as good as it gets."

According to a national newspaper gossip column the following morning, 'Mr Barwick and his wife had celebrated their big news with a slap-up meal in London's West End'.

Well, everything is relative and it depends whether you think a couple of packets of Chicken Tikka Masala and a bottle of Frascati bought from the local *Tesco Metro* constitutes a world of wild high-living but that's what we actually had.

In all seriousness, we had prepared ourselves as a family for a significant level of scrutiny and interest. I'd sat down with my two teenage boys, Jack and Joe, then 15 and 13 respectively, and told them that while in his new job, their dad was going to be in the papers, and on the television, on a reasonably frequent basis and that invariably it would be pretty unkind (if not necessarily unfair) stuff. I told them it was all part of the business I was now in, and indeed part of the business I had just left, and so they must promise not to take any of it to heart because I promised I wouldn't either.

Indeed, I also reminded them that once our front door was shut, life in our house would be exactly as it always had been. So, I routinely expected to be ignored by my two teenage boys and barked at by the dogs! And, in turn, my wife Gerry expected her viewing of Inspector Morse to be rudely interrupted at a critical crime-solving moment by her husband slapping on *Ceefax* to see if Liverpool had equalised in the last minute at Bolton.

My home, and the stability, love, affection and humour of my nearest and dearest, were a huge part of me being able to enjoy my time at the FA – and get as much pleasure as was possible in a role with so much professional scrutiny and public expectation.

Mind you, I fully accepted that the media would chase down leads and stories, drive agendas and campaigns, hit out at prominent individuals and, on occasions, take no prisoners. It was their job.

I didn't expect to be spared and I wasn't... but I didn't intend to be permanently scarred by the experience either... and I'm not.

So how did I get on? Well, firstly I found the staff at the Football Association to be absolutely a delight to work with. They just wanted to get on with their daily duties and for one of their bosses to actually stick around for a bit.

On my first day at Soho Square, I took the time to shake hands with every member of staff and told them I intended to be there for some time. And they responded really positively.

In the wider reaches of the game there was an understandable balance of supporters and sceptics to my appointment. If somebody had walked in off the street and told me how to run the television business I might have reacted similarly.

But, boy, was I enthusiastic. I felt I understood the game; knew its history and current narrative; knew and liked lots of people in it; felt I was recognised publicly and professionally as a 'football man'; understood the role of the media; had been involved in rights negotiations; had attended plenty of World Cups and European Championships and indeed employed plenty of former England managers in my previous professional life in television. All in all, I thought I had enough in my locker to have a decent stab at the job.

Once in the game I did find some of the politics surrounding the sport to be testing and, at times, difficult. I found some individuals less interested in the sport and more interested in the power and profile it brought them but I also met many really decent and highly accomplished people, and found the game itself at every level, 'from the mud to the stars', fun to be around.

And, I did make sure I got to see plenty of the type of football I'd played *in*, as well as the type of football I'd watched being played. In truth I was in my element. I built up a good rapport with the FA board and the FA councillors – many of whom I still consider to be friends, and tried to understand the positions taken on each and every issue by the various sides of the game – sometimes fair and right, sometimes unfathomable and unreasonable.

I tried to take a mature view of our role in world football and felt our 'cradle of the game' line had run its course, as has been subsequently proved.

I was concerned by the lack of ethnic diversity at the top of the domestic game and, by the fact that by introducing a second woman onto the 100-strong FA Council I had helped double the number of females on that particular body.

I wrestled with how the FA could find a way of having a positive relationship with the Premier League – a league that it had histori-cally helped create – then watched as the huge share of the game's riches were gobbled up on top players' wages.

A Premier League, by the way, I had a huge enthusiasm for – a week-by-week sporting saga that transfixed both our nation and many countries the world over. And whose clubs had become investment targets for foreign plutocrats.

I felt that a legitimate ambition should be for a strong FA and a strong Premier League and I didn't feel that such strength should be the sole preserve of one organisation or the other.

In believing that, I hit on a phrase that the FA should 'lead the national game and partner the professional game'.

I thought that was a realistic approach to a complex situation in which the professional game – the 92 Premier League and Football League clubs – helped raise the lion's share of the FA's revenue through its players and teams making the FA's commercial and broadcast contracts so enticing.

And we were able to land big deals – and then redistribute the spoils around the whole of the game. The professional game, the Premier League and its member club in essence felt that in allow-ing their assets to be commercially exploited, it had essentially done its bit for the wider game and that in other matters it should enjoy significant autonomy in running its own business.

However understandable that ambition, the sport itself – across the world – worked to a hierarchical system that demanded that FIFA, the game's much-criticised world governing body, sat above confederations, confederations regulated associations, who in turn had the duty to govern and regulate their own domestic game – and the leagues and players in it. Mind you, not every association had such a powerful and commercially successful league to deal with as the FA did. In fact, none of them did.

I understood very quickly there was something of a turf war in English football and beyond, and that not every decision taken in football would necessarily be to the benefit of the game as a whole, but just part of it.

*   *   *   *   *

I enjoyed working with FA people like Simon Johnson, a former colleague from ITV who I brought to Soho Square; David Davies, my old mate from BBC – a powerful ally in my early days; Sir Trevor Brooking, and his passionate views on the way his beloved sport should be developed; Hope Powell, a key driver of the women's game; Messrs Hill and Hall – the two Jonathans – contrasting characters but great operators in commercial affairs and football regulation respectively.

Then there was Alex Horne, the FA's finance director and its future General Secretary and, of course, Adrian Bevington, then the FA's director of communications now managing director of Club England, a brilliantly intuitive colleague who really under-stood his job and the sport, and a real player when the chips were down. Adrian is a man I consider to be a good friend. I was also ably supported by my assistant Nicki Clarkson who always provided an honest and caring sounding board.

I also had regular dealings with the likes of Richard Scudamore, the Chief Executive of the Premier League and Andy Williamson, now Chief Operating Officer of the Football League. We had fortnightly Friday breakfast meetings held at Soho Square to discuss common issues and problems.

Invariably, Richard wanted the meeting's first word, last word and, well, just about every other word in between – and quite often he warranted having them. A hugely talented executive, he knew his stuff so would get more and more frustrated if anybody else held the floor for any length of time. "Richard, just have another bacon sandwich," I would suggest to him.

Richard has been instrumental in making the Premier League a roaring global success. He is a powerful, committed, solely-focused advocate for his league, which is now one of world sport's big success stories. Such competitiveness did make it difficult on occasions to find a common position on significant matters.

It would, however, be great to see him spread such talent across the wider issues and fortunes of the English game at all levels some time in the future.

Andy is a real 'football man'. He warmly welcomed me into his industry and I often felt I could ring him up at the Football League for advice without sensing he would use the call to score points. A good man.

And there are lots of decent people on the amateur side of the game too – individuals who recognised that they had to protect the integrity of their own level of football. People like Roger Burden, John Ward and Michael Game; people who have given service yet only taken pride – and a blazer – out of a lifelong commitment to the game.

My working week probably involved me watching two or three games, something that strangely had not been normal practice for some of my predecessors or for some of my senior colleagues. I used the games to garner industry information, hear problems first-hand, meet football people *and* watch the sport – at every level. And show that we cared.

One football ground I was only sparingly seen at was Anfield. I felt that it was only right and proper to put my 'public' support of Liverpool on hold. It was already known in the game that I followed the Reds, with no comeback, but I still think I owed it to the sport to be seen as fair-minded. For nearly four seasons, therefore, I was a very infrequent visitor to Anfield.

Indeed, I held my visits back for Champions League games and made sure I also attended those of other teams including Manchester United, Arsenal and Chelsea. I was also at Goodison for Everton's Champions League qualifier against Villarreal.

Mind you, I still had my fair share of 'high days and holidays' with Liverpool whilst in office. After all, they did reach two UEFA Champions League finals, a European Super Cup, an FA Cup final, a Carling Cup final, a Community Shield match, an excursion to the World Club Championship, and a couple of FA Youth Cup finals – and it was part of my job to be there to see them.

And I did see them compete in one game at Anfield that tested my long-held loyalties – it was the Reds' FA Cup fourth round tie against Blue Square South's Havant and Waterlooville.

I had been at the Hampshire club's FA Cup third round replay against Swansea and witnessed first-hand the uncontained joy the Havant supporters had expressed as the final whistle confirmed victory and their date with destiny with mighty Liverpool.

I always made it my business to try and go to a game in each round of the FA Cup, starting in August with an extra preliminary round match. I went to one game at Ashford Town in this round, and an excited club official asked whether he could announce my arrival on the tannoy. I looked around the ground and told him that rather than going to all that fuss it would probably be easier for me to go and shake hands with the other 46 people in the ground!

Anyway, my match-choice on FA Cup fourth round day in 2008 was a most unlikely pairing – Liverpool v Havant and Waterlooville. As I walked past the Anfield Road end, the 6,000 fans from Hampshire were entering the stadium – they were *so* excited. If anybody wants to question the modern validity and relevance of the FA Cup this was an occasion to knock their arguments for six.

After I left the FA I had a short period on the board at Hampton and Richmond Borough Football Club, a team in the same league as Havant, and it gave me further understanding of just what that occasion at Anfield must have been like for all those connected with the Hawks, as they styled themselves, on that day.

As well as the actual incredulity of playing LIVERPOOL at ANFIELD, there was a financial pay-day which would be a debt-clearer and club builder for years to come.

When 'You'll Never Walk Alone' was played before the game the *whole* crowd sang the famous anthem, the red scarves – and, those of yellow and blue from Havant held out-stretched. One of their club officials sitting by me sang it whilst bawling his eyes out.

Preliminaries over, Havant then went out and gave Liverpool – 122 places above them in football's league ladder – the shock of their lives TWICE. Richard Pacquette gave the non-leaguers the lead, the Anfield Road went bonkers; Lucas levelled it, then Alfie Potter, who spent the first half terrorising Liverpool and the second man-marking Steven Gerrard so he would be near him to swop shirts, put Havant ahead again.

And for the first time in near 50 years of supporting Liverpool

I thought *I hope Havant win* – or rather, *I want Liverpool to lose.* Wearing my FA hat, I thought a result as extraordinary as Havant beating Liverpool would travel around the world faster than a speeding bullet and help restore the FA Cup's unique position in football. And the damage to Liverpool's reputation would only be temporary.

As I was mentally rehearsing my post-match public stance – 'Good for the game... great for the FA Cup...' Liverpool equalised for the second time on the stroke of half time.

Yossi Benayoun followed that goal by scoring two more in the second half, Peter Crouch rounded off the second half goal glut, Alfie Potter got his name in the papers – and Gerrard's shirt – and everybody went home satisfied. Although there was one FA chief executive just slightly peeved that an all-time cup upset had not transpired... Mind you, Liverpool were knocked out in the next round by Barnsley and still haven't made their debut at the new Wembley. Remember, the fans dubbed the old one 'Anfield South', the Reds played there that often.

The 2008 FA Cup final itself was ultimately between Portsmouth and Cardiff City and the final was at Wembley – the new Wembley – for the second year running, after a seven year gap.

I was delighted to be able to invite Sir Bobby Robson to be our Guest of Honour at that final. I had known Bobby for over 25 years and always found him and his family to be an absolute delight to be with. By now, he was in the grip of the latter stages of terminal cancer but still managed to get out of his wheelchair and walk out on the pitch to meet the finalists.

The crowd rose to him in a sustained and heart-felt ovation and he later told me just how much he had enjoyed that special day at the new Wembley Stadium. His last visit there.

The completion of the Wembley project, from building site to finished and open stadium, fell in my shift and at times was very problematical. Multiplex, the Australian constructors, had hit a number of big problems and the cost (to them) and the completion date kept slipping by weeks and months... and more.

Eventually, they, and we, were on the home straight and due to some sterling and inspired work by colleagues like Alex Horne, Roger Maslin and Scott Martin, we got there.

So, on FA Cup final day, May 2007, it had been my privilege as CEO of the FA, and Geoff Thompson, the Chairman of the FA, to accompany Prince William, the new President of the Football Association, on to the Wembley pitch – nowadays, thankfully perfect. We stood behind him as he declared the new stadium open. It was a genuinely special personal moment and one I did wonder what my late father would have made of.

I had also commissioned, on behalf of the Football Association, a painting of the big day.

Sure, there would be thousands of television and still photograph images of the occasion but I thought a painting – like the one produced for the 1962 FA Cup final that hung in the FA boardroom, would be a unique treasure of the big day. Accomplished artist Nick Botting completed a triptych – a painting on three panels – of the moment when Chelsea's Didier Drogba scored the match-winning goal against Manchester United in front of nearly 90,000 fans. A story goes that once Roman Abramovich heard about the painting he made an offer for it. My understanding is it still remains the property of the FA.

Six days after that cup final the first full international was staged and we invited Brazil to be England's opposition. I had made sure in the contract they wore their famous yellow shirts against us as they had occasionally played at Wembley in blue.

The first international, at the new Wembley, also gave us a chance to celebrate the stadium's rich sporting history. My dinner guests that evening were the legendary British boxer, Sir Henry Cooper and his wife, Lady Albina.

They were delightful company, and Sir Henry was patience personified as for the millionth time he told an enthralled set of diners about the night at Wembley in 1963 when he sent Cassius Clay crashing to the canvas with one of his trademark left hooks. Sadly, Sir Henry and Lady Albina are no longer with us.

In charge of England that night against world champions Brazil was Steve McClaren, a talented English coach who had enjoyed successful spells with Sir Alex Ferguson at Manchester United, and as boss of Middlesbrough, before assuming control of the senior side after the 2006 World Cup.

Steve's selection had not been universally well-received; as much a criticism of the recruitment processes itself as of the person who came out of it as the eventual winner.

At one stage it had looked as if Sven's successor might actually have been Brazilian World Cup-winning coach Luiz Felipe Scolari, but that possibility failed to materialise.

Following Sven's 'Fake Sheikh' escapade – in which, you may remember, he was caught in a Sunday newspaper 'sting' in Dubai – the FA had deemed it appropriate that the Swede step down after the World Cup in Germany and for his successor to be in place before the tournament.

However, the procedure for selecting his successor, of which I was a central figure, was fraught with problems and leaks, went on too long, was too public and had too many people getting themselves involved in the decision-making process.

The heavy criticism that came our way was valid.

In June 2006, I set off on my seventh professional World Cup assignment – four with the BBC had been followed by two with ITV and now I would attend my latest one as a member of the England party itself.

For me, being on the 'inside' of an England World Cup campaign, rather than pointing cameras and microphones at it was another unique experience.

Being part of that exaggerated joy of victory and the absolute desolation of defeat. And getting first-hand experience of just how long those days are before the tournament starts and then the rhythm of life in the training camp between your own matches once everything's underway.

And, of course, living every kick of every match. I always found myself a complete bundle of nerves while watching the games. Before our last group match against Sweden, the chairman of the 2006 World Cup organising committee, Franz Beckenbauer, came over and theatrically took hold of my wrist. "I am checking your pulse, Brian, because I saw you at the first two games and you looked so tense!" he joked. I was. Not least because I knew all the time how much it mattered to an expectant nation back home.

We travelled from Luton Airport to Baden-Baden carrying the country's hopes and then returned to Stansted Airport disappointed a month later, beaten quarter-finalists (again) having lost to Scolari's Portugal on penalties (again).

So now, Steve, Sven's assistant, stepped up and was in charge of getting the England team to Euro 2008, the next tournament. Qualification was the minimum requirement and, famously, it all came down to the last group match against Croatia at Wembley in November 2007.

The Croatians had already qualified, we just needed a point... but it was a very nervy occasion.

Indeed, at the pre-match function FA chairman Geoff Thompson had wished England coach, Steve *McQueen* and the players all the best for the game! I think by the end of the evening we all wished for a Great Escape... but it wasn't to be. We lost 3-2 on a filthy night and on a rotten ice-rink of a pitch. We were out.

Steve was castigated as the 'Wally with the Brolly' and I later reflected that only at Wembley would umbrellas even have been close to the dug-outs. The FA staff used to have them there on stand-by to protect dignitaries from the rain, if and when they went out to meet the players or stand for the anthems. A well-meaning gesture, which I always turned down. In the heat of battle and 'lost' in the game, Steve picked one up – and the rest is history.

It was a tough time. The following day Steve, now back in English football at Nottingham Forest, was relieved of his duties – and along with other FA board colleagues I faced a very hostile media conference in Soho Square. I apologised personally and publicly for our non-qualification and meant it.

I knew it wasn't good enough. The atmosphere in the room was electric – thankfully the chairs weren't.

The football world never stops... so within two days I was off to South Africa and the draw for the 2010 qualification groups. A loud gasp went around the room when England drew Croatia. Again.

Ten months later, we played Croatia in Zagreb, now under the coaching regime of the famous Italian coach, Fabio Capello.

We had recruited him after taking the thoughts on board from many luminaries in the game including the late Sir Bobby Robson, Sir Alex Ferguson, Sir Bobby Charlton, Arsene Wenger, Franz Beckenbauer and Michel Platini – as well as centrally involving our own Sir Trevor Brooking. We wanted to know what they thought could be done to improve the England national team set-up – and what type of coach could help us achieve it.

They explained the *type* of coach they felt would suit the special demands of the England job and provided us with some names –

outstanding coaches like Marcello Lippi, Jose Mourinho and Fabio Capello were amongst those consistently mentioned and, in due course, we went about our recruitment business. We decided, on this occasion, the nationality of the manager was not necessarily to be a barrier to appointment.

This time, too, the process was shorter and more private – and, within weeks, it ultimately came down to Capello and FA officials – myself included – meeting at Wembley in December, 2007.

Within days he was introduced to the massed ranks of the media as the new England coach.

The initial meeting had gone well, held in a hospitality suite in a deserted stadium. I had the blinds on the windows facing the pitch pulled tightly shut. Not for reasons of intrusion but just because I knew what lay behind them.

Sure enough, at the end of our two-hour session, Fabio implored me to open the blinds so he could see the famous Wembley pitch – a pitch he had actually scored on many years before.

With great reluctance, I opened the blinds and revealed the world-famous Wembley pitch converted to 'a figure of eight' with tarmac, sand, tyres, bridges and bumps for a forthcoming motorsport fandango – the *Race of Champions*. His face was a picture.

Capello's appointment was a big relief for me personally. I found this period in the job really tough. The public scrutiny was intense and I also had the further private issue that my elderly mother, now in permanent ill-health, had become very sick.

Indeed, between interviewing Capello, having his appointment approved by the FA board, then introducing him to a largely receptive and positive media as the new England coach just a few days later, I had rushed up to the north-west from London to sit quietly with my brother David and share my mum's last moments at her hospital bedside. David had spent the previous couple of years selflessly tending to her every need.

With typical Scouse resolve, although unconscious and fading fast, she had stayed with us until her two sons were re-united with her and then slipped away at around three o'clock on a Saturday afternoon. She always had perfect timing.

On reflection it was probably the most emotionally-tangled week of my life.

My mum had been a fantastic and super-loyal advocate of my career choices. If my dad was more naturally cautious, I often felt I was doing a little bit of the high-flying for my more ambitious mum, who would have loved some of life's opportunities that had come my way. She was proud of me – but then I was proud of her.

* * * * *

We famously won 4-1 in Croatia on September 10, 2008 – the date of the match had been burnt into my brain since the draw ten months before. A virtuoso performance from England and a hat-trick by Theo Walcott had put our old nemesis to the sword.

It was the most satisfying moment of my three-and-a-half years in the job and I was caught on camera jumping out of my seat and punching the air as Theo's first goal went in. I knew I was not observing the right protocol... but, blow it. I was up out of my seat another three times that night.

And, by now, I was on my own home straight at the FA as the previous month it had been announced I would be stepping down from my role as chief executive.

A new independent chairman now headed the organisation and wanted to change the FA's approach to running its affairs – and that meant new people and a new chief executive. Despite fantas-tic support from FA board members, for which I remain grateful, it was obvious to me that my time in the job was up.

The role had tested me, to the full at times, but I had enjoyed its breadth, its intensity and its challenge. I also enjoyed helping make football such a positive force for good.

The sport, with its huge following, did have the ability to 'get' to young people, disadvantaged people and socially-challenged people which is why Downing Street called us on a regular basis to try and help them make an impact in areas of concern like anti-racism, knife-crime, literacy, obesity and social inclusion. Probably only the music industry could have such a similar effect.

During my time at the FA I did actually spend some time with the senior political figures of the period. Prime Minister Tony Blair invited Gerry and me to have dinner at Chequers with him – an informal occasion. We were joined by three or four other couples, all of whom had Merseyside connections.

I spent a lot of the evening talking to Tesco boss, and Evertonian, Sir Terry Leahy, the upshot of which was the huge supermarket chain getting behind Sir Trevor Brooking's brain-child of the Skills Programme, helping youngsters develop basic ball skills and an early enjoyment of playing the game.

Then Gordon Brown was a guest at one of the FA's regular private dinners for 'movers and shakers' which I instigated on my arrival at Soho Square. Brown, a great football fan, came alive when asked to regale us with stories of his favourite team, Raith Rovers. He loved it and was one of the last to leave that evening.

And current Prime Minister, David Cameron, was my guest at the ill-fated match against Croatia. Then Leader of the Opposition, he turned up a little late for the pre-match function and a trifle wind-swept. Mind you, he had cycled all the way from Westminster to Wembley in torrential rain.

Canny politicians will always stay close to the game despite one leading Government minister recently describing football as the country's 'worst governed' sport. Nobody is denying it has some serious issues but I think 'best-loved' and 'most influential' may also describe the game's real impact on the nation.

In the position of CEO of the FA you have a brief chance to make a difference and I felt that championing something like the FA's Respect Campaign would act as a guide to youngsters taking up the game in the future, influence over-excitable, or just plain abusive match-attending parents, and help the referee get a fairer deal – both in the park and the Premier League.

Despite the occasional high-profile incident that threatens to undermine the campaign's principles I am pleased it continues to grow and am told it is having a positive impact.

The announcement of my own impending departure from the FA was due to be made on an August afternoon the day after England's first international of the 2008/2009 season against the Czech Republic at Wembley.

However, the story was leaked out before then. In fact, just before the match itself started. I was able to tell my mate Andy, my guest at Wembley for the evening, it wasn't going to be a good night for picking his nose in public as we were sure to be on camera. He didn't and we were – several times.

I went into work the following day and was the subject of an impromptu press conference on the steps of our Soho Square office. I was happy to answer the questions posed. Then, as should be the case, the story moved on to who would be the next man in.

Me, I enjoyed a gentle glide into departing the FA, travelling to the big England games – we won the next five on the trot that autumn – enjoyed a well-attended farewell party, and tried to say goodbye personally to the many people I had met whilst in the job.

I was genuinely disappointed to leave. I had enjoyed working for the organisation even through some tough times and still retain my affection for it.

I also felt I'd given the place some much-needed stability and visible leadership when it most needed it.

Of course, my time there wasn't perfect and I accept that, but I had done my best, fronted up for the organisation when required, cared passionately about what I did – and left Soho Square, as one journalist kindly put it with 'my reputation and my sanity intact.' Just!

* * * * *

And now I could return to watching Liverpool and supporting the team properly. Indeed, in a gesture that was genuinely thoughtful and appreciated, Liverpool's CEO Rick Parry rang me the day after my departure from the FA was announced to check I was ok.

Once that was established he then asked me which game I was going to see that weekend. "I don't know, Rick, as you can imagine I haven't even looked at the fixtures."

"Well, I do. You are coming *home* to Anfield – and David (Moores) and I look forward to seeing you." A lovely thought.

And so I went up for the match, Liverpool v Middlesbrough, with my FA colleague and Boro' fan Adrian Bevington and, on route from the car park to the ground, every other person seemed to stop me to wish me well.

To end a difficult personal week on a positive note, Liverpool came from behind to win 2-1, Liverpool and England's Jamie Carragher and Steven Gerrard appropriately scoring the goals.

18

Spanish America

It was on the flight to Athens for the 2007 UEFA Champions League final against old adversaries AC Milan that I took time to reflect on the upturn in Liverpool's fortunes in the previous couple of years.

This, after all, was the second Champions League final for the Reds in three years – an achievement way beyond the wildest dreams of Liverpool fans and a return to the heady days of the late '70s and early '80s.

I suppose I had become one of those Reds fans who feared all that heady stuff was behind us. After all, it had been 20 years since Liverpool's last appearance in the major European club final before, in 2005, on an unforgettable night in Istanbul, we had turned the football world upside down and added European title number five with that remarkable comeback.

And it had been over 25 years since we'd won the title. Indeed, the actual competition had changed its name and re-invented itself since we last lifted the championship trophy (still the most elegant) which was now the preserve of the second tier of English football. But whether as the original championship, or the brand spanking new Premiership, neither had passed our way since 1990. I've already suggested reasons why I feel this was the case but now on a flight to Athens I just sat back and reflected on the upturn in our fortunes.

And a lot seemed to hinge on the impact of one Rafael Benitez Maudes, born Madrid, April 1960 – Rafa, to the fans.

A good, if unremarkable, player had turned into a hugely successful coach. With Valencia, he had over-achieved in the face of the twin Spanish giants Real Madrid and Barcelona, landing two La Liga titles in three years and also the UEFA Cup.

It underlined Benitez, the chess-playing tactical master, was a top-class coach and Liverpool beat off stiff opposition to bag his services in June 2004.

He came as a replacement for Gerard Houllier so I suppose the wine in the boardroom changed from French to Spanish, as did the coaching staff and the playing staff – and the songs sung in their praise.

By the time the squad for Spain's ultimately successful tilt at Euro 2008 was named four years later, there were more Liverpool players in it. We had a total of four – compared to Barcelona, three, and Real Madrid, two. Astonishing, really.

England may not have been at Euro 2008 but Liverpool were and, indeed, a Liverpool player, Fernando Torres, scored the winning goal in the final.

By 2007, the journey thus far with Benitez had been sensational. An unforgettable Champions League success in the first season; UEFA Super Cup, FA Community Shield and FA Cup in his second term, and now a second Champions League final.

Chelsea had once again been beaten, again at the semi-final stage, this time on penalties – another absolutely mega Anfield night, and the running score between our man and their man, the mercurial

Mourinho, was edged in our favour. Benitez had master-minded wins over him in two Champions League semi-finals and an FA Cup semi-final to this point (Luis Garcia, we salute you). Mind you, Mourinho had bagged the Carling Cup in Cardiff. It was turning into a right royal rivalry.

As I say, our opponents in Athens would be AC Milan, the team whose hearts we had broken in Istanbul. Their coach Carlo Ancelotti would, ironically, end up at Stamford Bridge himself.

The Istanbul game had been simply sensational; a wind-swept, barely finished stadium way out of town hosted a game from the gods.

It was the ultimate '*I was there*' night – and I *was* there – six finals out of six – and, this time, as a member of football's top table. No pilchard sandwiches on this trip.

On the morning after the game, I headed back to London and started the ball rolling in trying to secure a place for Liverpool in the following season's competition. I relayed a message of congratulations from the then President of the FA, the Duke of York, up to Anfield and then, in the evening, watched enviously as the television pictures were broadcast of Liverpool's triumphant homecoming which looked absolutely magnificent.

For me, the following day was another flight, this time to Chicago, to join up with the England tour party.

We were playing the US national team in the original 'Windy City' and then Colombia in New Jersey.

When I arrived at the hotel in Chicago I was surrounded by members of the travelling party wanting to talk about all things 'Istanbul' and get a first-hand report on the great night from somebody who had actually been there.

Coaches, players and support staff alike, they all wanted me to re-live the match. So off I went... and I think I even added a few new things for good measure.

Two games, two wins in the States, but I left for home still needing to be convinced that football, the world game, can ever truly settle and thrive in the land of opportunity. I certainly hope it does – it deserves a chance.

However, it seems almost impossible to shift baseball, American football, NBA basketball and NHL ice hockey off the sports pages and if it is shifted, the space is filled by the college versions of the same sports. It is a tough nut to crack. But that doesn't mean American sporting entrepreneurs were oblivious to soccer and weren't looking alluringly at its commercial charms.

And so, on their way to Athens two years later, were two American businessmen, who were themselves on a crash course in understanding what the world's greatest game was all about and, also what ownership of one of world sports' greatest institutions actually meant.

Tom Hicks, a tall Texan, and George Gillett, from America's mid-west, had paired up to buy Liverpool Football Club earlier that year. They were Liverpool's new owners but ultimately only for what proved a short and deeply acrimonious period.

At one point, it seemed the club was destined to be bought by Dubai International Capital. Indeed, I was introduced to their representatives at a third round FA Cup tie with Arsenal at Anfield in January 2007.

As both the FA Chief Executive and a Liverpool fan I was probably a perfect pre-match dinner guest for Liverpool officials to parade in front of their determined suitors – and I left that evening thinking the club was heading for Middle-East ownership.

Whatever my concerns, I did recognise that a major injection of foreign capital, from a responsible source, was needed to help Liverpool to be able to compete on and off the field with clubs also the recipients of foreign wealth.

But that deal didn't happen and a month later Liverpool was bought by the American consortium of Hicks and Gillett.

Two different characters in both style and stature – with one common bond – football was a whole new ball game to them. In what seemed a last-minute switch in choice the Liverpool hierarchy went west rather than east.

I went to Liverpool's last 16 Champions League match against Barcelona that month and was introduced to them as 'the Chief Executive of the Football Association' and a 'lifelong supporter of Liverpool Football Club'.

They almost stood to attention – football 'top brass' – the game's 'Commissioner' as they saw it. I used the opportunity to explain to them what I felt, both professionally and personally; that they had a genuine responsibility to the club and its supporters.

I told them that they were now the guardians of something more than a brand, more than an asset, more than a name on a balance sheet, more than part of a foreign investment portfolio.

They were involved in something that was at the very heartbeat of thousands of people's lives. Something that was uniquely part of Liverpool life, something that had been passed down generation to generation. Part of what made people's daily lives tick.

Indeed, part of my own personal history.

They nodded in all the right places but I wondered whether they really 'got' it.

Indeed, at the end of the game I turned around to them and explained that the Anfield crowd was going mad with delight because we had knocked Barcelona out of the competition. They looked a little confused as we had actually lost the game 1-0.

"Away goals," I said. Their mutual look of bemusement gave me a clue that this might be a long journey of discovery.

The crowd then broke into a hugely emotional post-match rendition of 'You'll Never Walk Alone' – another unique Anfield bonding session between the supporters and the club they loved. Tom Hicks and George Gillett raised their pristine new scarves and attempted to join in.

At the end of the song I looked at them, pointed to the jubilant crowd and said: "This is what you've bought and this is what you must look after." They earnestly nodded in agreement.

We lost the final in Athens. It was a game where Liverpool never really got going and Milan won without ever having to go through the gears. No penalty shoot-out dramas this time. Filippo Inzaghi scored the Italian club's two goals with a late consolation from Dirk Kuyt.

I actually spent a lot of that evening watching the crowd at the Liverpool end of the ground rather than the game. I was concerned at just how over-crowded it looked compared to every other part of the ground. I spoke to Rick Parry, who was also distracted from watching the game by monitoring the crowd movement – it would seem that all the Greek hosts' promised checks and balances regarding ticket ownership and such-like had just been woefully inadequate on the night.

The defeat spared Liverpool another trek to Japan to play in the World Club Championship. I'd been there with them in 2005 and seen the Reds beat Deportivo Saprissa of Costa Rica (I know!) ahead of a narrow defeat in the final by the Brazilians, Sao Paulo.

The tournament lacked the style and gravitas of the Champions League and always will in my view. But as Jamie Carragher rightly said, 'try qualifying for it'.

Benitez had put together a side that could do a job in Europe – he forensically looked at the opposition and set up his teams to beat them – over two legs. And his record was exceptional.

Indeed, before he left Anfield the club reached the semi-finals of the Champions League again in 2008, and then the quarter-finals in 2009. In a remarkable sequence of matches, it was Chelsea again who they met at these crucial stages. This time the Londoners had the upper hand – and the games were spell-binding.

What Liverpool fans really, really wanted though was to win the league title again.

Since Kenny Dalglish had last delivered it in 1990, Souness, Evans, Evans and Houllier, Houllier and now Benitez had tried and failed and we were all getting tired of successive managers publicly conceding the title race before we had even unwrapped our Christmas presents – and 'planning for next season'.

Meanwhile, our arch-rivals had steadily closed in on Liverpool's record of 18 titles, season after season, ultimately surpassing it. The closest the Reds came to winning it under Rafa Benitez was in his penultimate season – 2008/9 – when the Reds claimed runners-up slot, four points adrift of their Mancunian rivals.

High-spots that season included a league double over Chelsea, strong results against Arsenal and a memorable 4-1 league win over Manchester United at Old Trafford. Earlier that week, I had gone to Anfield with Fabio Capello and his Italian sidekick Franco Baldini and witnessed the Reds' 4-0 annihilation of one of Fabio's former clubs, Real Madrid. I also made them both stand to attention for the Kop's pre-match rendition of 'You'll Never Walk Alone'.

Despite all this, the Reds dropped too many league points at home against teams we would have expected to beat.

Frustrating.

The season's last home game against Tottenham Hotspur marked Fernando Torres' 50th goal in just two seasons – and, more importantly, a chance to bid farewell and thank you to Sami Hyypia.

For me, Hyypia is one of the Reds' finest players in the past half-century. A real old-fashioned professional footballer if you like – low on profile, high on commitment – he was simply immense and had been a brilliant signing by Gerard Houllier.

I don't think I was alone that day at Anfield in being frustrated in how long it took Rafa to actually get Sami on the field from the subs' bench against Spurs.

However well-meaning and for whatever reason, it was odd to keep him back for just the last ten minutes or so – the crowd wanted longer to say a proper farewell to such a distinguished player.

And there was nothing else on the game.

*   *   *   *   *

By now, there was a serious undercurrent of unrest amongst the Liverpool supporters and the state of the club. They had totally and understandably lost confidence in the American owners, who seemed to have lost faith in each other.

They had sent the club spiralling into debt – promised to build a new stadium that remains unbuilt and every time they visited Anfield, which was more and more infrequent, it involved something close to a military operation to get them in and out without incident.

This was not what Liverpool Football Club was about. It was not what the loyal fans wanted. They were seeing their club put at risk, held up to ridicule and were not standing for it.

It was a complete mess.

Now a free agent again after leaving the FA, I resumed my regular trips to Anfield but felt there was a huge cloud ready to break over the club. It was the 'storm' of the club's seminal anthem.

In time, it was duly announced that long-serving Rick Parry was leaving the club. David Moores had already stood down as the club's chairman. I had always found these two men both good to work with and to be around.

David, a genuine Liverpool fanatic, was always ready with a warm welcome and cared passionately about the club. Rick was a steady, experienced and caring influence, uncannily in the professional style and image of his predecessor, Peter Robinson.

For some fans, however, the pair remain targets for blame for the late turn in the road that brought Tom Hicks and George Gillett to Anfield. I speak as I find, and I like both men.

Neither is there on matchdays now, which I think is unfortunate and I hope that will change one day.

Rafa's time in charge of the club – and at times it seemed exactly that – finally came to an end when he left by mutual consent in June 2010.

He came close to getting it right, it seemed to me, and had Liverpool in his heart but the turmoil off the pitch was a troublesome back-drop and his rotation and natural caution against some of the Premier League's weaker sides proved frustrating.

Again, like his predecessor Houllier, Rafa's work in the transfer market was a blend of the 'quite brilliant' and the 'cor blimey'.

Certainly in Reina, Alonso and Torres, he signed three very special Spanish talents, backed up by the likes of Argentinian Javier Mascherano and Holland's Dirk Kuyt. But there were other players bought who were simply not good enough for the club – or the challenge it had been set.

*   *   *   *   *

The removal of Hicks and Gillett from Anfield became as big a target for the fans as winning the Premier League itself. The fans at Manchester United were equally fired up about their American owners but were winning trophies in the meantime.

Liverpool, our club, deserved better than the trip it was being taken on. It needed something to happen and quickly. We wanted our club back.

It took strong campaigns from the fans, a determined financial institution in RBS, and some key senior individuals at the club to close a deeply troublesome chapter in the club's history.

Martin Broughton, the new club chairman (and Chelsea season ticket-holder), Christian Purslow, a lifelong Reds fan and the club's managing director, and Ian Ayre, the club's commercial director and long-standing Liverpool fan, were ultimately the high-profile trio who had 'their day in court' and wrested control of the club away from Hicks and Gillett. It was a headline news story, and for thousands of Liverpool fans a moment of sheer relief.

Not quite Istanbul – but perhaps will, in time, be seen as its off-field equivalent.

19

The Magic Thread

This year, I will make my way to Anfield on a match day and watch Liverpool's latest home game some 50 years after watching my first one there.

And I will step into the ground with the same level of enthusiasm I took into Anfield all those years ago – but probably not the same short trousers and duffle coat. It may be half a century later, but the same sense of anticipation will be there. I love going to watch a game of football.

I will want Liverpool to win – and win well. And, as well as the programme, I will take some type of memory away from the game to go alongside the hundreds of others I've stored up and down the years.

When I first watched Liverpool back in 1961, Bill Shankly was already beginning to weave his extraordinary magic. This was the breakthrough season – the campaign that put the Reds back where they belonged. In the top division.

As things get underway in the 2011/12 season, another Scotsman, Kenny Dalglish, has restored a sense of purpose and pride at Anfield and put a smile back on the face of the club. And the fans, in turn, are ready again to play their part in helping him build on the terrific progress made in the first half of the year.

My half century of years watching Liverpool has given me so much enjoyment, excitement and fulfilment.

The journey has been an emotional one which I have tried to bring to life and share with you.

Obviously this has been my own personal 'take' on the matches, victories, goals, stars and laps of honours I've witnessed with the Reds and, of course, everybody has their own special memories – of their own time and, indeed, their own team.

We are dealing with a sport that never stands still. The game itself has changed beyond all recognition in the past 50 years – some things by necessity, others by design.

When I first started going to the match there were no substitutes, red cards, shirt sponsors, televised live league football; linesmen were called linesmen – still are really, and the two now bizarrely behind the goal would have been arrested for invading the pitch; half time was 10 minutes; shin-pads looked like tank traps; fans would sit or stand – not sit and stand; everybody did the Pools; the game had lots of 'one-club' servants; there were huge attendances; famous stadiums with famous names; there were no millionaire footballers; few if any foreign players or foreign owners; the players were 'closer' to the fans; Burnley, Ipswich Town and Everton were amongst eight teams who could, and did, win the league championship in the Sixties; only the English champions entered the European Champions Cup; the FA Cup was truly world famous, the only live club game on television – had the weekend to itself – and was won, over a ten year span, by eight different clubs.

Football's prizes were spread around – the game was much more egalitarian. Oh, and there was no sign yet of the prawn sandwich brigade… but plenty of dodgy pies. And we won the World Cup.

Spin forward 50 years and the game is still truly engaging, but different. Football in this country is blessed with some outstanding English players, thankfully now both black and white, but they are fewer in number. Some foreign players playing in the Premier League have genuinely graced the sport, lifted our spirits whilst others have flattered to deceive – and taken the money and run – not very fast, not very far and not very often.

The best stadiums are now state-of-the-art and safer. And expensive. The game must continue their current hard work in making sure future generations of supporters are given their chance, 'first-hand and close-up', of falling in love with the game.

And while it is gratifying to know 'our' game is a global smash-hit – and it's genuinely really popular – let's make sure that it's not at the expense of 'our' fans and 'our' players.

After all, such global appeal failed to transfer itself into genuine political influence and votes, either in trying to win a World Cup bid – where we bafflingly failed to get beyond the first round – or in winning support for a highly principled stand at the 2011 FIFA Congress. That said we must continue to take our place at troubled FIFA, and currently that's between our alphabetical neighbours El Salvador and Equatorial Guinea, and work from within that flawed organisation to affect positive change and higher standards of governance.

In my old hunting ground, coverage of football on television has gone from black and white to colour, from widescreen to HD, from HD to 3D, from terrestrial to digital, from your telly to your mobile phone. But one thing hasn't changed; a good game is a good game and a bad game is a bad game and the viewer knows the difference.

I think advances in broadcast technology have really enhanced the look, style and feel of the English game – pioneered by the BBC and ITV and led in latter years by SKY Sports. And I do genuinely think we are world-class at it – and so does the world. The English game's broadcasters – across all channels and platforms – should be proud of that.

There is, however, too much football on British television. Anything and everything seems to get air-time somewhere. Fans now need a 24-hour clock as much as a fixture list. Or that's what my mates keep telling me.

And, of course, certain televised games – too many – are hyped up to within an inch of their lives. A Europa League Group game against third-rate opposition is just that – no more – and, once again, a savvy audience knows which games are 'big-time' and which aren't. Go easy on the hard-sell chaps.

The media are still a vital part of the game's messaging, be it in print or broadcast – and lots of the journalism, at its best, is still sharp, opinionated, intelligent and informed – and occasionally painful if you are on the end of it. But the in-vogue 'Breaking News' should do what it says on the tin – and not be wasted on a cured in-growing toe-nail or a League Two loan-signing. It's good that radio has made such a strong comeback – but stations need to cherish their broadcasters ahead of the next loudest mouth.

And the game has to develop a mature approach to the rapid growth of social-networking. Properly used, it is a fantastic way of players getting closer to the ordinary fans. After all, they are unlikely to share a bus to the ground with the supporter anymore – unless the fan is driving it – and our young population is both conversant and confident in their use of these new forms of contact. Critically, they are tomorrow's supporters.

The top clubs in our game have become the target for foreign plutocrats determined to get on board with the heady combination of social appeal and business possibilities that ownership of a Premier League 'brand' can bring. Each case should be taken on its merits, of course, but the fans' welfare in all of this must increasingly be taken into consideration – after all they are the ones who will still be there when pieces have to be picked up. As Liverpool fans know only too well.

The club v country debate will remain a lively one. We all want a brilliant weekly digest of top-class domestic league and cup football – and as I've hopefully illustrated in the preceding pages I do understand the intensity of following your own club side and that its success is clearly, for many, their first priority and first love. But many people, me included, also want the national side to win the World Cup.

I just sense at the moment these are difficult, even impossible, mutual objectives to achieve in the way the game is currently structured. And certainly our abject performance in South Africa adds fuel to that argument.

Let's hope the Football Association's new coaching and educational centre – St George's Park at Burton, due to be open next year – is a conduit for a more positive future and the creation of world-class performance. I wish it luck.

And let's not forget. Be it 1961 or 2011, we still have a sport which is the envy of every other one, has the widest appeal and the greatest impact.

When I was at the FA I regularly told audiences that the English game had 37,000 clubs, two-and-a-half thousand leagues and that some five million people were engaged in football each weekend – playing, coaching, refereeing, spectating, reporting, administrating, viewing, listening, reading... and now blogging and tweeting.

Those numbers aren't getting smaller and gives the game a unique chance to do some of the good things which it does – often with little or no recognition. But that's its privilege.

It's a game that became a sport, a sport that became a business and a business that's become a global industry – but let's remember, it is still a sport and it remains vibrant, exciting, vital and imperfect. Like life, really.

*   *   *   *   *

Life for me after the FA began with a decent rest and a chance to catch up with family life. Jack, a mean rugby player, was off to Manchester University to study Neuroscience – Gerry and I were thrilled and proud but none the wiser. He has since successfully graduated in a subject which probably won't clog up too many Sunday lunch conversations going forward.

Joe, a tricky and talented footballer, is now at Leeds University studying Economics. In his last year at school, he went on a football tour to Brazil and I went with him. The teachers had asked for some parental support in man-marking the 25-strong school party and four dads pitched up.

It was fantastic to share our sons' experiences and cheer them on from a South American touchline before going on to watch some football at the world famous Maracana Stadium.

I have been back to Brazil recently, this time with Soccerex, the football industry's leading convention business – and this time we were treated to a gala dinner at the summit of Rio's Sugar Loaf Mountain.

Top of the bill was an on-stage appearance of the famous Brazil World Cup-winning side of 1970. For those people of a certain vintage, like me, they are still a fabulous memory.

Indeed, Carlos Alberto, their captain and scorer of the famous fourth goal in their 1970 World Cup final win over Italy – still amongst my favourite all-time goals, was there and is, like me, an ambassador for Soccerex. So it is a delight for me to be able to boast I am now in the same team as him. I don't think Carlos Alberto necessarily sees it as a similar honour.

Talking World Cups, my son Joe and I went to the World Cup in South Africa hoping that we would witness a great England adventure. Like thousands of travelling fans, and millions more watching at home, we were bitterly disappointed by what we saw.

I went back out to South Africa to see the final itself and was pleased when Spain finally overcame a Dutch side more intent on stopping the opposition playing than creating opportunities themselves. I was pleased too that Howard Webb and his English colleagues got given the final – but, Webb, a great referee, had to call on every ounce of his experience to handle such a tempestuous game.

In late 2008, I had been gratified to be approached by Sir Howard Newby, Vice-Chancellor of the University of Liverpool, who offered a post in the academic institution's School of Management which I was delighted to accept.

So, on various days through the academic calendar, it is as Professor Barwick, a Visiting Professor of Strategic Leadership that I attend the university and help students chiefly on the MBA Football Industries course.

These are young people from all over the world, who see their future careers in the football industry, either back home where they come from or in the wider world and it is hugely rewarding to meet and work with them.

Along with other talented colleagues, I am delighted to work with Dr Rogan Taylor, a Liverpool fan, who has been so committed in helping and publicly taking a stand for the many people affected by the Hillsborough disaster.

Former Liverpool captain Phil Thompson also comes in to

engage the students with insights into the world of professional football and tales of his days as an Anfield great.

The big personal professional move my wife, Gerry and I made after the FA was to open our own business – Barwick Media and Sport – a consultancy dealing across the two huge industries in the company's title.

It is another learning curve for us and a new adventure, but things seem to be going well. We enjoy our wins – big or small – and our reputation and client base is growing quickly.

Away from professional duties, I am delighted to do some work for the Bobby Moore Cancer Fund and have agreed to get involved in a community football project in Liverpool, Little League Sports, which helps to give some much-needed stimulation and fun to local young people by providing them with week-long football camps in school holidays.

And I was absolutely delighted to be asked to become the patron of the Liverpool County Football Association late last year.

This is the organisation which is the parent body for all the football clubs in the area from Liverpool and Everton through to the type and level of football team I turned out for many years ago.

It was a real honour to be so publicly recognised by the sport I love, and in the area that had so much to do with nurturing my lifelong affair with the world's greatest game.

*   *   *   *   *

Now, finally if I was to list my ten favourite things about English football, I'm pretty sure watching an evening match at Fulham's Craven Cottage would be high on that list.

And it would nudge itself a little further up the rankings if the game was being played either at the start or end of the season, was full of great goals, involved a spectacular Liverpool win – and had a wonderful sunset over the River Thames thrown in for good measure. In May 2011, we just got all of that as Liverpool turned in a tremendous performance to beat Fulham 5-2.

The Dalglish-rejuvenated team were full of energy and imagination. Argentinian Maxi Rodriguez scored his second hat-trick in three games, Dirk Kuyt became the first Liverpool player to score in five consecutive Premier League games in the same season and the Reds' new star, Uruguayan Luis Suarez scored the final goal and, more importantly, ran the Fulham defenders ragged from start to finish. He is special. To top it all off, Jamie Carragher became the Reds' second-highest appearance maker behind Ian Callaghan.

It was a really outstanding performance from Liverpool, which was rapturously received by a huge travelling contingent and also acknowledged warmly by a knowledgeable home support.

Liverpool just kept driving forward; brilliant passing and moving, and the score in their favour on the night could have been absolutely anything. It was a genuine privilege and pleasure to see the team playing with such style.

Three days after the virtuoso display at Craven Cottage, it was finally announced Kenny had been confirmed in his post as the full-time manager of Liverpool – with a three-year contract. Another positive sign and one much appreciated by players and fans alike. As already discussed, he has been the alchemist who has conjured up a complete change in atmosphere at and around the club. His appointment of Steve Clarke has also been well-judged.

The recruitment of the commercially-savvy and committed Red, Ian Ayre as the club's managing director and the experienced Damien Comolli as the club's director of football, helping to spot future signings, have been further indications that the club is regaining its sure-footing following the trauma and damage of the previous regime at the club. These opening key strategic appointments made by the new owners of the club augurs well and underpins their declared public desire to take Liverpool Football Club forward, and in so doing, build a positive future for the club, both on and off the field.

John W. Henry and Tom Werner, of the Fenway Sports Group, have brought their Stateside sporting experience, know-how and success to the fore as they make their early moves in creating a new era for the club.

These Americans have learnt from others' mistakes and have eased themselves into their ownership with a delicate balance of decisive action coupled with humility and honesty.

They have listened... and listened, and then acted with a sureness of touch and they have also shown the correct blend of sporting intuition and intelligent commercial edge.

They have also understood quickly that the big stretch of water between us and them carries with it different cultures and concerns. They must be patient as they get to grips with all the special vagaries of English football.

In short, the owners of the world famous Boston Red Sox baseball team and now owners of the world famous Liverpool Football Club have made a good early impression – and most importantly, they are welcome.

We all know there is a journey the club has to go on to restore itself to former glories. First thing has to be create a team, and, indeed, a squad these days, that is capable of truly challenging for the Premier League. Of winning our own domestic league.

For me, this clearly must be the number one ambition for the club. Not just to chase down another club's achievement, but to put us back where we belong. It seems unbelievable that we haven't lifted that main prize since 1990.

In those days we had become very blasé about another title – not now. The roof would come off the Kop if we lay to rest that two-decade embarrassment. As I say, number one priority.

Of course, then there is Europe. A place in the UEFA Champions League has to be earned. There is no longer a shoe-in for the Premier League's 'big four' – there is no longer just a 'big four'. Each season, that level of European qualification is going to get tougher but it must also be a central target for the club.

Then we can make an impression on the competition itself.

After all, success in European football is a unique part of our club's DNA. It is what makes Liverpool special – no need to create a 'European' history – we have one – and a special one.

It is also about time we played at the new Wembley Stadium before it is no longer new. After all 'Anfield South' now sounds a little dated. Let's get to an FA Cup final or Carling Cup final – let's take those competitions seriously and give our fans a day out and then go on and win the trophies themselves.

And it is time to play with our famous style and confidence – both home and away in a manner that takes the initiative away from the opposition and the breath away from our fabulous support.

We will leave the tactics and team formation to the experts but I think we all want to see the team 'go for it' when they can. The first half of this year suggests that Kenny Dalglish shares that philosophy.

The recent breakthrough of local Liverpool lads in the first team has been a real unexpected bonus. As a fan brought up on Smith, Lawler, Callaghan, Thompson, McManaman, Fowler, Gerrard and Carragher, I am really pleased to see some new young Scousers coming through and wearing the shirt with such obvious pride. When they kiss the badge they mean it. Let's hope the club continues to champion local talent ahead of ageing imports.

Big decisions need to be made about the stadium. Of course, it would be sad to leave Anfield, but if it takes the club forward so be it. If the decision is to stay at Anfield then the great old stadium needs a proper re-fit, a significant plan for expansion, modernisation (big screens) and some urgent *TLC*. If that's difficult to achieve, think again. We must not fall behind – absolutely respect the past, but push on for the future.

My deep regard for the club remains undiminished although I must admit it took a buffeting through the Hicks and Gillett tenure. The club means so much to me, as it does for so many people.

Like every other Liverpool fan – indeed, every other football fan whatever your team – this magnificent game we all love weaves a magical thread through your whole life – indeed, *my* own life – from boy to man.

So many great memories, so many special individual moments to remember, favourite players, favourite matches, crazy journeys, match mates, rotten decisions, dodgy grub, talking points, arguments with friends, collecting stuff, daft superstitions and habits.

I will still find a way of getting the latest Liverpool score or result as soon as possible no matter what event, personal or professional, is keeping me away from the game.

It all adds up to a complete and harmless addiction... actually something that is very good for you.

I intend remaining a Liverpool fan – and a football supporter – for the next 50 years, so watch out for volume two in 2061!

Meanwhile, thanks for spending some time in my company; it has been a privilege and a pleasure to have you along.

Up the Reds!

Stoppage time

The venue, the sun-drenched world famous Copacabana Beach in Rio de Janeiro; the occasion, the last day of my son Joe's school football trip to Brazil.

In a lads, dads and teachers kick-about at the end of the tour I had finally emulated footballing greats like Pele, Jairzinho, Zico and Ronaldo by scoring a belting goal on the beach in Brazil.

Eventually.

A diving header actually, top corner of the net – Tony Hateley style. I glowed with pride – and sunburn.

"Right, that's it guys – he's finally headed one in, we can all go back to the hotel at last," said the bronzed beach-bum we had hired that morning to put us through the footballing tricks and feints passed down from one Brazilian generation to the next.

"I thought he was never going to score." I heard him say to his mate.

"Who?" his mate inquired…

"The fat old guy who thinks he's Pele."

Index

INDEX

Sport Media

Other publications produced by Sport Media:

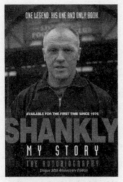

The real man behind
the legend

50 years of Ian
Callaghan's Liverpool

Best-selling story of
LFC's chief scout

Honest and amusing
tales from an LFC hero

Stories of the famous
Kop, told by Kopites

Alan Hansen's hilarious
collection of injury mishaps

Outrageous collection of
footballers' what not to wear

**All of these hardback and paperback titles, and more, are available to order
by calling 0845 143 0001, or you can buy online at www.merseyshop.com**